The New HIKING the Monadnock Region

The New HIKING
the Monadnock Region

44 NATURE WALKS AND DAY-HIKES
IN THE HEART OF NEW ENGLAND

Joe Adamowicz

University Press of New England

Hanover and London

Published by University Press of New England,
One Court Street, Lebanon, NH 03766
www.upne.com

© 2007 by University Press of New England
Printed in the United States of America

5 4 3 2 1

LIBRARY OF CONGRESS CATALOGING-IN-PUBLICATION DATA
Adamowicz, Joe.
The New Hiking the Monadnock Region : 44 nature walks and day-hikes
in the heart of New England / Joe Adamowicz.
    p.   cm.
Includes bibliographical references and index.
ISBN-13: 978-1-58465-644-9 (pbk. : alk. paper)
ISBN-10: 1-58465-644-1 (pbk. : alk. paper)
1. Hiking—New Hampshire—Monadnock, Mount, Region—Guidebooks.
2. Trails—New Hampshire—Monadnock, Mount, Region—Guidebooks.
3. Natural history—New Hampshire—Monadnock, Mount, Region.
4. Monadnock, Mount, Region (N.H.)—Guidebooks. I. Title.
GV199.42.N42M663 2007
917.42'9—dc22   2007014750

Every attempt has been made to verify the accuracy of the information
included in this book. Because changes can occur, please consider calling
ahead to confirm any information that is crucial to your plans.

 green
press
INITIATIVE

University Press of New England is a member of the
Green Press Initiative. The paper used in this book
meets their minimum requirement for recycled paper.

Contents

Preface

I first became interested in hiking the Monadnock Region while poking around the backroads in my 1970 Chevrolet Impala. Hills would suddenly come into view, then just as suddenly disappear as the road twisted around the next turn. One day I decided to explore a few of those mysterious green bumps on foot.

Maybe it was on Gap Mountain in the soft rain when I first discovered the gentleness of the region, or perhaps I found it watching cloud filaments drift over toy villages before evaporating into a deep blue sky. I don't know why exactly, but there is an intimacy here among the distant white-steepled churches and long-forgotten stone walls that you won't find on the frost-fractured summits of Mount Washington or Lafayette. Neither will you find peak-baggers or people in a hurry. What I think you will discover, however, is a greater appreciation for nature.

Acknowledgments

Thanks to the following people: Debra DeCelle, Robin Chouiniere, Gene Chouiniere, Elizabeth Howes, Curtis Carroll, Stephanie Wells, Brenda Clarke, Kathleen Flammia, Kathy Cleveland, Ben Haubrich, Helen Van Ham, Bruce Scofield, Michael Walsh, Andrew Zboray, Jim Bearce, George Johnson, Dwayne Denehy, Bob Spoerl, Jonathan Nute, Stephen Walker, Marshall Davenson, Valerie Vaughn, Chris Ryan, Jessie Salisbury, Bob Saudelli, Ralph Crowell, Dick Jenkins, Jim Orr, Jay Hewett, Steve Dermody, Ted Bonner, Denny Wheeler, Geoff Jones, H. Meade Cadot, Jr., and Brian Woodbury.

J.A.

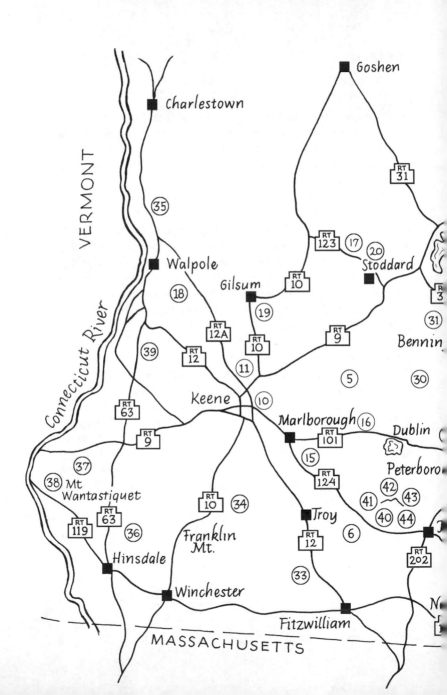

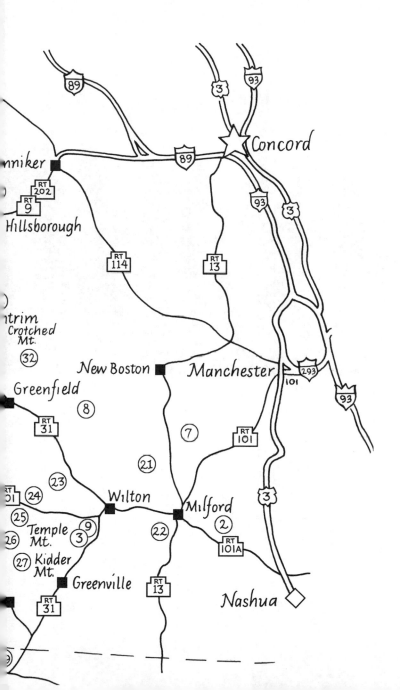

Atop Mount Monadnock.

Introduction

This book is about small mountains and gentle hills, places for the most part that can be easily hiked by families with children. There are a few hikes that are more challenging, and they are indicated as such. Some of the hikes in this book will take you to wildlife sanctuaries where you are apt to see a graceful blue heron stalking its dinner or a broad-winged hawk with its fantail soaring slowly above a craggy mountain peak. Other hikes explore kettle holes, ponds, hemlock forests, waterfalls, or old cellar holes on long-abandoned roads.

The Trails
The trails are marked with a single blaze of paint on trees or rocks, with a double vertical blaze to indicate a trail junction or turn in the trail, or with stone cairns or signs. These markers are maintained by various local and regional environmental groups such as the Friends of the Wapack, The Nature Conservancy, Harris Center for Conservation Education, Trailwrights, the Society for the Protection of New Hampshire Forests, Audubon Society of New Hampshire, and the Appalachian Mountain Club. Highest and lowest elevations are also given, and each trail description begins with an approximate distance and time (round trip). The routes return you to your starting point via a loop or by following the same trail in reverse. As with all hikes, allow extra time for resting, eating lunch, poking around an old cellar hole, watching birds, identifying plants, and of course, admiring the views.

The Hikes
The hikes are listed in ascending order of difficulty: starter, easy, moderate, and difficult. The ratings are arbitrary, but in general the starter and easy hikes involve gentle terrain or minor elevations; moderate hikes require some exertion and a few difficult stretches. Those hikes rated as difficult involve significant elevation gains.

Hiking Preparations

Before you hit the trail, here are some basic rules of hiking: First and foremost, always be mindful of the risks of the outdoors. Getting lost is a potential danger wherever you hike, even on the lower elevations of southern New Hampshire. Plan your hike before you set out, using a good map showing the direction that leads to the nearest road in the event you do become lost.

If you ever get lost, sit down to rest, calm down, and figure out your location. Back up to relocate your last trail sign. If you still cannot figure out your location, generally the shortest way out is toward any road, building, smoke, vehicle noise, or other signs of "civilization." Walls and fences usually lead somewhere, and although this may be only to an abandoned farm, it is probable that an old path will lead from there to a road. Natural signs show direction: Vegetation tends to be larger and more open on northern slopes and smaller and denser on southern slopes. Following waterways downstream also leads toward settlements.

Another option is to try to find an identifiable landmark by climbing to the highest elevation in the immediate area. Lakes, mountains, roads, and towns can be seen from above. If any of these methods fail, establish a home base. The worst thing you can do is to wander aimlessly. Remember—if you give prior notice to someone of your hiking plans, searchers will know where to come looking for you.

Get some basic experience in map- and compass-reading. The maps in this book are adequate illustrations, but learning how to read a topographical map will improve your hiking enjoyment and safety. Depending on a GPS (global positioning system) unit or cellular phone to call for help is not a substitute for being prepared before you set out. Never put your complete faith in something that runs on batteries (batteries die and chips fail). Rely on a map, a compass, and common sense. You can purchase topographical maps at outdoor stores, or you can order USGS maps from the government by contacting the U.S. Geological Survey Information Services, Box 25286, Denver, Colorado, 80225 (1-888-ASK-USGS; www.usgs.gov). Ask for a state index and price list for New Hampshire and the pamphlet describing how to read maps.

Respect the weather. Conditions can change at a moment's notice, especially here in New England when the seasons are in transition. Whenever there is doubt that the weather is changing for the worst, it is best to turn back rather than risk uncertainty. If you are on a mountain, you should immediately head for lower safer terrain when thunderclouds begin forming, or when you hear thunder. High, pointed terrain is the worst place to be. Standing on a ridgeline, you are the highest object, and lightning is more likely to strike the tallest object in a given area (in this case, you). Stay away from lone trees. You are hundreds of times safer in a forest than you are standing next to a tree in an open field.

Many people prefer to hike in the cooler days of autumn when the air has been cleansed of heavy haze and pesky insects; and trails are illuminated by the brilliant colors of the forest canopy. But remember, falling leaves on the trail can make it difficult to follow, and November brings with it hunting season, so wear something bright orange. The spring is a great time to visit a waterfall and see wildflowers, but be careful of trails with stream crossings and be prepared for mud.

Prior to embarking on your trip, notify someone of your destination and the time you plan to return. Be aware of when the sun will set. If you are with a group, stay together and do not leave the marked trail or "bushwack" for short cuts. Walk only as fast as the slowest member of your party. Consider joining a hiking organization. The Audubon Society and the Appalachian Mountain Club (AMC) sponsor a series of programs and events through regional chapters.

For even the most innocuous of hikes, wear a good pair of boots with ankle support and sturdy nonslip soles. Although tennis shoes are tempting and adequate for many of these walks, it is too easy to turn an ankle and the chance is not worth taking. A pair of lightweight boots weigh less than three pounds and are generally made of a combination of leather and breathable fabric. You are less likely to get blisters wearing lightweights and each step is easier and more flexible; but they take forever to dry and do not provide much ankle support. All-leather boots offer excellent ankle support and foot stability on difficult terrain. And they are usually more waterproof and durable than synthetic boots. The rubber-lug boot sole, which should feel hard and knobby, keeps your feet from slipping on the trail. Sturdy Vibram soles are excellent for this.

When you try on boots, wear the type of socks you will be using on the trail. Lace up the boots and stand up. They should feel snug around the ball and instep of your foot but loose enough to allow you to flex your foot forward. Your heel should be held firmly in place. If your feet easily slide forward when you walk, or you are able to move your heel from side to side, try a smaller size. If your toes make contact with the front of the boot without much forward movement, try a larger size. Break in your boots first before wearing them on the trail.

Shirts and T-shirts are acceptable for summer hikes, but carry a windbreaker or light jacket in case of foul weather. A heavy-duty garbage bag, such as a lawn or leaf bag, can protect you from the elements in an emergency situation. Cut an 8-inch slit about eight inches down from the closed corner, and pull it over your head, using the corner as a hood. Cut two small holes for your arms. For late fall or early spring hiking, jackets, sweaters, and knitted hats and gloves are the order of the day.

Think in terms of layers and loose fits. Layering clothing allows you to adjust what you are wearing to suit the temperature conditions. In cold weather wear polypropylene or a polyester knit next to the skin, wool layers or lightweight polyester fleeces over your undergarments as an insulating layer, and a waterproof and windproof layer on the outside. Wearing an outer layer of nylon or breathable fabric such as Gore-Tex is a good idea, especially if there is exposure to wind, which will rob your body of heat through convection. Cotton clothing can be very uncomfortable when wet and can lead to cooling and lowering of body temperature, which in turn leads to hypothermia. Wear a base layer made of a fabric that wicks away moisture from your skin. You dehydrate more easily in cold weather, so drink as much water as you would on a hot day.

Some recommended items to take along, in addition to a map and compass, include a good daypack to carry everything, an extra pair of socks to keep your feet happy (socks can also double as mit-tens), and plenty of water (two quarts per person for longer hikes—drink often to stay hydrated). If you are hiking under the hot sun, take extra water so you can drink six ounces every 15 to 30 minutes. Do not drink from streams or lakes. Even the clearest streams contain *giardia lamblia*, a waterborne intestinal parasite causing stomach and internal discomfort. Some springs are safe for drinking but as a rule, you should purify water by boiling at least two to three minutes or by adding purification tablets.

Other items to bring are matches in a waterproof container, insect repellent, a pocketknife, ribbon to mark trail intersections if you feel uncertain about the path, a field guide, a whistle in case you become separated, tissues or toilet paper (kept dry in a ziplock bag), bandanna, sunscreen—even on cloudy days the dangerous rays of the sun are still there—sunglasses, mini first aid kit, medications, tampons, and a small flashlight with extra batteries. If nature calls, find a location at least 200 feet from any water source and the trail. Dig a 4-inch by 4-inch cathole for human waste; fill and cover with dirt when done. Seal used toilet paper in a plastic bag and pack it out.

Bring high-energy snacks—food that is rich in carbohydrates, such as raisins, crackers, apples, chocolate, nutrition bars, cheese, trail mix, and dried fruit. Avoid diuretic foods such as coffee and soda with caffeine or sugar, which cause your body to lose water and nutrients.

A nondigital watch can be used as an emergency compass by pointing the hour hand toward the sun. (South will lie in the middle of the angle formed by the hour hand and the numeral "12" on the face of the watch. North will be at the point opposite it.) Other items that will enhance your hiking experience are binoculars, altimeter, camera, magnifying lens, measuring tape, notepad, and pen.

A word about hiking with dogs. Many people wouldn't think of hiking without their faithful companion. But some dogs will (quite naturally) chase wildlife, defecate on the trail, scare other hikers, or otherwise get into trouble. So it's best to find out about an area before bringing along Rover. (Dogs are not permitted on Mount Monadnock.)

If you do take your dog hiking, insure his safety and health by

On the trail to Pratt Pond.

providing adequate water. Be aware that rough footing can cause paw injuries. And clean up after and keep constant track of the whereabouts of your dog. Check your dog for ticks, especially eyelids and ears where there is less hair, and it is easier for deer ticks to attach.

Hiking with Children

If you are hiking with youngsters, take advantage of their natural curiosity by providing opportunities to satisfy their imagination. You might suggest that they keep a notebook illustrated with sketches of plant characteristics such as color, arrangement of flowers, and the number and shapes of leaves. Children can translate into picture form what they experience through their sense of touch and vision. Firsthand written observation will help them build on their own experience better than trying to keep what they see in their heads. You will be surprised at how your children's observation skills will improve.

Give kids something to do by playing games on the trail. Play "20 questions" or engage them in a scavenger hunt. Suggest things to look for, such as deer tracks, acorns, birds' nests, leaves, cones, a piece of bark, or a spider's web. Make a connection with nature by using all five senses. Create a game based on things they hear, touch, or smell. Spring odors will be very different from those in the summer or fall; see if your children can tell you why. Count the animals you see or hear. Imagine which tree you would like best as a home if you were a squirrel. Listen for natural sounds such as a crow's caw, a chipmunk's twitter, wind creaking through trees, water splashing and trickling over rocks, or the crunch and crack of leaves and sticks underfoot. Look under logs and poke around in nooks and crannies. Can you tell the red oaks from the white oaks? (Red oak leaves are bristle-tipped at the ends of the leaf lobes. White oak leaves are rounded or serrated).

Young children might enjoy bark rubbings. Place a piece of paper against a tree, and gently rub it with a crayon. Kids will also have fun with a magnifying glass looking at rocks, water, moss, and fungi, and using tools like binoculars, containers, and nets. Bring a guidebook so they can look up things they find. When hiking with children, don't be overambitious in your itinerary. Be flexible and allow them time to explore. Choose an appropriate hike with achievable goals, and set a pace that is comfortable for everyone. Remember, a hike is not a race. Plan frequent stops for resting and snacking.

Set good examples. Pick up any trash. Carry out what you carry in. Even those things that seem harmlessly biodegradable may break-down much slower than you think, so take banana and orange peels

Unusual double formation of paper birch.

with you. It is smart to pack lunches in roomy plastic bags that can also serve as refuse bags.

Even young children can carry a lightweight waist pack. Older children can follow the hike on a map, or chart directions with a compass. Plan an interesting destination such as a waterfall, pond, stream, or wildlife-viewing area. Getting wet while exploring is inevitable, so it is a good idea to bring along a change of clothes. Consider inviting along a friend of the same age. With young children, gaining the summit is not as important as having fun. Children under five can walk on their own for about an hour or less. It is natural for young children to walk a short distance and then stop to explore.

Some recommended hikes for young children include Shieling Forest (Boulder Trail); Harris Center (Dandylyon Trail); Rhododendron State Park (Rhododendron Loop Trail); Bear Den Geological Park; Edward MacDowell Lake (Wetland Wander Trail); Sheldrick Forest; McCabe Forest; Heald Tract (Pond Trail); dePierrefeu-Willard Pond Audubon Wildlife Sanctuary (Mill Pond Trail); Betsy Fosket Sanctuary; Sucker Brook Cove; Ponemah Bog; and Beech Hill.

If you are bringing a baby, select a specially-designed child carrier that has good head and neck support, secure safety straps, and a storage compartment, and feels comfortable on your back. Bring along extra diapers, towelettes, a bottle, and a waterproof bag to carry out soiled diapers.

At the end of the day check yourself, your children, and your pets for bugs that bite. Ticks, for example, like to attach at the hairline, in and behind ears, armpits, groin, and back of knees and legs. Although ticks are most common in grassy areas, they can also be found in the woods. Most ticks that humans come into contact with have the general appearance of a flat seed before gorging. Look and feel for unfamiliar dark spots or bumps. To remove ticks, do not pull off with your fingertips. Barbs on the proboscis (feeding snout) become embedded in the victim's skin, so even if you pull off the body the head remains. Using tweezers, grasp the head as close as possible to where it is attached, and pull back slowly and firmly until the tick is extracted. Wash, rinse, and disinfect the area. Apply an antibiotic ointment.

The Geological and Cultural History
of the Monadnock Region

Located in the quiet corner of southwestern New Hampshire, the Monadnock Region is a gently rolling land of wooded hills, old country roads, and sparkling lakes, with mountain laurel that blooms on roadside slopes in late May and June. The area roughly stretches from Hinsdale, Chesterfield, Westmoreland, and Walpole, along the Connecticut River on the west to Milford and Wilton on the upper reaches of the Souhegan River to the east. It is bounded to the north by the hill towns of Antrim, Hillsborough, and Deering, and on the south by Rindge and New Ipswich along the Massachusetts border. Three of the hikes—Ponemah Bog and Joe English Reservation in Amherst, New Hampshire, and Mount Watatic in Ashburnham, Massachusetts (which marks the beginning of the Wapack Trail)—are located in towns considered by most people to be just outside the region. The walks are close enough in location and in spirit, however, so that they are included here.

The Monadnock Region is old in terms of settlement. Most of the towns date back to the mid-1700s and have attractive, quiet village greens, white clapboarded buildings, photogenic churches and meetinghouses, and well-kept historic homes you will want to visit before or after you complete your hike. In spite of the gravelly till spread throughout the land by the glaciers, agriculture played an important role in the formation of these communities, and swift-moving streams once powered a variety of small mills.

A primeval forest of pine stretched from the river valleys to what is now Canada, and lumbering was an important industry for more than a century. Brick, glass, furniture-making, leather-tanning, and quarrying for soapstone and granite also contributed to the early economies of the Monadnock Region. Between 1790 and 1866, the region had several glass factories, including glassworks in Lyndeborough, Temple, Stoddard, and Keene. With the development of water power, paper, textile, and other manufacturing industries flourished on the banks of the region's rivers.

Beginning in the mid-1800s, many farmers left their rocky plots of land for the deep, fertile soil of the west. The pastureland, once dotted with sheep and cattle, began reverting to forest. Today, old stone walls hidden deep in the woods are the only evidence of the people who once cleared the land. Vestiges of the mill history can be found in the dams and brick buildings along the Contoocook, Ashuelot, and Souhegan Rivers.

The development of the railroad in the mid-1800s gave an economic boost to tourism, and the towns surrounding Mount Monadnock drew summer visitors from New York, Boston, and Hartford. Lodging for visitors was provided by resort hotels, private homes, boardinghouses, inns, and farmhouses. With the development of the automobile at the turn of the twentieth century, Monadnock became a popular destination for day trips and hikes up the mountain.

Geologically, the Monadnock Region is classified as an "upland," a landscape of wooded rolling hills, ponds, lakes, and low mountains whose surface elevation range from 700 to 1,400 feet above sea level. Above this level, a few solitary hills stand like islands overlooking the sea, remnants of ancient mountains whose fortunate locations far away from main streams enabled them to survive erosional forces better than the surrounding rock. The most famous of these

Old stone walls are a common sight in the woods of New Hampshire.

Mount Monadnock. Photograph by Curtis Carroll.

Island hills is, of course, Mount Monadnock, the imperial example that gives the region its name. ("Monadnock" is now the term that is used by geologists for any such isolated remnant mountain.)

Mount Monadnock is like a kindly grandfather watching over the hills, villages, and towns in his broad shadow with an ever-vigilant eye. It is impossible to drive for any distance in the region without glimpsing Monadnock. Its craggy peak and long northern ridge rise over the forest on the opposite shore of Dublin Lake, poking above the ring of hills encircling the ancient glacial valley of Keene. You can see Monadnock etched like a slate blue-gray pyramid on the sky as you round the curve beyond Temple Mountain in Peterborough Gap on Route 101, and descend into the Contoocook River Valley.

The bedrock foundation of the ancient hills of this region is made up of metamorphosed rock that is the result of uplifting and folding from the pressurized forces deep within the earth that began more than two million years ago. This was followed by another period in which the land rose and was sculpted by vast sheets of ice advancing and retreating from the north. Meltwater streams carried away thousands of cubic feet of rock material, sand, clay, and silt, while boulders gathered up by the moving ice were strewn nearly everywhere. Geologists refer to such boulders as "glacial erratics."

The springs, swamps, bogs, lakes, and ponds were also the result of the glaciers' handiwork, making the region an ideal summer va-cationland with opportunities to canoe, camp, pick blueberries, bi-cycle, fish, ride horseback, hunt, picnic, or visit a covered bridge, a small museum, or annual and seasonal fairs and events. Despite its location—only 30 miles west of the urban sprawl of southern New Hampshire—the Monadnock region remains largely unspoiled, and it is a premiere area for wildlife. Moose, bear, deer, fox, fisher, coyote, and bobcat can all be seen here.

Hiking Trails of the Region

A number of the day hikes in this book are located on well-known footpaths that traverse the region. The Metacomet-Monadnock (M-M) Trail begins in southern Massachusetts near the Connecticut state line, and continues along the traprock ridge bordering the Con-necticut River, over Mount Tom, the Holyoke Range, and the North-field Hills in Massachusetts before entering New Hampshire at the wooded town of Richmond. The M-M Trail crosses New Hampshire Route 119 to continue northward on old roads, then ascends Little Monadnock Mountain and Gap Mountain before terminating on the summit of Mount Monadnock.

Mount Watatic in Ashburnham, Massachusetts, marks the be-ginning of the Wapack Trail, the oldest interstate hiking trail in the Northeast. Originally used to drive cattle from Massachusetts to the then-pastured slopes of the Wapack Range, the footpath was blazed out in the 1920s and follows a long ridge along the eastern edge of the Monadnock Region. For many years the trail was neglected but has enjoyed revived popularity, thanks in large part to the Friends of the Wapack, volunteers who maintain, blaze (with yellow trian-gles), and clear the trail of blowdowns and brush. From the sum-mit of Mount Watatic, the trail descends northwest past abandoned ski slopes and into the Watatic Wildlife refuge area. The trail enters New Hampshire and continues its 20-mile-long bumpy journey past stonewalls deep in the woods, old cellar holes, woods roads, abandoned pastures, and beaver ponds.

The Wapack Trail moves along a skyline route over the open summit ledges of New Ipswich and Barrett Mountains, with a detour to Kidder Mountain, and Temple Mountains. Boston is visible from some points along the ridge, with side views of farms, fields, and the forested Souhegan, Nashua, and Contoocook River Valleys along the way. The trail ascends Pack Monadnock and terminates on Old Mountain Road beyond the north slope of North Pack Monadnock Mountain in Greenfield. There are numerous entry points on the Wapack Trail, for it crosses several roads. A good portion of the footpath passes through privately-owned land. Camping is available nearby at the Windblown Ski Touring area on Route 124 in New Ipswich (To make reservations, call 603-878-2869).

The Monadnock-Sunapee Greenway is a 49-mile hiking trail linking Mount Monadnock with Mount Sunapee in Newbury, New Hampshire. Blazed in white markings and developed by the AMC and the Society for the Protection of New Hampshire Forests, the route begins at the summit of Mount Monadnock on the Dublin Trail and continues north, following abandoned roads, pastures, and wilderness trails through small towns, open hardwoods, towering pine, and hemlock forests, state parks, and the Monadnock Highlands (Pitcher Mountain) that divide the Connecticut and Merrimack River drainages.

The majority of the corridor crosses privately-owned land, and it is protected by conservation easements between the Forest Society and more than 80 private landowners who have worked with the Forest Society's Land Protection Department, as well as through the statewide Land Conservation Investment Program (LCIP). The Monadnock-Sunapee Greenway Trail Club coordinates the Greenway's maintenance. All three of these trails lend themselves well to extended hikes, and provide excellent opportunities for day hikes because they cross numerous access points along the way.

Mount Monadnock

Mount Monadnock is the crown jewel of the region and can be approached from four different towns: Jaffrey, Dublin, Marlborough, and Troy. Monadnock State Park in Jaffrey (603-532-8862) comprises more than 5,000 acres, with the Park Headquarters located on the southeast hip of the mountain. There is a $3 service charge per adult; $1 for 6 to 11 year olds, with camping year round, and no pets are allowed. There are five major trails that lead to the summit and nearly two dozen connecting trails (totaling 40 miles of trails) that make it easy to climb the mountain without using the same route twice. The most popular sites to begin hikes are on the Old Toll Road and the State Park Headquarters, which offers the most variety of loops. The Marlboro Trail begins off Shaker Farm Road South, 2.1 miles west of the Old Toll Road trailhead. The Pumpelly Trail begins off Lake Road; the Dublin Trail begins off Old Troy Road, located off Lake Road.

The most popular trails—White Dot and White Cross, approximately 2 miles each—are also the most direct. The White Dot begins near the Warden's office in the state park. The White Cross branches off the White Dot Trail at Falcon Spring (the Spring), then joins the White Dot Trail well above the timberline about 0.25 mile from the summit. The Old Toll Road leads 1.2 miles to a large clearing where the Halfway House Hotel burned down in 1954. Several connecting trails lead from the clearing to subpeaks and the summit. You can have more of a "wilderness experience" by hiking many of the rarely-used trails. Excursions should start at the visitor's center in the park headquarters (open mid-April to Veteran's Day), where you will find a model of the mountain, displays of history, flora, and fauna. Trail maps are available along with a skyline panorama map—a useful tool for identifying towns, lakes, and other mountains from the summit. A fixed compass is painted on the summit, and a ranger is often stationed on the mountaintop to provide interpretative information, on Saturday and Sunday, from late May to late October.

On a clear day it is possible to identify the Atlantic Ocean and points in all six New England states and New York. The Society for the Protection of New Hampshire Forests (SPNHF) owns the largest portion of the mountain, with State of New Hampshire and town

Enjoying the view atop Mount Monadnock.

of Jaffrey owning the remaining tracts. (In 1884 the town of Jaffrey, which was the first to protect land on the mountain, located the heirs of Reverend Laban Ainsworth—Jaffrey's first minister who bought 200 acres including the summit—and persuaded them to deed the land back to the town.)

The area is administered by the State of New Hampshire, Division of Parks and Recreation, by lease arrangements. The park was designated a National Natural Landmark in 1987. The Park Headquarters area is located off Route 124 In Jaffrey, providing camping (28 sites), picnic area, visitor's center, toilet facilities, and parking. For reservations, call 603-271-3628. Plowed parking is provided for winter hiking and cross-country skiing (12 miles of trails). Winter camping is permitted, but the campground road is not plowed. The park manager is present on a full-time basis throughout the winter, and the park is staffed for visitors on weekends and holidays. Mount Monadnock hosts approximately 100,000 visitors every year, making it one of the most climbed mountains in the world. Columbus Day weekend is the most popular three-day period at the mountain.

STARTER HIKES

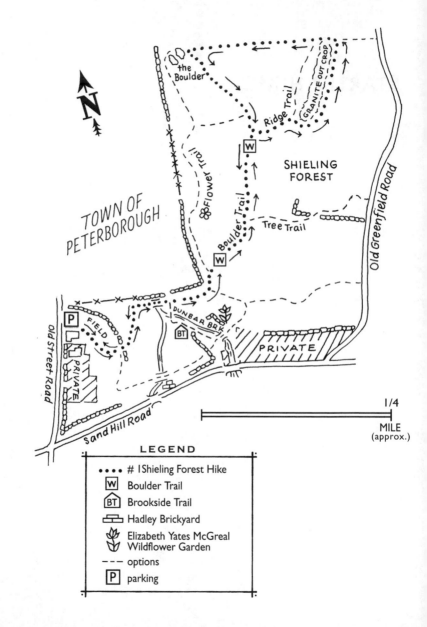

the Boulder

Ridge Trail

GRANITE OUT CROP

SHIELING FOREST

Flower Trail

Boulder Trail

Tree Trail

TOWN OF PETERBOROUGH

W

W

P

FIELD

PRIVATE

DUNBAR BRK

BT

PRIVATE

Old Greenfield Road

Old Street Road

Sand Hill Road

N

1/4

MILE
(approx.)

LEGEND

• • • • # 1 Shieling Forest Hike

W Boulder Trail

BT Brookside Trail

Hadley Brickyard

Elizabeth Yates McGreal
Wildflower Garden

— — — options

P parking

1

Shieling Forest

Rating: An easy walk on a well-marked loop trail that leads to a glacial erratic, with side paths to a wildflower garden and a tree-identification trail. An excellent introductory hike for young children.

Distance: 1.5 miles

Hiking Time: 1.5 hours

Lowest Elevation: 760 feet

Highest Elevation: 860 feet

USGS Map: Peterborough North

Other Maps: New Hampshire Department of Resources and Economic Development map; Peterborough Conservation Commission Trail Guide

Trailhead: Peterborough, New Hampshire

The Shieling Forest is a pleasure to hike any time of the year, for each season bringing its own subtle beauty. With its behemoth Ice-Age boulders, stream-side wildflower garden, and easy walking trails that carry the hiker past a variety of plant and wildlife habitats, it is an ideal place for young families to cut their hiking teeth. Although it is not a state park (Shieling Forest is maintained by the New Hampshire Division of Forests and Lands), it does have limited picnic facilities, and "well-mannered" dogs (on a leash) are welcomed. There are also opportunities for showshoeing and cross-country skiing. For information about Shieling Forest, call 603-431-6774. Trails and forest are open seven days a week, dawn to dusk.

A network of over 2 miles of self-guided trails winds through 48 acres of forested ridges and valleys that were donated to the state in 1980 by the late Elizabeth Yates McGreal. This long-time resident of Peterborough was a conservationist, historian, and celebrated writer best known for her Newbery Award-winning children's book *Amos Fortune, Free Man*, about a freed slave who lived in Jaffrey.

Mrs. McGreal also established a trust fund to help defray the maintenance and operation costs of the property, which includes her former renovated 1789 house, office headquarters building, and Forestry Learning Center. A large map in a glassed-in bulletin board outside the Center building details the forest pathways, and a mailbox contains copies of the trail guide/map. The Forest Learning Center includes an exhibit area and library, and presents a variety of workshops, from pruning to basic orienteering, as well as tree- and wildflower-identification.

Access: The trail can be reached by taking Route 101 West from Milford. Three miles west of Miller State Park, turn right onto Old Street Road. Use caution because it is a sharp downhill turn. Continue 1.7 miles to a stop sign (Sand Hill Road). Continue straight for another 0.2 mile.

Description: Begin by heading east across a small field in the direction of an unusual tree for a New Hampshire setting: a white mulberry tree. Although the Chinese import looks out of place among its hardwood and evergreen counterparts, it has adapted quite well to its environs, and in late July produces a crop of creamy white berries that are a favorite with the birds. After stepping through a gap in a stone wall and descending a set of brick stairs, you'll walk down a steep bank through a red pine forest devoid of a plant understory— pine is not shade-tolerant so it tends to grow dense.

White paint marks on the trees identify the way and signposts point out the various trails. At the bottom of the hill the trail crosses Dunbar Brook on a wooden footbridge. Beyond the brook, the Boulder Trail continues straight ahead (east), but before you continue, take some time to visit the Elizabeth Yates McGreal wildflower garden (along the Brookside Trail) and Hadley brickyard.

You can get to both of these points of interest by crossing a second footbridge to the right and south. The Brookside Trail leads to the spectacular McGreal wildflower garden maintained by the Peterborough Garden Club. Almost 100 varieties of wildflowers, shrubs, ferns, trees, mosses, and groundcovers can be viewed here, including trillium, Solomon's seal, hepatica, and wild sarsaparilla, but also the more unusual spice bush and swamp azalea. But sure to stay on the mulched pathways as this is a delicate area. Markers identify the plants, and stream-side picnic tables and benches are provided for relaxation.

Brickyard Road leads south to the site of the former Hadley family brickyard at the edge of a large planting of red pine. Brickmaking was once a prominent industry in Peterborough. According to town histories, all but one house built in the town between the years 1800 to 1870 were fashioned from bricks made locally. (Peterborough used to be known as "Brick City.") If you look closely along the banks of the stream, you can detect pieces of red brick shimmering through the clear water.

Return to the footbridges and continue on the trail to the boulder that rises gradually past a picnic area and stand of white pines nearly 100 feet tall. In the colonial period, trees such as these were valued for their use in the making of masts for the British royal navy. At one time, 400-year-old Eastern White Pines grew as high as 200 feet and reached up to 10 feet in diameter. A three-striped "broad arrow" mark hewn by an axe was used to reserve the giant trees for the king, and tampering with the conifers resulted in fines and floggings.

Just beyond the pines you'll pass the Flower Trail junction on the left. The Boulder Trail continues through a stand of old sugar maples. Once a productive sugar operation, many of the trees were destroyed in the Hurricane of 1938. Shortly, the Tree Trail (a 10-minute walk which identifies several hardwoods species by small signs) enters to the right. The white-blazed Boulder Trail continues through a magnificent grove of Eastern hemlocks. Hemlocks make excellent screening, serving as a windbreak to provide protection, travel lanes, and food for wildlife. The cones of the hemlock are among the smallest of all tree cones, about .75 inch long, maturing in one year and falling in the spring to provide feed for squirrels who feast on the seeds. Arched by dollops of newly fallen snow or spread like feather dusters, the short, dense needle-branches of these trees are a treat to experience any time of the year.

"The Boulder," Shieling Forest, Peterborough.

Just past the hemlocks, turn right onto the Ridge Trail, which carries you through a beautiful open beech forest and a large granite outcrop that was once the site of a quarry. On closer inspection, you can see that some of the blocks of granite have drill holes. Near the outcrop, look for an interesting dead red oak tree sliced by a grooved lightning scar running up its entire side.

After 0.15 mile you will reach a junction. Turn left to follow the trail that parallels a stone wall. After 300 yards you will come to the boulder. This stupendous erratic was transported here by the retreating glaciers from the Mount Ascutney area in Vermont 18,000 years ago. Centuries of weathering and frost action have resulted in splitting the huge rock in two. At least 30 feet high and equally as long, it attracts young and "young at heart" climbers who may wish to spend time exploring the bumps and crevices of these giants before turning left to follow the Boulder Trail back.

Sightseeing: If you have time, you may want to visit the Wheeler Trail on 45 acres of town conservation land in Peterborough. The

0.62-mile long white-blazed trail follows a meandering stream and loops back to a starting point. A side trail leads to a pond. The parking area and trail sign are located on Route 101, at 0.2 mile downhill from the Route 123 turnoff to Sharon.

Consider a visit to the Casalis State Forest, which comprises 230 acres of forests, trails, ponds, and streams. Birdwatchers can observe waterfowl, flycatchers, wood duck, Virginia Rail, eastern wood duck, pewee, and common yellow throat. Beyond the pond are ample opportunities for exploration on old roads. Casalis State Forest is located on Route 123 1 mile south of the Route 101/123 junction. Look for a sign and parking area on the left side of the road. For information, call 603-464-3453.

Also nearby is the 175-acre Fremont Conservation Land, a 2-mile, out-and-back trail that will take you through an open field and forest, and an enormous glacial erratic, "the Rock." To reach the trailhead from the junction of Routes 101 and 202, travel south on Route 202 for 0.9 mile then turn right onto Old Jaffrey Road, across from Noone Falls. The trailhead is 0.5 mile on the right. Map and trail guide are available in the mailbox near the parking area.

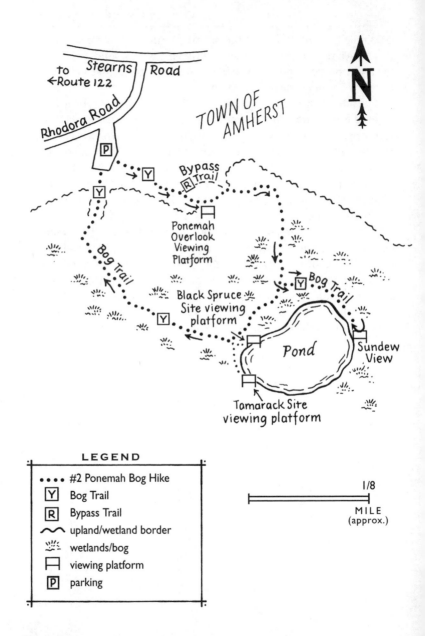

to
←Route 122

Stearns Road

Rhodora Road

TOWN OF AMHERST

N

P

Y

Bypass Trail
R

Y

Bog Trail

Ponemah Overlook Viewing Platform

Y Bog Trail

Black Spruce Site viewing platform

Y

Pond

Sundew View

Tamarack Site viewing platform

LEGEND

•••• #2 Ponemah Bog Hike
Y Bog Trail
R Bypass Trail
‿ upland/wetland border
⸰⸰⸰ wetlands/bog
⊟ viewing platform
P parking

1/8

MILE
(approx.)

2

Ponemah Bog

Rating: An easy boardwalk stroll over the quaking mat of a kettle-hole bog that is home to leatherleaf, cotton grass, pitcher plants, sundews, and other curious insect-eating plants.
Distance: 0.75 mile
Hiking Time: 0.5 hour
Pond Elevation: 210 feet
USGS Map: South Merrimack
Other Maps: Audubon Society of New Hampshire Field Guide map
Trailhead: Amherst, New Hampshire

Ponemah Bog is operated by the Audubon Society of New Hampshire and is open year-round from dawn to dusk, with no charge to visit the bog. The entire 0.75-mile trail (including the pond loop) takes only half an hour to complete, but you will want to spend extra time exploring the wealth of curious plants and savoring the solitude of the otherworld of the bog.

Like all kettle-hole bogs, the Ponemah Bog will one day complete the natural pond succession to become dry land. The encircling mat of sphagnum moss will inexorably squeeze in on the three acres of open water where partial decay and burial will convert it to peat. In time, trees and shrubs will gain a foothold on the organic foundation to wipe away all evidence that a glacial lake ever existed here. But the good news is that you have more than a few centuries to visit before all this takes place.

Ponemah Bog is a legacy of the Ice Age. About 13,000 years ago, when the last glaciers retreated north, huge blocks of ice were left embedded in the ground. As the climate warmed and the frozen chunks melted, the earth caved in to form steeply-sloped depressions known as kettle-hole ponds. At Ponemah you'll find these examples of the special vegetation able to adapt to this nutrient-poor habitat: the pitcher plants, sundew, and bladderwort (all of which

Ponemah Bog, Amherst.

feast on insects), bog laurel, sphagnum moss, rhodora, tufted bog cotton, leather-leaf, and waterwillow.

Ponemah is a special place to visit in late spring when the vegetation is in full bloom. While one area may bloom earlier than another, you'll see a riot of pinks, yellows, lavenders, and bright whites. In the fall, blueberry bushes and red maples provide vibrant color. The bog is also special in winter when russet-colored blankets of leatherleaf sprawl across the marsh and the moss freezes into delicate white filigrees like icing on a wedding cake. In winter, you can look for interesting plant patterns frozen beneath the surface that look like flowers encased in a glass paperweight. You'll see sphagnum moss spreading like a spongy pale green blanket, or massed in yellow and maroon mounds along the shoreline. Melting crystals of ice glitter like jewels between the dense hummocks of grass. Listen to the delicate crinkling of ice melting as the sun climbs higher in the afternoon sky. As you approach the pond loop, tamarack and black spruce stand naked in black silhouettes against the sky and the pond surface sparkles in the late afternoon sun like a fire. The bog appears lifeless, but there are frogs, insects, and turtles resting beneath the frozen surface or hidden in crevices.

Access: Ponemah Bog is located in Amherst, New Hampshire. To get there from the Manchester area, take Route 101 west to Milford and take the Route 101A Exit. Continue on Route 101A east for 0.7 mile to the Route 122 junction. Turn left onto Route 122 north and take an immediate right onto Stearns Road. Continue on Stearns Road for 1.1 miles to Rhodora Road (right), which turns into a dirt road after a short distance. Park near a trailhead sign.

Description: The yellow-blazed trail begins at the parking area on the high ground of an upland forest. The familiar birch, maple, and oak grow here but so too does pitch pine—a three-needled conifer with deeply furrowed bark more common to sandier southern soils of New England. Pitch pine produces closed cones that remain on the trees for years.

Be sure to keep an eye out for chickadees, jays, titmice, a variety of sparrows, thrushes, and other birds. You're likely to hear the persistent tapping of a woodpecker or you may spy a raptor searching the landscape for unsuspecting rodents. At first it may sound like you are on a neighborhood stroll as voices from children playing in the back yard of a nearby residence drift toward you from the edge of the woods. The aroma of sweet fern scents the air, and in the spring, ferns curled up like fiddleheads and the membranous pink globes of lady slipper poke up from the wet ground at the edge of the trail. Ponemah Bog has quite a collection of native orchids, including whorled pogonia, ladyslippers, and liparis. There are 35 native species of wild orchids in New Hampshire.

Shortly, the trail branches to the right to lead to an observation platform. This perch allows a good view of the subtle colors of the low brush and tawny grasses stretching to the open water in the distance. Looking out at this sparse expanse of stunted trees and shrubs, it is hard to imagine that this was once a 100-acre lake. Return to the main trail. Soon you'll walk by a marsh that bursts with clouds of pink Rhodora in May. Rhodora is especially showy because its flowers appear before its leaves unfold.

You will step onto a boardwalk as you approach the vast expanse of the bog mat. Here you will find wiry-stemmed leatherleaf, also called Cassandra, a low shrub with tough leathery leaves and white bell-like flowers hanging in lines of a dozen or more underneath its stem in the spring. In June, you will see bog laurel that displays a pink cup-like flower. As you continue on the boardwalk, swampcandle and white tufts of bog cotton show themselves among the floating web of sedge and moss that is thick enough to allow shrubs and birch, pitch pine, and other trees to take root.

A few minutes later, the open water of the bog appears in the distance. You may want to reach over to squeeze a spongy mass of pale green sphagnum moss. Some species of this moss can absorb well over 10 times its own weight in water. Sphagnum was dried and used as a diaper material by the Native Americans and as a surgical dressing during World War I. Sometime in the 1940s, the bog was used to harvest peat moss, which develops from sphagnum. Peat was cut with a shovel and hauled to a drying shed, where it was ground and then shipped to greenhouses to be used for the propagation, growing, and shipping of plants.

Turn left at a junction as you approach the pond. You'll notice a distinct spring to the wooden planks as the thickness of the mat tapers toward the edge of the pond. Follow the boardwalk to an observation platform. Look for grass pink, a showy pink-flowered member of the orchid family, and the unusual insect-eating plants that are much smaller than their *Little Shop of Horrors* reputations. The showstealer has to be the remarkable pitcher plant. The delicate paper-thin green- and red-veined leaves of this vessel-like plant secrete a fragrant syrup that insects can't resist. Once an insect is caught, the slippery hairs around the lip of the leaves, like the withes of a lobster trap, hasten the victim's trip downward. Digestive juices do the rest.

You will have to bend down to see the red sundew plant, which resembles a tiny burdock. Lured by the false "dew" on its round leaves, the insect is wrapped by small hairs and then digested by the plant enzymes. Another insectivorous plant grows here—the slender yellow bladderwort whose flowers resemble snapdragons.

Ferns, leatherleaf, bog laurel, and bog rosemary present a visual treat of contrasting summer greens. Yellow pond lilies bob on the rippling surface of the water. Also thriving in these boggy conditions are the feathery tamarack (American larch), red maple, and black spruce, a small tree with dark cones and thin, grayish, scaly bark. The cones of the black spruce may remain on the tree for decades. The only conifer to shed its needles each fall, tamarack does not reach great heights growing through the wet moss of the bog. Its long tough roots were used by the Native Americans to sew together their birch-bark canoes. Return to the junction and continue on the boardwalk to the other viewing platforms. Toward the end of the pond loop, the boardwalk continues through brush before taller conifers signal you are approaching higher ground and the end of the trail. Several minutes later you'll find yourself back at the parking area.

Sightseeing: After your hike you may want to visit the town of Amherst, with its colonial-period houses and village center that is listed on the National Register of Historic Places. Once a shire town and a main stop for the old Boston stagecoach, Amherst was also the site of New Hampshire State government for a short time, sharing that honor only with Concord and Exeter. The old brick Courthouse (built in 1823), a simple Georgian structure that today serves as the town hall, was once the scene of much judicial activity when Amherst was the shire town of Hillsborough County. It sits to the east of the pear-shaped Common and immediately behind it is an old cemetery. On the Common remains a somber reminder of the past—a large square stone or granite "whipping block" with a sinister iron ring attached to the top of it.

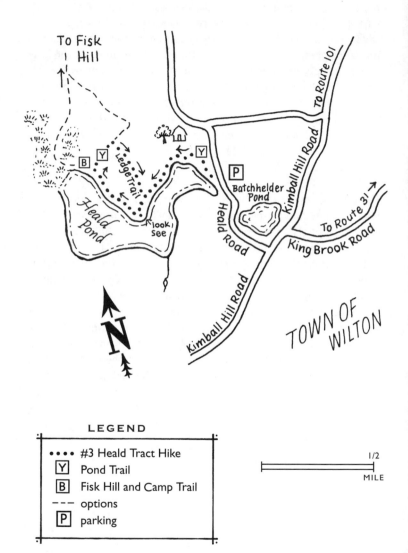

To Fisk Hill

To Route 101

Ledge Trail

To Route 31

Heald Pond

look see

Batchhelder Pond

Heald Road

Kimball Hill Road

King Brook Road

Kimball Hill Road

TOWN OF WILTON

N

LEGEND

•••• #3 Heald Tract Hike
Y Pond Trail
B Fisk Hill and Camp Trail
- - - options
P parking

1/2
MILE

3
The Heald Tract

Rating: An easy forested walk past a variety of wildlife habitats
    along the edge of a flood-control wildlife pond.
Distance: 2 miles
Hiking Time: 1 hour
Pond Elevation: 835 feet
USGS Map: Greenville
Other Maps: Heald Tract map; town of Wilton recreational trail
    map
Trailhead: Wilton, New Hampshire

This summitless hike features meadows, wetlands, old cellar holes,
ponds, orchards, wildlife habitats, an abandoned farmstead, blue
heron rookery, and a magnificent airy grove of beech trees. Located
on the Wilton-Temple town line, the Heald Tract is a preserve of the
Society for the Protection of New Hampshire Forests (SPNHF). Donated in 1986 by the Heald Trust, the property has grown to 1,024
acres and encompasses 10 miles of footpaths and trails for passive
recreation and nature learning opportunities.

    The centerpiece of the Heald Tract is a 69-acre wildlife pond, the
result of a food control and watershed protection project completed
in 1964. The pond here is the haunt of many species of waterfowl
during the seasonal migration periods. Waterproof footwear is advisable as the trail is sometimes wet. Canoeing and boating are not
allowed, but foot trails lead to fishing areas. The Heald Tract is open
year-round. For information, call 603-224-9945.

Access: To reach the trailhead, take Route 101 west to Route 31 south
in Wilton. Continue on Route 31 south toward Greenville for 2.5 miles.
Turn right onto King Brook Road, a pleasant uphill drive of 0.9 mile
that winds alongside a tumbling brook bordered by feathery hemlocks. At the road's end, turn left onto Kimball Hill Road. Continue

uphill for 0.1 mile, and turn right at a big red barn onto Heald Road. Drive 0.3 mile past a Heald Tract Forest Society sign and park at the second pull-off on the right. This area is rich in mountain laurel, an evergreen shrub with spectacular white and purple clustered flowers that blooms from early June to early July. You can see mountain laurel along Route 31 from Wilton to Greenville and south to the Massachusetts border, as well as along Route 123 through Mason and Route 101 from Milford to Peterborough.

Description: The 2-mile long Pond Trail, blazed in yellow, begins opposite the parking area. After moving through a stand of white pine with an impressive understory of mountain laurel, the trail follows the north shore of the pond for nearly 1 mile. Sedges, reeds, and the spikes of cattail grow here in the shallow water. You will also see partridgeberry, leatherleaf, arrowwood, Canada lily, and polypody ferns before the trail widens as it moves through a grove of hemlock. In August, the New York ironweed displays its brilliant hairlike clusters of lavender flowers on the bank near the dam site and flood control monument. Ironweed gets its name from the rigidity of the stem.

A long, sloping stone wall rambles along a hillside. It is believed that these walls were originally built to mark the boundaries of once-open fields and pasture, now overgrown by woods. Just beyond a huge, gnarled white pine, the trail moves through an open field, then swings down to a pond. Near an abandoned beaver lodge, purple pickerel weed and jewelweed brighten the water's edge. Jewelweed has particular value for hikers because its tiny pendant-like orange flowers can be rubbed on the skin as an emergency antidote to poison ivy. Coincidentally, jewelweed often grows near poison ivy.

Just ahead, the trail emerges at a clearing. To the right, two old deteriorating barns sit on the slope of a hillside orchard. In late May, viola and wild strawberry grow in the marshy area near the pond here. In late summer, you'll find the soft, bristled, purple flowers of the Joe Pye weed (*Eupatorium purpureum*) that are especially attractive to butterflies. According to folklore, Joe Pye was an Native American medicine man who lived in colonial Massachusetts and used the

Heald Pond, Heald Tract, Wilton.

plant to cure typhus fever. Colonial settlers named this plant ague weed, Indian sage, gravel root, and kidney-root (the last because it was said to dissolve kidney stones).

The trail re-enters the woods and moves past a shoreline boulder outlook where you can sit and contemplate the rippling waters, the delicate yellow blossoms of water lilies, and the twittering chorus of insects and birds. As you continue on the trail, look for club moss blanketing the forest floor with its tiny brown cone-like spore cases and erect, branching stems. Club moss is also known by other names, such as crow foot, wolf's claw, standing spruce, and ground pine. In the United States there are about 50 types of club mosses, which are not true mosses but rather primitive vascular plants. Because of their extreme resistance to water, club moss spores, in powder form, are used not only as a coating for pharmaceutical pills to keep them from sticking to each other when placed together but also to disguise their taste. Quite flammable, the spores were also used before the advent of electricity to produce special effects in theaters and in fireworks. Although it is hard to imagine from its low height, the ancestors of this 6-inch evergreen plant once grew to heights of 100 feet in primeval swamps. Today, coal is produced from the remains of such swamps, and many states have laws protecting this important ground cover. The club moss has a creeping stem running beneath dead leaves that prevents soil from being washed away.

Shortly you will come to the Pond Trail/Ledge Trail junction. (The Ledge Trail is your return route.) Approximately 100 yards from this junction you will see a double blaze. Head left to take a short detour to an overlook at the edge of the pond, a perfect spot to enjoy lunch and the solitude of your surroundings. There's a good chance you will see a wood duck or blue heron, or hear the hammering of a pileated woodpecker as it seeks insect larvae in the bark of dying trees. After a rest, return to the (yellow) Pond trail to follow the shoreline with its broken stumps and grasses.

The trail parallels a stone wall. After moving past a high, abandoned beaver lodge, in a few minutes you will come to a junction with the blue-blazed Fisk Hill Trail. Continue on the yellow Pond Trail, moving uphill to the right and east. A three-minute walk will bring you to the ledge cut-off on the right. This 10-minute walk takes you past hemlock, an airy grove of beech trees, and scalloped ledges, and brings you back to the Pond Trail junction. Turn left to retrace your steps back to the parking area.

Optional Extensions: If you have time, take the 3-mile Fisk Hill and Camp Trail, blazed in blue. This 2-hour walk will lead you on an adventure over the slopes of Fisk Hill, then on to an orchard with a great view of the Lyndeborough Mountains, Joe English Hill, the Uncanoonucs, and Crotched Mountain to the north. The trail continues northerly and goes down into the woods past a beaver pond with a blue heron rookery, where nests sit atop dead trees. The trail moves onto a camp lot and 3-acre pond held back by a cut-stone dam, past a series of cellar holes off an old road, magnificent open beech woods, an orchard, and briefly along the shoreline of Batchelder Pond, before ending at Heald Road near the parking area.

Another hike, the yellow-blazed Pratt Pond Trail, features stone railway culverts, waterfalls, and the remains of the stone foundation of an old potato-starch mill. Years ago starch from potatoes was used for sizing (smoothing and stiffening) cotton cloth and for thickening puddings and sauces.

This 5-mile route begins off Kimball Hill Road (0.7 mile from the junction with Heald Road) near an old cellar hole. The trail moves onto the bridge at Route 31, crosses the Souhegan River, and continues through the 1,000-acre Russell Abbott State Forest to Pratt Pond. The foundation remains of the old starch mill are located on Starch Mill Brook, which flows from Pratt Pond in Mason, New Hampshire.

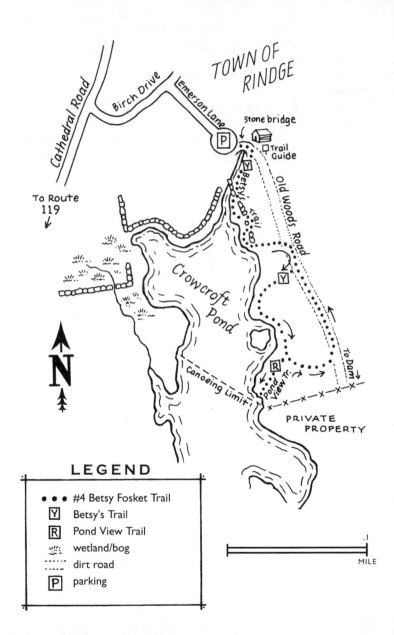

Cathedral Road

Birch Drive

Emerson Lane

TOWN OF RINDGE

Stone bridge

Trail Guide

To Route 119

Betsy's Trail

Old Woods Road

Crowcroft Pond

Canoeing Limit

Pond View Tr.

To Dam

PRIVATE PROPERTY

N

LEGEND

● ● ● #4 Betsy Fosket Trail

Ⓨ Betsy's Trail

Ⓡ Pond View Trail

wetland/bog

dirt road

Ⓟ parking

.1

MILE

4
Betsy Fosket Sanctuary

Rating: A short, easy walk along the edge of a pond past hemlock
and tall white pines, with an opportunity to see a variety of
birds, wildflowers, and wildlife.
Distance: 0.6 mile
Hiking Time: 45 minutes
Pond Elevation: 1,170 feet
USGS Map: Peterborough South
Other Map: Audubon Society of New Hampshire Field Guide
map
Trailhead: Rindge, New Hampshire

The trailhead for the Betsy Fosket Sanctuary of the Audubon Society
of New Hampshire is located at the end of Emerson Lane—a residen-
tial area of contemporary homes, manicured lawns, and driveways. It
is an unlikely start for a nature hike, for at first you may feel you are
going out for a neighborhood stroll. But soon after crossing a stone
bridge and entering the woods, all vestiges of civilization are quickly
left behind as hemlocks, tall white pines, birds, wildflowers, and a
pond appear. If you are lucky you may spy an otter, mink, or red fox,
or discover bottled gentians hiding away in lush vegetation along
the trail. The Audubon Field Guide notes that bottled gentians grow
along the trail from August through October. The gentian is easy to
recognize but hard to find. The leaves grow in pairs on opposite sides
of the lower stem but are whorled near the top. Looking very much
like little narrow blue barrels pinched off at each end, the clusters
of 1- to 2-inch blue flowers must be sought out in their own special
haunt—the moist ground of wet roadside banks.

On moist summer days, you can see a variety of fungi sprouting
from the forest floor, and Indian Pipe, a small perennial plant often
found in dark hemlock because it uses fungi instead of sunlight to
make its food.

Crowcroft Pond, Betsy Fosket Sanctuary.

Access: The 35-acre, heavily-wooded Betsy Fosket Wildlife Sanctuary is located at the northeast corner of Crowcroft Pond in Rindge, New Hampshire. From the junction of Routes 202 and 119 in Rindge, go east 1.5 miles on Route 119 to a yellow blinking light and then left on Cathedral Road. After 0.5 mile, at the Cathedral Estates sign, turn right onto Birch Drive. Continue 0.3 mile and turn right on Emerson Lane. Park in a cul-de-sac at 0.1 mile.

Description: After crossing a stone bridge, you will notice a log-cabin home at the end of a driveway. Look right for the yellow-blazed "Betsy's Trail" just beyond the brown Audubon Society of New Hampshire sign and mailbox, where you can pick up a trail guide. Large hemlock trees immediately curtain off the outside world to create a palpable sense of peace and quiet. After briefly moving downhill and following the small stream that flows from Emerson Pond, you will step through a gap in a stone wall and come to Crowcroft Pond.

The old dam at the outlet of Emerson Pond dates back to the late eighteenth century and has been in ruins for many years. Crowcroft Pond was created when the water of Emerson Pond was diverted through a meadow. In the summer, pickerel weed (*Pontederia cordata*) with its spiky carpet of blue flowers and white water lilies choke the coves and fringes of the pond. Pickerel weed—also called Dogtongue (the Native Americans knew it as *wampee*)—got its name because it can usually be found where pickerels swim and lay their eggs. Common most everywhere in the shallow waters of ponds, pickerel weed is likely to dominate if given the opportunity. Only the cattail seems able to hold its own against it.

There is a good view to the southeast of the pond here. In the distance you may spy canoeists paddling in and out of the quiet coves along the shoreline. Crowcroft Pond is privately owned. Canoeing is allowed, but restricted to the northern third of the pond.

For the next several minutes the trail continues along the shoreline, crossing stone walls several times and winding through groves of hemlock. Chipmunks scurry underfoot and along stonewalls; red squirrels chatter their warning and scold you from their treetop perches. Look for mounds and depressions in the forest floor—evidence of pillowing and cradling here indicating storm-damaged trees. This wavy topography occurs when a tree is blown over and its root system is ripped from the ground. After the tree decays, a "pillow" or mound of dirt adhering to the woody parts of the upward root system is left in place, and a depression or "cradle" remains in the area where it was lifted.

As you continue, look for sphagnum moss growing along the edge of the water. The forest floor is rich in a variety of groundcovers: clintonia, bunchberry, wild sarsaparilla, wood sorrel or wild shamrock, star flower, wild lily-of-the-valley, and partridgeberry or twinberry (the small, round, evergreen leaves are always in pairs, and there are two blossoms). The common name, partridgeberry, is derived from the fact that the berries are eaten by several species of birds, including grouse, quail, and wild turkey. Partridgeberry is a distinctly North American plant. Its nickname, "squaw vine" was coined by colonists who saw Native American women using it. The plant was used to treat menstrual cramps and pain, regulate menstruation and relieve heavy bleeding, and induce childbirth and delivery.

Shortly you'll reach a woods road. Turn right. The trail briefly follows the road, then turns left into the woods to parallel it. A short time later, re-enter the woods to the right. (Your return route, Betsy's Trail, continues left). Step through another gap in a stone wall, and continue along the shoreline for a chance glimpse of a painted turtle sunning itself on a half-submerged log. The trail turns left back into the woods, then moves toward the shoreline again where you will see a small pine tree-topped island that is popular with red-breasted nuthatches, hairy woodpeckers, and black-capped chickadees.

The route continues on an easy walking surface of pine needles to a red-blazed connector trail leading to an outlook beyond a stone wall on the shoreline. Turn left to rejoin the woods road back to complete the loop to the parking lot. At this point you can also turn right (south) to follow the road for 10 minutes to a wood plank footbridge and the dam site that creates Crowcroft Pond. The Audubon Society does not own this property, so be respectful of the property owner.

Sightseeing: If you have time after completing your hike, consider visiting the Cathedral of the Pines. This simple outdoor memorial to the American War dead consists of a stone altar, bell tower, and wooden bench set against spectacular backdrop of Mount Monadnock. To get there, return to Cathedral Road and continue north for one mile. For information, call 603-899-3300 or 866-229-4520; or go to www.cathedralpines.com.

Annett State Park, picnic sites, and walking trails with a 0.25 mile trail leading to Black Reservoir within 1,494 acres of woodland, is 1 mile north of the Cathedral of the Pines. Pets are allowed. For more information, call 603-271-3556.

Another point of interest, the 1796 Second Rindge Meetinghouse, is located in Rindge Center. It is one of the largest buildings of this type in northern New England, and one of the few remaining meeting houses still used as a town building and church. To get there, return to the blinking yellow light on Route 119 and drive 0.5 mile up Payson Hill Road.

The Stearns-Lamont Forest is also nearby. To get there from the blinking yellow light, drive west on Route 119 for 1 mile. The 123-acre forest is located on the left; enter the forest at a gate near the small pond.

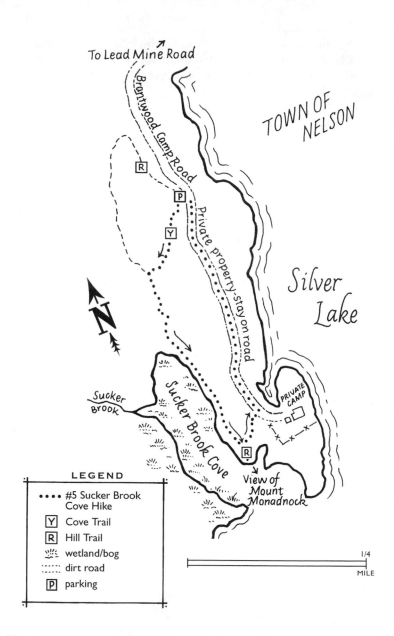

To Lead Mine Road

Brantwood Camp Road

TOWN OF NELSON

R

P

Y

Private property - stay on road

N

Silver Lake

Sucker Brook

Sucker Brook Cove

PRIVATE CAMP

R

View of Mount Monadnock

LEGEND

• • • • #5 Sucker Brook Cove Hike

Y Cove Trail

R Hill Trail

⚘ wetland/bog

⋯ dirt road

P parking

1/4

MILE

5
Sucker Brook Cove, Silver Lake

Rating: An easy woodland walk that leads to a boulder perch with
   an outstanding view of Mount Monadnock across Silver Lake.
Distance: 0.75 mile
Hiking Time: 45 minutes
Pond Elevation: 1,319 feet
USGS Map: Marlborough
Trailhead: Nelson, New Hampshire

Mount Monadnock is a spectacular sight from any direction, but especially when seen rising above Silver Lake. You can take in this sight
by walking on an easy woodland trail to a boulder perch at the Audubon Society of New Hampshire's Sucker Brook Cove Wildlife Sanctuary at Silver Lake in Nelson.

Access: To get to the trailhead from the Manchester area, take Route
101 to Dublin. Just beyond the red buildings of Yankee Publishing, the
white-steepled community church, and the Dublin Fire Department,
turn right onto Dublin (New Harrisville) Road and continue 8 miles
to Nelson Center. (Notice, when you first start out on Dublin Road,
the great views to the south and east of the Wapack Range, Crotched
Mountain, Skatutakee, and Thumb Mountains). In Nelson Center go
south on Leadmine Road. After 0.3 mile, just beyond a cemetery, bear
right. Continue 0.6 mile to the private dirt access road for Brantwood
Camp (left). Continue 0.9 mile (the road is rough) past camp buildings to a small parking area.

Description: Beginning at the parking area, the yellow-blazed Cove
Trail leads uphill and south through a mixed understory of hobble-
bush. Bristly club mosses push up from the matted duff of the forest
floor. In summer, one inhabitant of the moist woodland is the para-
sitic, fleshy white Indian pipe (*Monotropa uniflora*) that grows 4 to 8

inches tall with nodding flowers, hanging slightly at an angle to give this odd, specialized plant the general appearance of a Native American peace pipe. It is also called ghost flower, eyebright, fairy-smoke, ice plant ("ice" because it is cold and resembles frozen jelly). It is also called a corpse plant because of its general bluish waxy, dead appearance, and its cool and clammy feel, and its tendency to decompose and turn black when handled.

You will soon come to a yellow-red trail junction. Continue left on the yellow trail downhill past gigantic boulders and into a grove of hemlock. A few minutes later you will get your first glimpse of 333-acre Silver Lake through a tangle of alder bushes. As you skirt the shoreline, the twittering of birds is a reminder that this is a wildlife habitat, and that you are here as a guest of nature. As you continue on the woodland path, look for a decaying log ruffled in fungi, clintonia, shamrock-shaped wood sorrel, and wild sarsaparilla.

After five minutes you will come to another yellow-red trail junction. The yellow trail on the left leads to the road back to the parking area, so turn right to follow the red path for a short distance to a cove with a spectacular view of Mount Monadnock, seven miles to the south. The shoreline boulders provide an excellent vantage spot to sit and enjoy Monadnock and the other sights and quiet sounds of the lake: the waves gently lapping the shore; swallows skimming across the surface of the water in search of insects; bumblebees working the bell-shaped flowers of high blueberry bushes that grow on the rocky shoreline along with Mountain Holly. Mergansers and loons also nest at this lake, and you may see a mallard duck, the most widespread duck in the northern hemisphere. The female mallard (hen) is a drab light brown whereas the male (drake) has an iridescent blue-green head, white neck band, and rust-colored breast. The underside of the male is white and his wings are a dark, smoky color compared to the mottled down feathers of the female. Both the male and the female mallard sport a speculum, a triangular patch of bright blue bordered in white, on their wings.

Sightseeing: You may want to visit the nearby towns of Nelson and Harrisville before or after your hike. Nelson is a handsome village laid out in 1752 and named for British naval hero Admiral Horatio Nelson. It has a beautiful town common, an old brick school house, and town hall reconstructed from an old meetinghouse (built in 1787), which is also used as a contra dance hall. There's also the Olivia Rodman Memorial Library, named for a nationally-known botanist (1845–1920), and a Greek-and-Gothic revival Congregational Church with a two-stage bell tower.

Along the way to Nelson, you may want to stop at Harrisville, designated a National Historic Landmark District, and one of the most beautiful mill villages in New England. With its original brick buildings reflected in the water of Harrisville Pond, Harrisville is a favorite subject of photographers and artists.

EASY HIKES

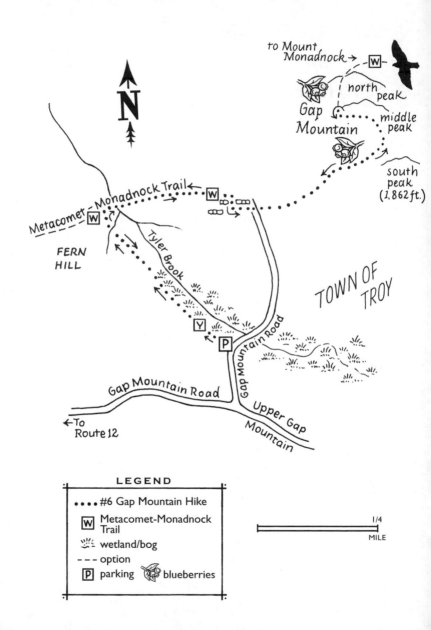

to Mount
Monadnock → W

north peak

Gap
Mountain

middle peak

south peak
(1,862 ft.)

Metacomet–Monadnock Trail ←

W

W

FERN
HILL

Tyler Brook

Y

P

TOWN OF
TROY

Gap Mountain Road

Gap Mountain Road

Upper Gap
Mountain

← To
Route 12

LEGEND

•••• #6 Gap Mountain Hike

W Metacomet-Monadnock
Trail

wetland/bog

- - - option

P parking   blueberries

1/4
MILE

6
Gap Mountain

Rating: An easy hike that follows a section of the Metacomet-
   Monadnock Trail through abandoned pastures, with rewarding
   vistas along the way, and a stunning view of Mount Monadnock
   from the summit.
Distance: 2.6 miles
Hiking Time: 1.5 to 2 hours
Lowest Elevation: 1,260 feet
Highest Elevation: 1,862 feet
USGS Map: Monadnock
Other Maps: New Hampshire State Parks Trail map; AMC
   Metacomet-Monadnock Trail Guide
Trailhead: Troy, New Hampshire

Comprising three low peaks and named for a gap between its southern and middle summits, Gap Mountain beckons the hiker with its
serenity and close-up view of Mount Monadnock. Except for one
rocky stretch, the trail to Gap's middle and northern peaks is mini-
mally demanding. In late summer, blueberries grow abundantly at
the top.

Access: The trail to Gap Mountain can be reached off of Route 12
in Troy, 1.5 miles south of the town common. Look for Gap Mountain Road just beyond the highway's town line marker for Troy-
Fitzwilliam, opposite Bowker Ville Road. After 1.0 mile you will reach
the parking area.

Optional Access: North approach. From Jaffrey drive for 6.2 miles
west on Route 124 to Bullard Road (formerly Old County Road). Continue on Bullard Road for 0.6 mile to parking lot. The trail starts off to
the right of a kiosk and after 50 yards merges with the white-blazed
Metacomet-Monadnock Trail. Turn west (right). At 0.2 mile you'll

cross a woods road and shortly afterward reach Quarry Brook. At 0.5 mile into the hike the trail begins a steady climb and after moving through an abandoned apple orchard reaches an open area of brush and rocks at 1 mile. Continue 0.2 mile to the summit of North Gap.

Description: From the Forest Society kiosk in the parking lot the yellow-blazed trail moves through a typical New Hampshire woodland of birch, beech, maple, and white pine. Soon you will see a marsh to the right. Though the terms "marsh" and "bog" are often used interchangeably, a marsh contains reeds, sedges, and cattail-to-maple woods vegetation, whereas a bog (acidic and nutrient-poor) harbors moss, health shrub, and spruce. The trail moves past impressive ferns and through an opening in a stone wall. Continue downhill and through a hemlock forest before approaching a junction with the white-blazed Metacomet-Monadnock trail at 0.4 mile. Continue (right) on the M-M trail past a stream and uphill through open woods laced with stone walls that once marked boundaries and pasture lands. Look for a big boulder in the woods to the right. This may be an example of glacier-transported haystack rock, or erratic. These solitary monolithic rocks bear no resemblance to local bedrock because they were carried and dumped by a melting glacier and moved miles away from their original location. Geologists identify erratics by studying the rocks surrounding them and the rock of the erratic itself.

About 15 minutes into the hike, you step through another opening in a stone wall and emerge at a field. Bear left and follow the stone wall to emerge at a woods road. The trail crosses the woods road and continues back into the woods to move steeply uphill. The path here is flanked by shoulder-high juniper and goldenrod in late summer, and before long you will reach a meadow populated by old apple trees. Gap Mountain was once open pasture and a valuable summer grazing area for cattle brought up from farms in northern Massachusetts. Beyond the abandoned pasture, the trail becomes deeply rutted and steepens, but is made easier by some finely-placed wood steps. The most difficult section of the hike, a series of flat, sloping, vertical rocks that may require hand and toe holds follow this sec-

View of Mount Mondadnock from Gap Mountain.

tion. You will then see the view opening up. Gap Mountain's 1,862-foot south peak, as well as Troy to the west, are clearly visible. A few steps beyond this outlook brings you to the middle summit and a striking view of Mount Monadnock to the northeast. Just west of Grand Monadnock lies Bigalow Hill, an elongated hill shaped by the erosional force of ice moving southeast during the last Ice Age. The glacial ice bulldozed up the north slope of the hill, polishing the rock, then slid down the south side, creating crags and steep cliffs. This polishing and grinding action carved out a hill shaped like a breaking wave, which geologists call a "sheepback" or *roche moutonné* (literally, "mutton rocks" in French). Ice also produced drumlins, which are rounded little hills composed of boulder-filled clay called "till." Drumlins were created when the till that the ice was dragging along got caught on protruding knobs of bedrock. The whole area that is east, southeast, and south of Mount Monadnock is populated with drumlins down to the border of Massachusetts.

The view to the south-southwest is of Little Monadnock Mountain, Rockwood, and Bowker ponds, and the church spires of Fitzwilliam. An excellent view of the entire 21-mile-long Wapack Range appears to the east. To the west you can see the town of Troy, sprawled out in the valley against a backdrop of distant Vermont peaks, several of which are scarred by ski trails. Troy is home of Troy Mills, the third oldest mill in the United States. In the nineteenth century, the mill was famous for making horse blankets, but today is no longer in the operation. From the middle peak, the Metacomet-Monadnock Trail continues northeast to Gap Mountain's north peak. With just a few minutes' walk, you descend the ledge area, walk past a boggy meadow, and then a stone wall. Return by the same route.

7

Joe English Reservation

Rating: An easy loop hike through evergreen and deciduous
  woodland to a beaver pond, with a chance to discover a wild-
  flower garden, as well as deer, fox, and other animals that make
  their homes here.
Distance: 1.8 miles
Hiking Time: 1 hour
Lowest Elevation: 350 feet
Highest Elevation: 400 feet
USGS Map: Pinardville
Other Map: Amherst Conservation Commission map
Trailhead: Amherst, New Hampshire

Joe English Reservation is located only 20 minutes from the bustle
of downtown Manchester. Managed by the Amherst Conservation
Commission and located in a valley between Mack and Chestnut
Hills in the northwest corner of the town, the 600-acre tract encompasses miles of wooded paths, clear flowing brooks, a beaver pond,
and lots of birds, wildflowers, and elbow room for those weary of
crowds and concrete. The short loop hike outlined here takes you to a
beaver pond, with an excursion to Lookout Rock, a large granite outcrop. Dogs are allowed.

Joe English Reservation is bounded on two sides by the 2,800-
acre United States government satellite tracking station in New Boston, which is a well-managed wildlife preserve in itself but closed to
the public. In the 1940s and 1950s the area was used as a practice
bombing range. Joe English Hill (1,240 feet) is located on the tracking station property about 3 miles north of Joe English Reservation.
Joe English was a real person, a Pennacook Native American named
Merrimacomet. "Joe English" was the derisive name given to him by
members of his tribe who banished him to New Hampshire for be-
friending the white settlers. According to legend, Joe was hunting

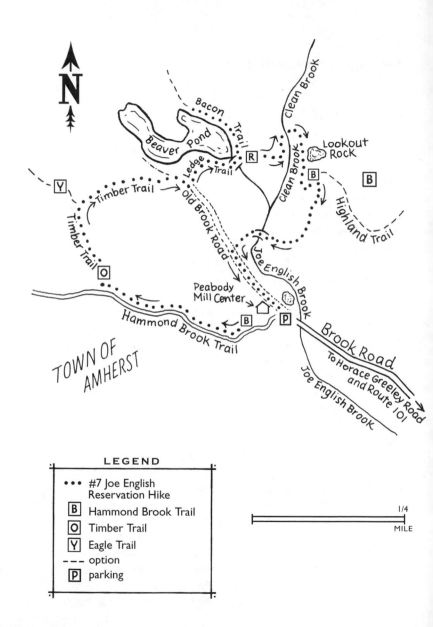

N

Bacon Trail

Clean Brook

Beaver Pond

Lookout Rock

Ledge Trail

R

Clean Brook

B

B

Timber Trail

Y

Old Brook Road

Highland Trail

Timber Trail

Joe English Brook

O

Peabody Mill Center

Hammond Brook Trail

B

P

TOWN OF AMHERST

Brook Road

To Horace Greeley Road and Route 101

Joe English Brook

LEGEND

••• #7 Joe English Reservation Hike

B Hammond Brook Trail

O Timber Trail

Y Eagle Trail

--- option

P parking

1/4

MILE

Joe English Reservation.

one morning and was surprised by a small group of Native Americans who were intent on capturing him. The braves chased Joe up the slope of the hill that now bears his name, confident he would not escape the rocky precipice that awaited him on the other side. Joe, who was known for being a swift runner, managed to escape by finding shelter under an overhanging rock. From his hideaway he watched his pursuers crash through the underbrush and tumble to their deaths over the steep rocks.

Joe English Reservation is home to a wealth of wildflowers. In the springtime bluets, meadow rue, hepatica, false hellebore, violets, lady slipper, trailing arbutus (Mayflower), dwarf ginseng, and jack-in-the pulpit bloom along the banks of the brooks, roadsides, and grassy areas. Spring is an ideal time to search for woodland wildflowers that peak in late April and early May. Sunlight passes through the branches of the hardwoods before the leaves emerge, warming and providing energy for nutrients in the soil. Later, when the leaves shut out the sunlight, these woodland plants go quietly to sleep. You may have noticed that many spring wildflowers are white. That's because they have been formed underground the previous year and no pigment has been developed. When the temperature becomes favorable, many of these flowers rise up into the light and air, and take on various hues, among them blue, red, or yellow. The best way to find wildflowers is to search out areas where there is light, moisture, and temperatures above freezing. Look for sunny spots in clearings or along road cuts and margins. Wildflowers in southern New Hampshire bloom in this order: April—arbutus, blood root, hepatica, marsh marigold, purple violet, shad bush; May—bunchberry, columbine, flowering dogwood, fringed polygala, wild ginger, hobble-bush, Lady's Slipper, nodding trillium, painted trillium, jack-in-the-pulpit; June—blue flag, bristly locust, June pink, mountain laurel, pitcher plant. Remember that many wildflowers will not survive after being picked and moved from their natural environment.

April is also a good month to seek out vernal pools—small woodland ponds that fill with water in the late winter and spring when the snow melts and it starts to rain and that serve as breeding sites for wood frogs and salamanders. The wood frog survives the winter buried under leaf litter by producing a glycogen substance that allows up to 40 percent of its body to repeatedly freeze and thaw without causing damage to the cells. About 2.5 inches long with a dark mask below the eye and a distinctive white line along the upper lip, the wood frog lays its eggs in communal nests, with each spherical, jelly-covered egg clump containing about 1,500 eggs. Male wood frogs make a sharp clucking sound to attract females, so large groups can sound like ducks quacking. Because vernal pools eventually dry up, they cannot support a population of fish that can eat eggs, which makes these temporary bodies of water good breeding areas for wood frogs. Another spring visitor, the peeper, has a high-pitched, short call that in chorus sounds like the ringing of sleigh bells. Though they are easy to hear, spring peepers are difficult to see because of their small size (only about 1 inch). If you ever come upon a thumbnail-sized frog with a brown cross on its back, however, you have found one. After a rainy day, look for delicate purple, scarlet, and maroon capped mushrooms hiding among the tall ferns. Others look like tiny orange fingers hugging the ground, pure white sponges, or wineglass-shaped. In June, mountain laurel with its showy large clusters of pink to white cup-shaped flowers bloom in profusion in the woods like mounds of snow.

Access: To get to the trailhead from the Manchester area, drive west on Route 101 to Horace Greeley Road (8.0 miles from the junction of 101 and 114). Continue on Horace Greeley Road for 0.4 mile. Turn left onto Brook Road. The parking area is 1.5 miles farther at the end of the road. The Peabody Mill Environmental Center, located at 66 Brook Road at the main entrance to Joe English Reservation, has a summer nature camp for children and is used for environmental education and as a meeting space for town organizations. For more information, call 603-673-1141, or go to www.pmec.org.

Description: The blue-blazed Hammond Brook trail starts southwest at a signboard (maps available) in the parking lot and enters a quiet forest of maple, beech, birch, and oak. Soon after, the path turns right to run along Hammond Brook, which is worth a detour to see the brilliant red Cardinal flower (*Lobelia cardinalis*)—the only wild lobelia—sprouting from the dry stream bed in late summer. Lifting its flaming clusters of two-lipped scarlet flowers, this 1.0- to 3.0-foot-tall striking plant seems to beg for attention. As red as a cardinal's robe, Cardinal flower is probably the most brilliantly colored wildflower.

After crossing a plank bridge, the trail continues to follow Hammond Brook. Dense thickets of mountain laurel flourish on both sides of the path. After crossing over a trickle of a stream on a small plank bridge, the path brightens as the woods thin out to a brushy area dotted with stubby pines. In late summer golden rod and wood aster grow here, and the air is thick with the aroma of sweet fern. Shortly after, the path turns right and you'll cross a small brook, continue on the Timber Trail through a corridor of mountain laurel, and then begin a gradual descent. Look for violets, dewberry, and gold thread here. The gold thread gets it name from the orange-colored creeping rootstalks, by which it spreads. The plant has rich, glossy, green leaves somewhat like strawberry leaves, and the dainty white flowers rise from the basal leaves to a height of 3 or 4 inches in earliest summer. Shortly you will come to the yellow-blazed Eagle Trail junction on the left—an interesting path that moves over hilly terrain past a Black Gum (tupelo) swamp. Tupelo is not commonly found in

New England. The leaves of this medium-sized tree turn scarlet in the fall and its blue-black berry-like fruit is a favorite of many species of wildlife. Soon after the Eagle Trail junction the trail widens as the footing changes to a dirt-gravel firmness. After walking past a low row of hemlocks that march off to the right, at 0.8 mile you will come to a junction with Old Brook Road, which was once a thoroughfare to the town of New Boston. Continue right on Old Brook Road for 50 yards. At this point, the leaf-matted, red-blazed Ledge Trail to the beaver pond (a three-minute walk) turns left into the woods. At the pond, cross a wooden King Post bridge and take the Bacon Trail that leads to the shoreline. Over the years the beavers have built a mud-and-stick dam across Joe English Brook, leaving as the food supply dwindled and returning when it had replenished itself. Poke weed, Carolina yellow-eyed grass, loosestrife, blueberry and hobble berry bushes, and the whorled leaves and pink flowers of sheep laurel grow along the edge of the pond, and a sea of pickerel weed spikes the shallow water. Stay for a while to keep an eye out for songbirds such as yellow warblers, nuthatches, and unobtrusive vireos whose persistent song give a better clue to its presence than its drab color and fidgety nature. From the distant woods you may hear the tapping of a hairy or downy woodpecker. Wood duck, Canada geese, and blue heron have also been known to visit the pond. When you have finished communing with nature, continue on the red-blazed Ledge Trail that heads into the woods beyond the footbridge. You'll cross Clean Brook then shortly afterwards arrive at Lookout Rock (wooded view). From Lookout Rock the trail drops down a hill. Turn right to join the blue Highland Trail, which shortly turns right again at another junction. Continue across Joe English Brook on a wooden footbridge to Old Brook Road. Turn left and walk 150 yards back to the Peabody Mill Environmental Center and parking lot. Stay on the lookout for wildlife on this final stretch, as you might spy a porcupine lumbering off in the woods as slowly as a tortoise.

Optional Extensions: Joe English Reservation offers many more miles of hiking opportunities in addition to the ones outlined here. The Plumb Trail is another popular route that offers good views northwest of Joe English Hill. The trailhead for the Plumb Trail is 0.8 mile up Chestnut Hill Road, with a small parking area on the left. Chestnut Hill Road is located off Horace Greeley Road about 1.0 mile beyond the Horace Greeley-Brook Road junction. The Highland Trial can also be accessed from Brook Road. The trailhead is located on the right side 0.8 mile from Horace Greeley Road. Park in the school bus turn-around 0.1 mile below the trailhead on the left side of Brook Road.

Sightseeing: If you are still in the mood for the outdoors, the B and M Trail offers another woodland walk nearby. This former Boston and Maine railroad bed stretches 2 miles between Walnut Hill Road and Baboosic Lake Road in Amherst. Along the way you will see a variety of birds and wildlife, marsh habitat, wetlands, and stone works from this surviving piece of railroad history. To get to the trailhead from the junction of Route 101 and Horace Greeley Road, travel west on Route 101 for 1.2 miles. Turn left onto Walnut Hill Road and continue 1.2 miles where there is limited off-street parking. The walk is a 1.5-hour round-trip.

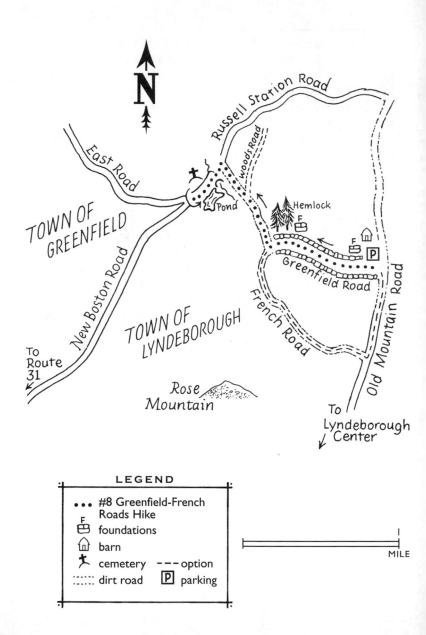

N

Russell Station Road

East Road

Woods Road

TOWN OF GREENFIELD

Pond

Hemlock

F

F

P

New Boston Road

TOWN OF LYNDEBOROUGH

Greenfield Road

French Road

Old Mountain Road

To Route 31

Rose Mountain

To Lyndeborough Center

LEGEND

••• #8 Greenfield-French Roads Hike

F foundations

barn

cemetery   --- option

.... dirt road   P parking

MILE

8
Greenfield-French Roads

Rating: An easy woodland walk along old town roads that will carry you past cellar holes, an old burial plot, and long-forgotten stone walls.
Distance: 3 miles
Hiking Time: 2.5 hours
Lowest Elevation: 830 feet
Highest Elevation: 1,000 feet
USGS Map: Greenfield
Trailhead: Lyndeborough, New Hampshire

Something about walking down old town roads like the Greenfield and French Roads in Lyndeborough can give you the feeling that, although you are alone, you are somehow connected to those who have traveled this way before. There are secrets here among the winding stone walls and cellar holes, and the stillness of the surrounding woodland offers opportunity for reflection. Located in the northwest corner of town, this hike traces these old thoroughfares to the New Boston Road in Greenfield and back for a 3.0-mile round trip. Depending on your appetite for exploration, you can complete the route in a few casual hours and return to your everyday world with a renewed appreciation for the past.

Access: To get to the trailhead from Manchester, take Route 101 west to Wilton. From the traffic island drive north on Route 31 for 3.6 miles to South Lyndeborough. At 0.5 mile beyond the village store, turn right onto Center Road. Continue 2.5 miles and turn left onto (Old) Mountain Road. After driving 2.5 miles you'll come to the French Road on the left. (This is wheret you would end the optional hike). Continue for 0.7 mile (the road turns into a dirt surface), and park in a grassy clearing (left) near a telephone pole and red-and-white sign ("Road Closed—Subject to Bars and Gates"). A small brown barn sits in a field across the road from the clearing. Make sure you pull your vehicle well off the road so as not to impede traffic, and please note that much of the property along the way is posted, so be respectful of landowners.

Description: The trail starts out on the old Greenfield Road. Generally, old town roads have stone walls to either side and that is the case here. You will immediately walk downhill (northwest) past a residence on the left. The branches of enormous beech, birch, oak, and maple trees reach to the sky, while ferns along the roadside put on their own brilliant display of rich green, yellow, and bronze in the fall. After crossing a small brook, you will notice a break in the stone wall to the left. Look opposite in the woods to the right for an old foundation made of smooth slabs of cut granite (close inspection reveals drill holes), with several white birch trees growing out of it.

Lyndeborough has a good number of old cellar holes like this one. Town histories report that many of the nineteenth-century settlers abandoned the stony soil of New England to settle in the Midwest, where there was deep, fertile soil. This particular cellar hole is all that remains of an old school house that has long since rotted away. Take time to step inside and look around. You can see a square formation of stone that was once a chimney. A little farther down the trail, look in the woods to the right for another old cellar hole.

The trail continues through a red maple swamp (ablaze in autumn, buggy in the summer), moves abruptly uphill, and five minutes later levels out. Look to the right. In a depression in the forest floor at a break in a stone wall beneath maple trees, mossy and gray-green stones are all that remain of an old barn foundation built of stone fitted together without mortar. Maple trees and a big mound of earth rise through the spaces where early settlers once lived. In between the foundations is a large pile of stones covering an old well.

At 0.6 mile, just beyond a residence to the left, the feel of the forest trail shifts to a country lane. You will pass through a grove of hemlocks and hardwoods bulging with odd shaped burls, then descend as the road crosses a brook. A beautiful display of hobble-bush (*Viburnum alnifolium*) is here in the spring, showing off its lacy white clusters of flowers in May. The name hobblebush comes from the hindrance to unwary walkers caused by the shrub's drooping branches. The trail moves uphill and comes to a Y junction with the French Road. Turn right and north. Signs in the woods note that this area is protected by the Francestown Land Trust. Originally the main road to Francestown, the French Road today serves only as a thoroughfare for wildlife—even moose tracks have been seen here in the winter. Stone walls continue to follow you at either side, and to the right is an old pasture overgrown by juniper. The French Road gradually declines, and in 5 minutes you will come to a fork. Stay to the left to follow the badly eroded road downhill. At this point the towns of Lyndeborough, Francestown, and Greenfield come together, although there is no sign indicating the boundaries. The road levels out and moves over a wet area as the forest canopy begins to open up.

A few minutes later you will come to a junction with Russell Station Road, a hard-packed dirt road. You are in Francestown at this point of the hike, but continue left (southwest) and a few steps will put you in Greenfield on the New Boston Road. Follow the New Boston Road downhill past a marshy area, and a culvert that channels a brook under the road, where you may spy a stilt-legged blue heron stalking its dinner. Otter have been seen here, too. An old graveyard soon appears on the right, sitting on a moss-covered hill behind some tall white pines, a rusted gate, and a stone wall. This, the Whittemore family cemetery, makes an interesting and peaceful place to spend a few minutes. Major Amos Whittemore, who fought in the Battle of White Plains during the Revolution, is credited with naming the town of Greenfield. A stately federal brick home built by the major still stands on the crest of a small hill a few hundred yards behind the cemetery at the end of a long dirt driveway and across from a field crisscrossed by stone walls.

The gravestones here are weather-worn and some are difficult to read. (One technique for deciphering well-worn script is to squeegee shaving cream over the lettering to make it stand out). Slate was the burial marker stone most used in the 1700s, until the advent of the railroads made it easier to ship granite. Some of the stone markers

Lyndeborough Cemetery.

have rounded tops, others are arched or even edged with an etching of hands pointed skyward, an elaborate willow tree (a symbol of bereavement) bending over an urn and a winged angel. The burial urn and willow tree motif became popular during the 1800s and replaced the winged effigy that represents spiritual uplifting. Other burial marker symbols included arches, crowns, doves, flowers, vases, and grapevines.

From the cemetery, the New Boston Road continues past a pond brimming with water lilies with Rose Mountain rising behind it. The road changes to a tarred surface 0.1 mile beyond the cemetery. This is the turnaround point of the hike. (From this point the New Boston Road continues 2.3 miles to Route 31 in Greenfield). Return to your car by the same route. Make sure to look for the French Road fork on the right at the crest of a small rise on the New Boston Road 0.3 mile beyond the cemetery. Retrace your path to the Greenfield Road junction and turn left for the 15-minute walk back to your car.

Optional Extension: You can bypass the Greenfield Road junction and continue straight and south on the French Road. Bear left at a fork at the top of a hill. A 25-minute walk will bring you back to Mountain Road. Along the way you will see a large cellar hole on the left side of the road, marking the residence of the French family for whom the road was named. Just beyond, at the bottom of a hill, look in the woods to the left for the remains of an old soapstone quarry. You can see the indentations in the ground where they dug for soapstone, a soft rock composed mostly of mineral talc. Soapstone, unaffected by high temperatures, makes a good insulator, and years ago was used to make sinks, table tops, stoves, and bed warmers. When you reach Mountain Road, turn left and walk 0.7 mile on the tarred and dirt surface back to your car in the grassy clearing.

Sightseeing: If you're looking for a small mountain to climb that offers wide views after your woodland walk, head back to Lyndeborough Center on Mountain Road. After just over a mile, look for a yellow blaze in the woods to the right and park off the shoulder. A 30-minute walk brings you to the top of Pinnacle Mountain (1,703 feet), sometimes called Lyndeborough Mountain. Nearby are Pinnacle's sister peaks, Rose and Winn Mountains. Mount Monadnock stands out prominently to the west, with distant views of the White Mountains.

If you have time, you may want to visit the sleepy hilltop community of Lyndeborough Center and view an interesting grave site and monument along the way. To get to Lyndeborough Center, return to Center Road, turn left and drive for 0.3 mile. About 0.1 mile before Center Road, turn right onto Crooked S Road to visit the tombstone marking the grave of Dr. Lorenzo D. Bartlett. Bartlett came to Lyndeborough in 1854 to care for a young woman named Ann Jones and a small child who had contracted smallpox. Although the treatment was successful for his patients, Bartlett himself contracted the dreaded disease and died at the age of 29. The townspeople were so fearful that the smallpox would spread, they insisted that he be interred outside of the town cemetery. The grave site is located 0.4 mile down Crooked S Road on the right side under a cluster of oak trees. The Woodward monument is located off Center Road at the foot of a steep hill at the corner of Herrick Road. A simple granite shaft memorial surrounded by an iron chain hung on four granite posts marks the spot where Christiana Woodward was killed after being thrown from a wagon on May 8, 1852. The fatal accident happened when Woodward was returning to South Lyndeborough from Lyndeborough Center where she and her sister-in-law, Huldah, had delivered the mail to the Center Post Office. After stopping to let her sister-in-law out, Woodward started on the road again, but the horse (which was blind) panicked when a harness loosened, and threw her onto a ledge as he ran away.

Before the railroad came through in 1870, Lyndeborough Center had a post office, dance hall, store, and tavern. Today, only the old town hall and United Church remain. Next to the church is the town pound built in 1774 of field stone with a sign stating that the structure cost "4 pounds legal money" to build. For more information on the history of town pounds, go to "Sightseeing" in Hike 43, Pumpelly Trial (p. 252). Across a field from the church, look for the gentle slope of Piscataquog Mountain (1,262 feet). Legend has it that silver was once mined on the ledges here and that one pair of buckles was fashioned from the precious metal.

Also nearby is Wilton, a hillside town nestled on the banks of the Souhegan River. In years past it was a manufacturing village; at various times boasting cotton worsted yarn and cloth mills, woodworking plant, box factory, machine shop, and boot and shoe-making businesses. The granite building stone and under-pinning were cut out of the ledge along the Souhegan River. In the town center you'll find the fortress-like town hall of granite and brick, a sophisticated example of Queen Anne architecture with a monumental, domed clock tower. This impressive building, which houses a movie theater in addition to town offices, was built on the site of the old Whiting Hotel, which burned in 1874 in a fire that destroyed all of Main Street except the old post office. Nearby are the Masonic Temple and the Gregg Free Library (which is on the National Register of Historic Places); the library's interior features a rotunda of Sienna marble and fine wood paneling of curly whitewood, sycamore, and mahogany.

At 3 miles north of Wilton's town center you will find Frye's Measure Mill, a manufacturer of wooden ware and colonial and shaker boxes, which is also listed on the National Register of Historic Places. The museum shop offers a variety of handcrafted products that are authentic survivors of ninenteenth-century technology and craftsmanship. They have been in the same mill, and with the same machinery, still partially water powered, since 1858. In the days before electricity, the owners used a one-cylinder steam engine for additional power and to heat the mill, kilns, and steam vats. The engine, which still remains at the mill, was made in Cambridgeport, Massachusetts, in 1871 and its main flywheel measures 6 feet in diameter. The engine also powered the sawmill, which was removed. To get to Frye's, drive north on Route 31 (Forest Road) for 1.5 miles to the Burton Highway. Fork left and continue another 1.5 miles. Mill tours are given at 2 P.M. on Saturdays from June to October. For information, call 603-654-6581 or go to www.fryesmeasuremill.com.

Nearby Barnes (Gaerwin) Falls is a beautiful waterfall on County Farm Brook. Gaerwin Falls was the site of the first mill in Wilton, and a popular spot for picnics, church parties, outings, and school reunions. You can see many pot holes and basins worn in the ledges by the force of the meltwater during the retreat of the glaciers. To get to Gaerwin Falls, turn left on the Isaac Frye Highway, 0.5 mile from the junction of Route 31 and Burton Highway. Continue driving on the Isaac Frye Highway for 0.5 mile. Just after a small bridge and Putnam Hill Road, look for a woods road where a cable is stretched across the road. Park on the shoulder of the highway. A 5-minute walk down past the Old Wilton Reservoir brings you to the head of the falls. Along the way, you will see tall pine, mountain laurel, and hemlock, which grows in cool, moist ravines and likes the north side of hills facing rain-bearing winds.

Wilton Center lies 1.0 mile farther on the Isaac Frye Highway. This village of beautiful homes, town hall, and the First Unitarian Congregational Church (built in 1860), was rebuilt as a replacement for the 1773 meetinghouse that burned in 1859. The "Yellow House" is an excellent example of country Federal architecture, and the "Red House" is the parish house for the First Unitarian Congregational Church.

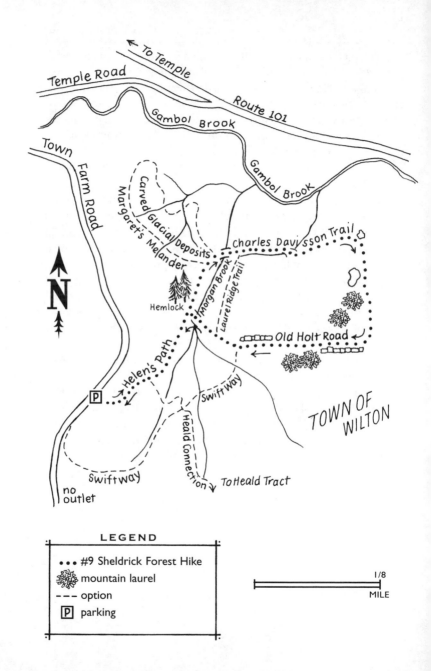

To Temple

Temple Road

Route 101

Gambol Brook

Gambol Brook

Town Farm Road

Carved Glacial Deposits

Margaret's Melander

Charles Davisson Trail

Hemlock

Morgan Brook

Laurel Ridge Trail

Old Holt Road

Helen's Path

P

Swiftway

TOWN OF WILTON

Heald Connection

Swiftway

To Heald Tract

no outlet

Swiftway

N

LEGEND

••• #9 Sheldrick Forest Hike

mountain laurel

- - - option

P parking

1/8
MILE

9
Sheldrick Forest

Rating: A short walk through a primeval forest with a rich glacial history, boasting towering pine and hemlock, stonewalls, boulders, and eskers.
Distance: 1.75 miles
Hiking Time: 1 hour
Lowest Elevation: 700 feet
Highest Elevation: 860 feet
USGS Map: Greenville
Other Maps: The Nature Conservancy map; town of Wilton recreational trails map
Trailhead: Wilton, New Hampshire

The small town of Wilton, New Hampshire, offers big hiking opportunities. One of the best nature preserves in the state is located in West Wilton, at Sheldrick Forest. This 227-acre tract of The Nature Conservancy offers 3.0 miles of trails and has six forest communities with streams, mountain laurel, and a variety of interior forest-breeding birds. While typical New Hampshire forests are just 50 to 100 years old, some trees on the Sheldrick Forest preserve (which is located between Town Farm and Russell Hill roads) have been around since John Adams was president and Napoleon was conquering Europe. The ecologically-rare forest had been slated for gravel- and timber-harvesting, and eventual development, but became a preserve of the Nature Conservancy in 1996 when old-growth trees were discovered.

Sheldrick Forest is also perfect for children. The trail has numbered interpretative points, with a self-guided brochure available at the kiosk. This 1.75-mile-loop hike starts in the parking area at a kiosk (which also contains a visitors guide and youth activity sheets on birds, insects, and trees) and includes views of old-growth trees, mountain laurel, and the old stonewall-lined Holt Road.

Access: To get to the Sheldrick Forest from Milford, take 101 west, past Wilton Center. Turn left, just beyond Gary's Harvest restaurant, onto Temple Road. Bear left across a bridge and then take the first left onto Town Farm Road. Continue 0.7 mile to the preserve entrance on the left.

Description: The hike begins at the kiosk, crosses a field, then enters the forest (Helen's Path) near the northeast corner of the parking field. The trail eases downhill, skirting the bank of Morgan Brook as it enters the Valley of the Giants (huge hemlock and pines trees). Neck-craning is required to fully appreciate these immense conifers, some of which are more than 200 years old. Shortly, you will pass the Flyway (connecting trail). After passing the Swift Way junction (right) the trail continues along Morgan Brook and connects with both Margaret's Meander and Charles Daivisson Trails. Stay right and cross Morgan Brook on a split-log bridge to begin a gradual climb on the Charles Davisson Trail, which shortly moves past the junction (right) with the Laurel Ridge Trail. The Charles Davisson Trail continues to parallel the brook, which you will soon cross again. As you move along the edge of a terrace above Gambol Brook, you will enter a stand of large hemlock and pine. Shortly you'll enter a magnificent stand of mountain laurel (*Kalmia latifolia*), whose pink and white blossoms are a striking contrast to the dark forests in which they grow. Mountain laurel has narrow shiny leaves from one to five inches long and sticky stalks that sometimes look like twisted canes. Eating utensils could be made from the shrub's fine, even-grained wood, which may be why Native Americans called it "spoon wood." When in bloom, mountain laurel is covered with showy clusters of pink flowers. After moving through a stretch of open forest you will again enter a stretch of tall pine and hemlock, then move up hill to reach a junction with old Holt Road, which is lined with stonewalls and mountain laurel, and punctuated by stone culverts. Turn west (right) to follow the ancient pathway to the intersection in a hemlock stand with the Swift Way. Step through a gap in a stonewall and continue downhill as the trail parallels a brook to the left. Cross the brook at Helen's Path junction. Take a left and retrace your steps to return to the parking lot.

The Charles Davisson loop is just one of many hikes at Sheldrick Forest. Margaret's Meander explores the carved glacial deposits in the northwest corner of the preserve, whereas the Laurel Ridge Trail follows a ridge above and to the east of Morgan Brook and offers views down into the valley. Sheldrick Forest also sits adjacent to the Heald Tract and a 0.9-mile connector trail joins the two preserves. The connecting trail starts off the Swift Way and joins the Heald Tract system at the Castor Pond Trail just north of "the Rocks."

Sightseeing: On the way to Sheldrick Forest, you may want to visit a memorial marking the spot where Captain Samuel Greele was killed by a falling tree on September 25, 1798, while riding on horseback to attend a public hearing in Wilton Center. Forty years after the incident, Greele's sons, Deacon, Samuel, and Augustus, commemorated the spot where their father died with a simple marble obelisk on a square base. To get to the monument, take Route 101 west from intersection with Route 31 for 0.7 mile. Turn left onto Russell Hill Road. The monument (surrounded by a rusted iron fence) is located 0.7 mile further under a grove of hemlock trees on the left.

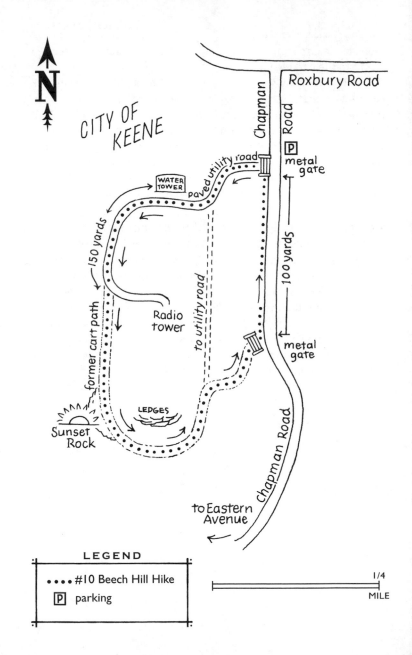

N

CITY OF KEENE

Roxbury Road

Chapman

Road

P metal gate

paved utility road

WATER TOWER

150 yards

100 yards

metal gate

former cart path

to utility road

Radio tower

LEDGES

Chapman Road

Sunset Rock

to Eastern Avenue

LEGEND

•••• #10 Beech Hill Hike

P parking

1/4

MILE

10

Beech Hill

Rating: An easy climb to open ledges and a bird's-eye view of the
city of Keene.
Distance: 1 mile
Hiking Time: 45 minutes
Lowest Elevation: 916 feet
Highest Elevation: 1,040 feet
USGS Map: Keene
Other Map: City of Keene map
Trailhead: Keene, New Hampshire

Some say at night that Keene's Beech Hill looks down on the likes of
Paris. The daytime view of the city is also a spectacular sight, even on
an overcast day. In 1890 Horace L. Goodnow built a 35-foot wooden
observation tower on the hill, and on Sunday afternoons the citizens
of Keene flocked to Beech Hill for the fabulous view. Afterwards, a
nearby picnic grove provided an ideal spot to enjoy lunch and the
cooling breezes. Although the "the Horatian Tower" and picnic grove
are no longer around, the panoramic vista from Sunset Rock continues to beckon hikers, and the ledges make a great lunch spot.

Access: From Manchester, drive west on Route 101 to Keene and take
the "Optical Avenue to Marlborough St." exit. Continue for 0.5 mile
and turn right onto Tiffin Street. At the end of Tiffin Street turn right
onto Marlboro Street and then take an immediate left onto Eastern
Avenue. Continue on Eastern Avenue for 0.1 mile and turn right onto
Chapman Road. After 2.0 miles you will reach a metal gate (left). Park
off of the right shoulder opposite the metal gate. Another starting
point is the return route for the hike outlined here—an old woods
road 100 yards south of the metal gate. The Beech Hill Preserve is
maintained by the City of Keene Parks and Recreation Department.
For information, call 603-357-9829.

Description: The trail begins on the paved utility road behind the metal gate. A brisk 3-minute walk up hill leads to a concrete water-storage tank surrounded by a chain link fence. From the water storage tank, continue on the paved road for 150 yards. Just before the road turns left and uphill to cable television towers, satellite dishes, and a red beacon light, a former cart path (dirt) leaves to the right from the pavement. A 5-minute walk down the leaf-strewn path under a canopy of beech, birch, and maple brings you to a grove of hemlock and the ledges (Sunset Rock) at the southern end of the ridge. The cart path continues into the woods. The view from Sunset Rock is stirring.

To the south, the runways of the Dillant-Hopkins Airport in North Swanzey lie against a backdrop of conical hills. Central Square, to the north, is dominated by the white spire of the United Church of Christ. The long, forested ridge of West Hill sits on the horizon to the west. From Sunset Rock, Keene looks like a toy town, and trucks and cars roll west on Route 101 like tiny Tonka toys. The bright green patch south of Route 101 is the artificial grass of the Keene State College athletic field.

Looking out at the sprawl of houses, brick factory, office buildings, and network of streets, it is difficult to imagine that the city was once the bed of a primeval lake. Take time to imagine the Paleolithic past, look for small planes circling on their approach to the airport or soaring turkey vultures, or just relax and listen to the birdsong or rustle of the breeze in the trees. When you are ready to return, continue on the cart path that moves into the woods beyond the hemlock grove. After 0.25 mile you'll reach a fork. Stay right (left leads back to the utility road) and continue downhill. Take an easy walk of 300 yards past ledges, boulders, and a beech tree rooted in the middle of the trail, to return to Chapman Road. Turn left for the 100-yard walk back on the paved road to your car.

Sightseeing: At the junction of Eastern Avenue and Chapman Road you can access the Keene Industrial Heritage Trail. After you climb Beech Hill you may want to bike, walk, or rollerblade this bike and pedestrian route, which is 1 mile long from Eastern Avenue to Main

Street in downtown Keene. (The paved path continues as the downtown Cheshire Trail from Main Street.) Look for a small gravel parking lot and two metal orange posts. Historical signs posted along the trail note that the mills bordering the former railway manufactured a variety of goods in the post–Civil-War industrial era, including woolen blankets, bicycles, automobiles, silverware, furniture, shoes, chairs, bricks, and toys. In late summer and fall, the red brick nineteenth-century buildings provide a striking background for the white Queen Anne's Lace, purple clover, yellow birch and goldenrod, and bright red fruit of the Staghorn Sumac that brighten the edge of the trail.

Robin Hood Park and Forest, hiking trails, pond, and recreation facilities is located on the lower slopes of Beech Hill. To get there from the metal gate, follow Chapman Road north for 0.4 mile to Roxbury Road. Turn left and continue on Roxbury Road for 0.3 mile to a stop sign. Continue (left) down a steep hill for 0.4 mile to Roxbury Street. Turn right and drive 0.2 mile on Roxbury Street to Reservoir Street. The parking lot is between the pond and the swimming pool. For more information, visit www.ci.keene.nh.us/parks/.

The Horatio Colony Trust Nature Preserve is a 415-acre privately held conservation trust on West Hill with 1.5 miles of trails with numbered stops that mark plant communities, geological features, and historical ruins. A guidebook is available at the trailhead map stand. To get there, turn south off Route 9 onto Daniel's Hill Road 1.2 miles west of the junction of Routes 9-10-12. Continue 0.2 mile to the parking lot.

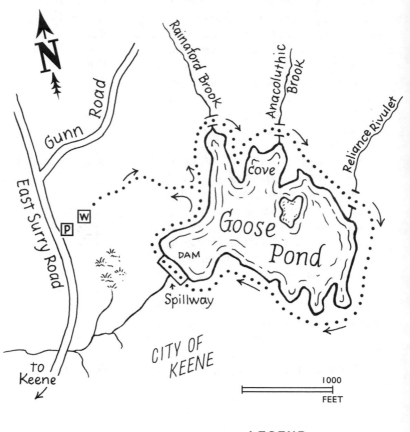

N

Gunn Road

East Surry Road

Rainaford Brook

Anacoluthic Brook

Reliance Rivulet

Cove

Goose Pond

DAM

Spillway

to Keene

CITY OF KEENE

1000 FEET

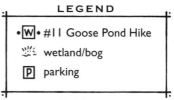

LEGEND

• W • #11 Goose Pond Hike

☼ wetland/bog

P parking

11

Goose Pond

Rating: An easy loop around a wilderness pond with an opportunity to see thick groves of hemlock, buffleheads, black ducks, and other waterfowl along the way.
Distance: 1.3 miles
Hiking Time: 1 hour
Pond elevation: 635 feet
USGS Map: Keene
Other Map: City of Keene Map
Trailhead: Keene, New Hampshire

A wilderness area in Keene? Just 3.0 miles north of the shops on Main Street, you will find the 500-acre Goose Pond preserve and recreation area. Through careful purchase and negotiated land protection, the city has guaranteed that the quiet coves, islands, inlets, and surrounding wooded hills of this vast tract will remain a wildlife refuge and source of enjoyment for future hikers, nature lovers, and bird-watchers. A popular place for the citizens of Keene to relax after a day at work, the walk around Goose Pond takes about an hour to complete, although numerous diversions will tempt you to extend that time. Along the way you will see a variety of birds and waterfowl, and may even get a glimpse of the deer, fox, raccoons, fishers, beavers, or minks who dwell in the wooded hills surrounding the pond. In addition to hiking, Goose Pond offers many opportunities to bird-watch, picnic, snowshoe, or cross-country ski in season. Hunting, swimming, and motorized vehicles are prohibited. Overnight camping and fires allowed by special permit.

Access: From the Manchester area, take Route 101 west to the Main Street exit in Keene. Continue to Central Square, go halfway around the rotary, and turn onto Court Street. Follow Court Street north for 2.1 miles to East Surry Road. The parking area is 0.9 mile farther.

Goose Pond.

Description: The white-blazed trail begins to the left of the parking area and quickly moves uphill past huge white pines with an understory of hemlock. In a few minutes you will descend into a clearing of meadow-sweet, brambles, and stubby pine before re-entering the woods and moving uphill again. A stone wall continues to follow you on the left, and polypody fern blankets the forest floor. You will soon glimpse Goose Pond off to the right, appearing through the lower branches of oaks and maples. Slender white birch trees bend gracefully toward the open water and highbush blueberry bushes, brilliant red in the fall, border the perimeter of the pond. Turn left to follow the path northeast along the shoreline. As you walk, look for the pileated woodpecker (*Dryocopus pileatus*) that feeds on the rotting stumps and decaying trees in the open beech and oak forest. A large, wary bird with a gray body marked with patches of white and a brilliant red crest, the pileated woodpecker flies with an irregular flap of its wings and has a distinctive cry—a loud, nasal *kuk-kuk*.

In a few minutes, you will walk under an arbor of feathery hemlock grown so thick with boughs that little sunlight reaches the ground. You will shortly approach the first of many hidden coves and inlets. Mallards rest here in the sheltered waters in the fall, so your sudden appearance may startle them into a frenzied flight as they whip the water with a flurry of wings. Canada geese, black ducks, buffleheads, and mergansers can also be seen here. The trail continues across Rainaford Brook, the first of three watercourses to cross, then circles along the shore of a cove where there are half-submerged trees with stubble branches and upturned root stumps. Continue walking through another grove of hemlock and beech trees. For an interesting view of the shoreline, follow the side trail that leads to the tip of the peninsula.

Return to the main trail to follow the shoreline of another cove where you're likely to see more ducks floating peacefully on the calm waters near a small island. You will shortly step through a gap in a stone wall. Look for an arrow on a tree that directs you (right) toward the shoreline. Use caution here as it is easy to go left instead. Whenever you are in doubt, stay in sight of water. After crossing Anacoluthic Brook and moving through another open beech forest, follow a side trail that leads (right) to another peninsula where there is a huge boulder and good view of a small island across a dark narrow channel of water.

Tall white pines and hemlock hug the shoreline as the trail moves past a hillside outcropping of ledge that has become a natural rock garden of wintergreen. Step on more stones to cross Reliance Rivulet as It dances down from the hillside to the left to enter the pond. In the fall, there Is an especially nice view southwest of the distant hills across the pond. From this point the walking becomes more difficult as the trail narrows and tree roots grow thick and high underfoot. After passing a boulder-studded cove, the path moves away from the shoreline to enter cool hemlock woods.

Several minutes later you will come to an earthern dam where a sawed-off stump provides a good resting spot to sit and enjoy the cooling breezes. The trail reenters the woods and widens. After 25 yards, look for a white trail marker painted on a tree. Be careful here. It is very easy to follow the park boundary and city access road. Instead, continue right and toward the pond, past a boggy area where sphagnum moss jiggles on the water along the pond's edge and stumps poke through the water.

By now you have undoubtedly noticed that Goose Pond is actually more like a lake in size (42 acres). Over 100 years ago the townspeople of Keene built two dams to double the surface area of the pond (a good part of the newly flooded area was formerly bog and forest). The impetus for the enlargement was the citizens' concern after the Great Fire of October 19, 1865, which destroyed a good portion of Central Square and exhausted the water supply of the town wells. The dams were built to enlarge Goose Pond and bring new water to Keene, and in November 1868 a pipeline of hollowed-out logs channeled water to the city's new fire hydrants. Although Goose Pond (on some old maps called Sylvan Lake) has not been used as a public water supply for many years, it remained a potential source of water for Keene until 1984. That year the city designated the 500-acre area for a wilderness park, never again to be used as a water supply.

After you walk past the boggy area, the trail continues along the shoreline through more massive hemlock and pine. Numerous shoreline outlooks provide especially good views of wooded hills to the northeast. You will soon come to a large cove, and step through a gap in a stone wall to emerge from the hemlock woods to a grassy clearing. Continue walking across a square block concrete dam and overflow spillway (the outlet flows into the Ashuelot River). Your hike ends 100 yards beyond the spillway, at the path on the left that leads back to the parking lot.

Sightseeing: To get to Beaver Brook Falls from Central Square in Keene, drive north on Washington Street for 1.3 miles and turn right onto Concord Road. Take an immediate left onto Washington St. Extension and continue 0.3 mile. Park where the road ends at a metal gate. A 0.8-mile walk up an abandoned section of the Old Concord Road, with good views along the way of Beaver Brook cascading down the gorge, leads to an overlook at the falls. At the falls use your imagination to examine the profile of a Native American inscribed in the ledges.

12

McCabe Forest

Rating: An easy walk through various forest communities, meadows, and fields along the Contoocook River.
Distance: 1.5 miles
Hiking Time: 1 hour
Lowest Elevation: 600 feet
Highest Elevation: 650 feet
USGS Map: Hillsborough
Trailhead: Antrim, New Hampshire

If you are looking for a good family hike, then you have found it at the McCabe Forest in Antrim, New Hampshire. A former farm that has a self-guided interpretative trail (guides available at kiosk mailbox), the 189-acre McCabe Forest has an easy, rolling terrain ideal for young hikers. The tract was donated to the Society for the Protection of New Hampshire Forests (SPNHF) by the McCabe family and is one of five wildlife habitat management demonstration woodlot areas in New Hampshire.

The hike outlined here is a 1.5-mile loop that leads to the banks of the Contoocook River and continues through such forest communities as spacious pine groves and flood-plain meadows that provide a habitat for a diversity of wildlife, before returning to the parking lot. It is advisable to bring waterproof footwear as sections of the trail are sometimes wet.

Access: From Manchester, take Route 101 west to Peterborough. Drive north on Route 202 east to Antrim. At the junction of Routes 31 and 202 in the center of the town, continue on 202 for 0.3 mile to Elm Street Extension Road (dirt). Turn right. The parking area and kiosk are 300 feet on the right.

Description: The yellow-blazed McCabe Forest trail starts east of the kiosk, moves downhill on a needle-softened path under towering

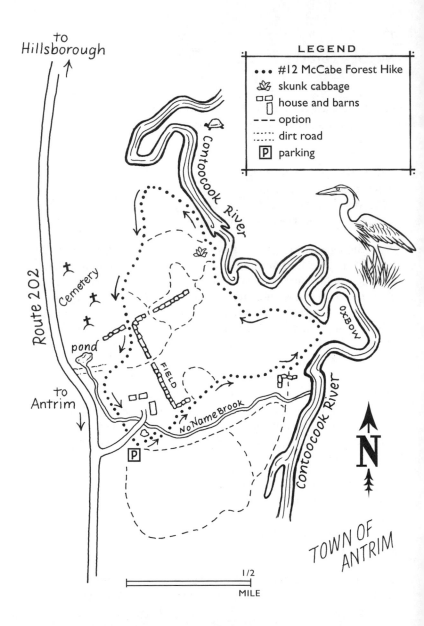

to
Hillsborough

LEGEND

••• #12 McCabe Forest Hike
🌿 skunk cabbage
🏠 house and barns
- - - option
⋮⋮⋮ dirt road
P parking

Route 202

Contoocook River

Cemetery

pond

to
Antrim

FIELD

No Name Brook

oxbow

Contoocook River

N

TOWN OF
ANTRIM

1/2
MILE

pines, and skirts past an enormous boulder to the left deposited by a receding glacier 12,000 years ago. The trail turns right and parallels rocky No Name Brook as you walk under dark hemlock. See the trail guide indicating that there was once a brickyard in the vicinity. After crossing the brook on stepping stones, you will emerge at a field. The walking is easy as you move through a gap in a stone wall and continue on the wide grassy path past apple trees that have been pruned back to enhance fruit production for wildlife. A nearby grove of aspen is a valuable source of wildlife food. Beaver eat the inner bark, and moose browse the foliage, strip the bark, and chew the twigs. As the trail runs along a stone wall and reaches the Contoocook River, keep an eye out for great blue and little green herons and otter that rest here. A small wading bird with a long neck, like the shaft of a javelin, the green heron is a stealthy hunter, standing at the water's edge, ambushing prey by extending its neck to quickly spear fish.

The path turns left and moves under tall pines as it parallels the river, which makes a number of wide turns, including one oxbow-shaped bend. Move through a grassy opening of shrubs and berries, and an impressive display of hobblebush, the follow the trail as it swings by the river again. Feel the acorns mix under your feet before you reach a fork (stay right) to cross a footbridge. Skunk cabbage (*Symplocarpus foetidur*) grows in the moist soil here in the spring. It is the first wild flowering plant to thrust itself above the ground and burst into bloom in the spring; it actually generates enough heat to melt the snow around it. The skunk part of the name comes from its disagreeable odor (which resembles decaying flesh); it lures insects that pollinate it. The cabbage part is from the large cabbage-like leaves. (Native Americans smelled the crushed leaves as a cure for headache). Instead of petals, the skunk cabbage has a single leaf-like sheath—a spathe—that is hood-shaped and maroon, streaked with greenish-yellow.

The trail moves past a huge pine tree before coming to another fork. Continue (right) along the river and past a grove of eastern hemlock (*Tsuga canadensis*), which shades the north end of McCabe Forest. Hemlock will take root only in soil that is moist with humus, and where the canopy of other trees already provides shade. The Eastern hemlock produces a great many seeds; Its small, reddish-brown cones cover the tree from the nodding top to the lowest branches, and its seeds are so tiny that as many as several hundred thousand go into a pound.

Take time to explore the grassy riverbank and watch the reeds waving in the lazy, tannin-colored river. Sit for a while and look for bottle green and metallic blue dragonflies as they helicopter past and land on half-submerged logs. Keep an eye out for painted turtles basking in the sun or snapping turtles surfacing and sinking in slow motion. Listen for the sudden splash of a fish breaking through the surface at the river's bend. When you are finished taking in the sounds of nature, return to the trail, which turns left at a yellow double blaze and moves over a wet area before continuing along elevated dry ground matted with pine needles and oak leaves. The path continues (right) past another junction and widens. After passing through a gap in a stonewall near a field, the trail proceeds uphill and turns right. Soon you will approach a small pond (right) with Route 202 about 50 yards beyond. Turn left for the 3-minute walk, which includes crossing No Name Brook, back to the parking lot. In the winter, when No Name Brook freezes, walk down Route 202 back to the parking lot.

13

Monroe Hill, Fox Forest

Rating: An easy walk along an old town road and forested path
that comes up to a lookout platform on Monroe Hill with views
of Crotched Mountain, Mount Monadnock, and the Contoocook
River Valley.

Distance: 1.8 miles

Hiking Time: 1 hour

Lowest Elevation: 800 feet

Highest Elevation: 1,210 feet

USGS Map: Hillsborough Upper Village

Other Map: New Hampshire Department of Resources and
Economic Development map

Trailhead: Hillsborough, New Hampshire

Located on the fringe of the Monadnock Region, Fox Forest in Hillsborough is 1,445 acres of undeveloped forest land. A total of 25 miles
of trails take you past old cellar holes, cemeteries, bogs, marshes,
ponds, old growth beech and hemlock, plus a black gum swamp and
a quaking bog.

Fox Forest began in 1922 as a gift to the state of 348 acres from
Caroline A. Fox, whose summer home now serves as the forest headquarters building. Fox Forest is the State of New Hampshire's forestry research station. It is operated by the Forest Management
Bureau, part of the Department of Resources and Economic Development, Division of Forests and Lands. Nearby is the Henry I. Baldwin
Environmental Center, which is used for forestry and conservation
meetings and environmental education. Trail maps are available at
the headquarters, which can be reached at 603-464-3453. No motorized vehicles are allowed in the forest.

Access: To reach the trailhead from Keene, take Route 9 north to Hillsborough. From the traffic signal in the center of Hillsborough, drive

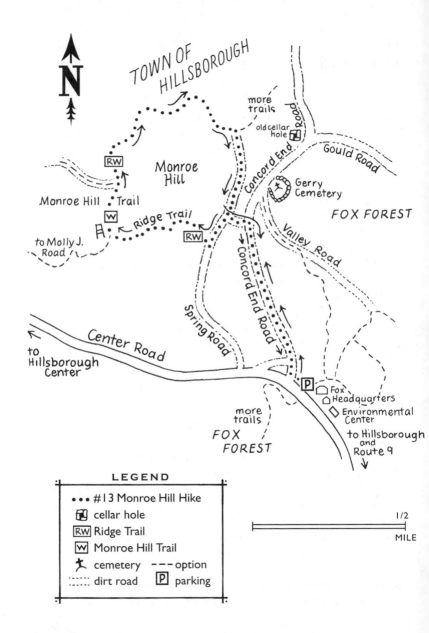

N

TOWN OF HILLSBOROUGH

more trails

old cellar hole

Concord End Road

Gould Road

Gerry Cemetery

FOX FOREST

Monroe Hill

RW

Monroe Hill • Trail

W

Ridge Trail

RW

to Molly J. Road

Valley Road

Concord End Road

Spring Road

Center Road

to Hillsborough Center

P Fox Headquarters

Environmental Center

to Hillsborough and Route 9

more trails

FOX FOREST

LEGEND

••• #13 Monroe Hill Hike

cellar hole

RW Ridge Trail

W Monroe Hill Trail

cemetery   --- option

dirt road   P parking

1/2

MILE

Concord End Road, Fox Forest.

north on School Street, which changes to Center Road. Fox Forest is 2 miles farther on the right.

Description: Walk north past the large dirt parking lot. The hike starts on Concord End Road (dirt). In the spring look for red trillium and wild oats that grow on the edge of the road and in the woods as you walk. After 5 minutes, you will come to a sign pointing the way (left) to the Ridge Trail marked in red and white blazes. The Gerry Cemetery is 200 yards farther on the right. An old cellar hole is less than a quarter mile still farther on the left.

Stone walls, weather-etched, lichen-covered, and colored an age-less gray, border the road you have walked. New Hampshire stone walls were built from the granite rubble left by melting glaciers during the Ice Age, long before the Anglo-European invasions of the seventeenth century. Most history books, however, tell us the story of the hard-toiling settlers who used the stones to enclose pastures and mark property boundaries in the days when farms and pastures were everywhere.

The pace of the walk quickens as the trail moves uphill. At the top of the rise, turn left onto Spring Road. In 150 yards, a sign points the way right to continue on the Ridge Trail. Keep walking uphill through a hemlock forest and past large boulders. Step through a gap in a stone wall for a second time, and walk past a grove of beech trees.

Beech trees are sometimes called "money trees" because when a scrunched-up ellipse-shaped leaf unfolds, it reverts to its original shape, much like a dollar bill does. Be on the lookout for beech trees with claw scratches and broken upper branches—signs that tell you a black bear (*Ursus americanus*) has been around.

Beechnuts provide an important food source for black bears in October, supplementing their omnivorous diet of squirrels, birds, eggs, fish, frogs, ants and their larvae, young bees, honey, and berries. A bear will find a comfortable seat in the crotch of a beech tree in order to reach out and pull back the limbs to strip the nuts. Don't worry—there is little chance you will come upon a black bear, as this large forest-dweller usually prefers his own company. If you do encounter a bear in a tree, he's likely to stay put. Bears learn to climb as a way to escape and hide from predators, not as a means of pouncing on prey or people. For more information on bears, go to "wildlife profiles" at www.wildlife.state.nh.us.

Beyond the beech grove, the trail winds gradually uphill. In five minutes you will reach the platform lookout in a clearing where you can stop for a view to the southwest of Crotched Mountain, Pack Monadnock Mountain, and Mount Monadnock. The twin summits of Riley and Gibson Mountains in Antrim rise in the foreground.

The Ridge Trail drops away from the tower to the southwest. Your route continues north on the Monroe Hill Trail, which is marked by white blazes. To the right in the woods is an enormous boulder that you may want to explore. After a few minutes, you will reach the Ridge Trail junction where a turn to the left would lead west to Molly J. Road. Instead, continue straight ahead (north) on the Ridge Trail. The white blazes will change to red and white as the trail continues downhill past hemlock trees and a boggy area. After crossing a stone culvert, the trail opens up into a woods road. Several minutes of walking leads you to the Spring Road junction. Continuing downhill on Spring Road brings you past a spring house on the right.

You will start to see white birch and quaking (trembling) aspen, which are known as pioneer trees because they rapidly seed in after a timber disturbance. In this area, the disturbance was the Hurricane of 1938, which destroyed over one million board-feet of timber in Fox Forest alone. It has been estimated that this hurricane uprooted or broke more than 275 million trees in New England.

Although aspen and white birch thrive in open areas with abundant light, they cannot compete with more shade-tolerant species such as oak, white pine, and hemlock, which reach greater heights and overshadow the pioneer trees. By the time the more timber-valued species are able to thrive, the aspens and white birch have come to maturity and declined.

Continuing along the trail, a few minutes walk from the spring house leads you back to the Ridge Trail junction. Turn left and walk back to the parking lot. This route is only one of many possible ones in Fox Forest. Another popular hike leads to Mud Pond, a quaking bog of sphagnum moss with insect-eating plants, In the eastern part of the forest. Consider exploring the "tree identification" and "mushroom identification" trails for your next trip to Fox Forest.

Sightseeing: Built in 1804, the Franklin Pierce Homestead was the childhood home of the fourteenth president of the United States and is located 3.0 miles west of Hillsborough near the junction of Routes 9 and 31. Franklin Pierce (1804–1869) was brought here by his parents when he was six weeks old, and spent his early years here. The Hillsborough Historical Society maintains and staffs the property (which has been restored to the Federal-style era) and is open for tours every day in July and August, weekends in June and September through Columbus Day (Sundays 1–4 P.M.). There is a nominal entry fee for adults (under 18 free of charge). To get to the Pierce homestead from the center of Hillsborough, drive west 1.4 miles on West Main Street to its junction with Route 202. Continue on West Main Street for 1.4 miles to the Route 9 junction. Continue on Route 9 west for 0.3 mile to Route 31. The Homestead is located 0.1 mile north on Route 31. For information, call 603-478-3165 or 464-5858, or visit www.franklinpierce.ws.

You may want to visit nearby Gleason Falls, where there Is picnicking, wading, and fishing. Also nearby is the site of one of the town's first grist mills. Built between 1830 and 1860 by Scotch-Irish masons who used rough, locally-hewn granite, three stone arch bridges are still in active use. The original stones of the Gleason Falls Bridge were hand-cut with a hammer and a wedge. To get to Gleason Falls from the junction of West Main Street and 202, drive west for 0.3 mile on West Main Street and turn right onto Beard Road. After 1.7 miles, Beard Road turns to dirt at the intersection with Jones Road. Continue another 1.1 mile on Beard Road.

14
Edward MacDowell Lake

Rating: An easy stroll along the shore of a reservoir with views of waterfowl and wildflowers.
Distance: 1.6 miles
Hiking Time: 1.5 hours
Lake Elevation: 912 feet
USGS Map: Peterborough, Marlborough
Other Map: U.S. Army Corps of Engineers map
Trailhead: Peterborough, New Hampshire

The Edward MacDowell dam on Nubanusit Brook in Peterborough was built between 1948 and 1950 by the U.S. Army Corps of Engineers as part of a network of flood-control projects in the Merrimack River basin. At 1,100 feet long, 25 feet wide, and 67 feet high, the massive dam and flood-control reservoir protects Peterborough, Hancock, Bennington, and other small towns in New Hampshire and Massachusetts, as well as larger cities such as Manchester and Concord, by holding back flood waters from the major tributaries of the Merrimack River.

The park offers 1,198 acres of land for recreation and the enjoyment of nature. There are opportunities here for picnicking, fishing, boating, hunting, cross-country skiing, snowshoeing, horseback riding, hiking, and swimming at a beach area (no lifeguards) at the edge of the lake. Dogs are allowed throughout the MacDowell area, with the exception of the beach area. The 1.6-mile round-trip Wetland Wander Trail hike outlined here follows an unpaved road along the eastern shore of Lake MacDowell, and offers good opportunities to see wildflowers and waterfowl. For more information, call 603-924-3431, or go to www.edward-macdowell-lake.us.

Access: From the intersection of Routes 101 and 202 in Peterborough, continue on Route 101 for 2.2 miles to the sign for Edward MacDowell

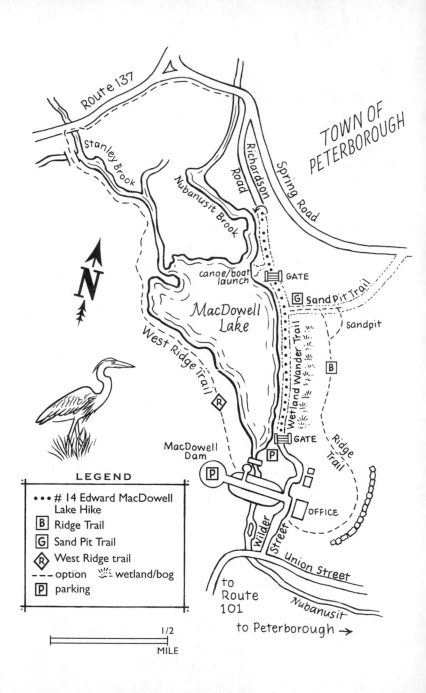

Route 137

Stanley Brook

Nubanusit Brook

Richardson Road

Spring Road

TOWN OF PETERBOROUGH

N

canoe/boat launch

GATE

G Sand Pit Trail

sandpit

MacDowell Lake

West Ridge Trail

B

R

Wetland Wander Trail

Ridge Trail

MacDowell Dam

GATE

P

P

OFFICE

Wilder Street

Union Street

to Route 101

Nubanusit

to Peterborough →

LEGEND

••• # 14 Edward MacDowell Lake Hike

B Ridge Trail

G Sand Pit Trail

R West Ridge trail

- - - option   wetland/bog

P parking

1/2
MILE

Lake. Turn right onto Union Street. Go 0.6 mile to Wilder Street (left) and continue uphill. After 0.4 mile you will come to the main building and visitor information board. Continue driving beyond the entrance gate downhill for 1,000 feet, to a picnic shelter and parking lot. (As you start downhill, the MacDowell Path, a short tree-interpretative trail that leads to the parking area, is on the right).

Description: This hike starts on the unpaved road (Wetland Wander Trail) that runs along the eastern shore of MacDowell Lake. The biggest draw of this short walk is the opportunity to observe the abundance of bird life in the wetlands lining the road: woodducks, mallards, mergansers, ring-necked ducks, and Canada geese. In October, a variety of sparrows including white-throated, and song and swamp, work the scrub shoreline area and you'll see Northern Flickers. Herons stalk through the marsh grass of these waters, there are osprey, and occasionally, reports of an eagle sighting. The vast network of marsh at the isolated north end of the lake make this a popular nesting area or regular stopover for a variety of waterfowl during their spring and fall migrations. To the west, beyond the rock-studded shoreline across the lake, moose, fisher, deer, mink, coyote, raccoon, red fox, and an occasional bear make their homes in the mixed forest. Soon after you start out, a good view of the Skatutakee Mountain shows itself to the north. As you continue, the "Pinnacle" in Dublin pokes into view to the northwest.

In June look for blue-eyed grass and clouds of bluets blooming along the road, and yellow (bullhead) pond lilies bobbing on the lake surface. The smallest of pasture wildflowers, bluets have a delicate pale bloom and usually form large clusters in early spring. Local names for the ubiquitous vernal flowers are innocence, Quaker ladies, nuns, and blue-eyed babies. Pickerelweed grows in abundance along the banks of the weedy lake, where arrowhead is also found. The white flowers of this appropriately-named plant begin to appear in July and may be found in bloom through August and September. Sometimes called duck or swamp potato because of the potato-like tubers produced along its submerged root system, arrowhead is a favorite with ducks and geese who feed on the starchy tubers. You will also find goldenrod, steeplebush (hardhack), Joe Pye Weed, and meadowsweet. Steeplebush is easy to recognize because of its wine-purple color. Meadowsweet is found over much of the same area as hardhack but its leaves are a little broader and its blooms are usually white. Buttonbush, identified by its ball-like flower and seed clusters that open up to fuzz as they ripen, also grows here. The fruits have some appeal to Mallard ducks.

At 0.5 mile you will come to a "beach" area on the left and will see another road that spurs off to the right. This is the (green-blazed) Sand Pit Trail that leads to Spring Road. The Ridge Trail, a (blue-blazed) rolling woodland walk through hemlock and beech, and past stone walls that leads back to Wilder Street below the park entrance, can be also be accessed off the Sand Pit Trail. Continue on the gravel road (Wetland Wander Trail), which becomes more wooded on the right. At 0.6 mile you'll come to a closed yellow gate; step around it to continue your walk. A road to the left leads to a boat ramp and parking area. MacDowell Lake (165-acres) is an ideal body of water for canoes and johnboats with trolling motors. Canoeists and kay-akers will find orange buoys marking the channel of Stanley Brook. The lake is shallow (3 feet deep on average; 8 feet deep at its low-est point) and ideal for fishing for hornpout, largemouth bass, pick-erel, and perch. Beyond the gate, there is marsh on both sides of the road that provides an ideal habitat for mallards to build their nests. Goldfinches, swamp sparrows, eastern kingbirds, owls, and pileated, downy, and hairy woodpeckers are other birds to observe. There is a chance you will see a red-winged blackbird lighting atop a cat-tail or bulrush, or hear his "konk-a-ree" call. If you look closely to the left and northwest, a small waterfall is visible at the upper end of the lake.

At 0.8 mile you will reach another yellow gate. (0.3 mile farther is Spring Road, an East-West road that leads to Route 137.) Turn around here to retrace your steps back to the picnic shelter. After the hike is finished, consider a walk across the 1,100-foot-long dam. Follow a set of concrete steps down the 67-foot high rock slope embankment to check out a marker on the gatehouse wall indicating the record high water level (946.8 feet mean sea level). The record was established during the 1987 April flood when a combination of melting snow and heavy rain filled the lake to 126 percent of its capacity. April of 1987 was the only period in the history of the dam when the water crested the spillway.

The 100-foot-wide spillway is located 3.2 miles upstream (northeast) of the dam at Halfmoon Pond in Hancock, and it empties into Ferguson Brook, which in turn flows into the Contoocook River. The overflow system for the dam works on the same idea as an old-style bathtub, where a drain near the top of the tub allows safe drainage and prevents water spilling over the sides if the tap is left running. Three 1.0-foot-thick steel gates that run down to the water level regulate the flow of the lake. The gatehouse channels water downstream through a concrete conduit that stretches several hundred feet under the dam. MacDowell Lake drains an area of 44 square miles—from the eastern slopes of Mount Monadnock in Jaffrey to Lake Nubanusit in Hancock—and the reservoir has a capacity to store 4.2 billion gallons of water. Five different lakes run into the reservoir. Prior to the creation of the system of reservoirs and local protection works, cities and towns in the Merrimack Valley basin experienced frequent and sometimes devastating floods. The Flood of 1936 and the Hurricane of 1938 were especially destructive. The Hurricane of 1938 alone caused 750 million dollars in damage and led to the creation of much of the U.S. Army Corps of Engineer's flood control projects.

Complete your walk to the west side of the dam where there is a circular parking area, restrooms, and picnic tables on park-like fields of grass. To the right of the restrooms, a red diamond-blazed trail leads to Route 137. By continuing on Route 137, Spring and Richardson Roads and the Wetland Wander Trail, it is possible to complete a 3.5-mile circuit around the lake.

MacDowell Dam is open 8 A.M. to 8 P.M. during the recreational season (Memorial Day to Labor Day), and sunrise to sunset the rest of the year. Tours of the dam and gatehouse are given periodically during the summer recreation season, along with interpretative programs on wetlands and forest-management techniques. Information is available at the project office where you can pick up maps and brochures, and view charts and aerial photographs of the dam.

Sightseeing: The town of Peterborough is worth a visit before or after your hike. A handsome town of dignified homes on hilly streets with a number of red brick buildings in the Georgian Revival style that are a favorite with photographers, Peterborough was the model for Thornton Wilder's *Our Town*. The Town House (on the National Historic Register), a monumental structure built in 1918 and a copy of Faneuil Hall in Boston, serves as the center for town meetings as well as cultural events.

A commercial and cultural center for the Monadnock Region, Peterborough is also the home of the famed MacDowell Colony and Peterborough Players Summer Theatre. The Peterborough Town Library was founded in 1833 and was the first free public library in the U.S. to be supported by taxation. In the 1800s, Peterborough was a prosperous manufacturing community with a dozen mills. The Phoenix Cotton Factory was the principal plant and it employed hundreds of people for well over 100 years until its demise in 1922. A tailrace below the mill ran in a wide stream in the lot below the Town House on its way to the Contoocook River. It conveyed water from the great mill wheel to supply power for a number of other businesses, which included a planing mill, shoe factory, and basket shop. For years the canal was called the "Little Jordan" because the Mormon and Baptist churches used the stream for baptisms.

An old mill and a school building have been moved onto land owned by the Peterborough Historical Society on Grove Street; they contain the historical and genealogical library, exhibits, and museum, which are open year-round, Monday through Friday, 10 A.M. to 4 P.M. and Saturdays, July and August. For hours, call 603-924-3235. Museum admission is $3; free for children under 12, PHS members, and research visitors. For more information, go to www.peterborough history.org.

Putnam Park is also on Grove Street, near the post office; It offers short trails that parallel the Nubanusit River and waterfalls.

15
Meetinghouse Pond

Rating: A pleasant woodland walk on the edge of a pond, with
    side trails leading to shoreline vistas and opportunities to view
    wildlife along the way.
Distance: 1.4 miles
Hiking Time: 1.5 hours
Pond Elevation: 1,096 feet
USGS Map: Marlborough
Other Map: Audubon Society of New Hampshire Field Guide map
Trailhead: Marlborough, New Hampshire

This is a pleasant woodland hike through mature stands of hemlock
and pine along the edge of a 45-acre pond, Kensan Devan Sanctuary, on the western slope of Mount Monadnock. The route outlined
here explores a rich variety of flora and fauna, and colorful mushrooms sprouting from the moist woods on the hemlock-lined shore
of Meetinghouse Pond. August is the month for the mushrooms, especially on a rainy day when the humidity level of the ground is high.
Bring along a mushroom book on this walk to identify the many varieties and their shapes, sizes, and colors. You will likely find milky
caps—a large, white-capped common mushroom that tends to
stain brown in age and has a cottony in-rolled margin. Milky caps or
Lactarius deceptivus ("deceptive milky") are so called because of the
milky secretion emitted if you score its gills. Young milky caps are
flat-topped with button-hole centers and edges that fold over. As it
grows older, the cap of this mushroom lifts up into a funnel shape to
resemble a goblet.

    Other mushroom species found here include the in-rolled-pax, a
brown pancake-like mushroom with a thick stalk and gills that stain
reddish-brown; the purple-capped mushroom; the yellow disc waxy
cap mushroom; and the destroying angel, a pure white mushroom
that grows beneath hemlock and belongs to the Amanita genus.

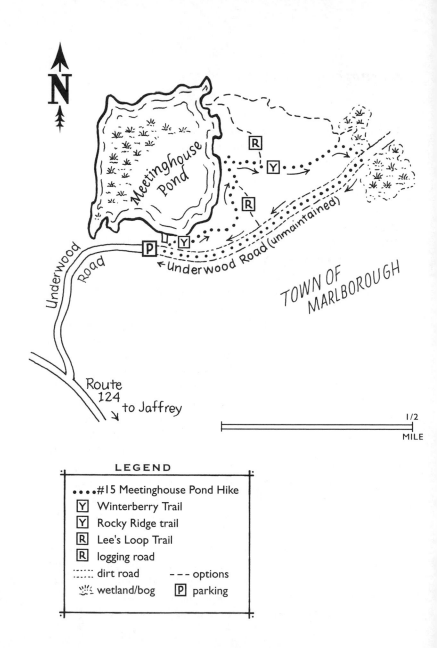

N

Meetinghouse Pond

R

Y

R

Y

P

←Underwood Road (unmaintained)

Underwood Road

TOWN OF MARLBOROUGH

Route 124 to Jaffrey

1/2 MILE

LEGEND

••••#15 Meetinghouse Pond Hike
Y Winterberry Trail
Y Rocky Ridge trail
R Lee's Loop Trail
R logging road
::::: dirt road   - - - options
﹋ wetland/bog   P parking

Amanitas contain one of the deadliest poisons found in nature: One cap of the *Amanita virosa*, or destroying angel, for example, can kill a person. Perfect white mushrooms are often poisonous and Amanitas are responsible for 95 percent of all mushroom poisonings.

How can you tell if a mushroom is poisonous? One of the many old wives' tales that describe how to determine the toxicity of mushrooms includes boiling them with a silver dollar. If the coin turns black, it means the mushroom is poisonous. Unfortunately, there is only one rule that can be applied to mushrooms: You have to know exactly what kind of mushroom you have picked to know if it is edible.

Despite their reputation, mushrooms do have a positive function. They work to decompose leaves and animal remains, and they release antibiotics. There would not be any forests if it were not for fungi that reduce dead timber and forest litter to essential humus on the woodland floor. Mushrooms lack leafy greens and are unable to manufacture starch, sugar, or other elements. They must absorb these nutrients from dead wood, leaves, or soils enriched by plant remains, softening and breaking down the wood. Without mushrooms and other fungi, we would have miles and miles of logs, without space for anything to grow. If you live in the Monadnock Region and are interested in learning more about mushrooms, you can join the Monadnock Mushroomers Unlimited, an organization of amateur mycologists who study mushrooms in their natural habitat. Contact Monadnock Mushroomers Unlimited, P.O. Box 1796, Keene, New Hampshire, 03431.

Access: From Manchester, take Route 101 west to the Route 124 junction in Marlborough. Turn south on Route 124 and continue for 2.3 miles to the dirt Underwood Road. Continue 0.5 mile farther to the parking area and boat landing.

Optional Access: For a more scenic route to the trailhead in the autumn, take Route 101 west to Route 137 to Jaffrey. From Jaffrey take Route 124 past lowlands ringed with fiery red maples, colorful hills, roadside yellow ferns, and purple asters. Route 124 also offers great views of the stony crown and broad flanks of Mount Monadnock.

Meetinghouse Pond.

Description: Before you begin your hike, take a short walk down to the pond to get a peek at the white and yellow water lilies and the water-loving plants growing on the shoreline, including sweetgale, high bush blueberry, maleberry, and mountain holly. The yellow-blazed trail starts near the shoreline in the woods to the right of the boat landing, and moves past ground cover of trillium, clintonia, bunchberry, and an impressive display of hobblebush with large, heart-shaped leaves at their base that turn bronze-red and purplish-pink in the fall. The shady shoreline of Meetinghouse Pond provides the ideal habitat for this viburnum, also called moosewood, which grows in dense thickets throughout the woods.

The trail soon swings away from the pond and leads uphill along the side of a ridge, as the footing becomes rocky. More hemlock enshrouds you as you step over a bed of moss-covered boulders; Note a large boulder to the right of the trail with a cluster of polypod fern clinging to its top. The trail turns left, back toward the pond, then moves through a gap in a stone wall and comes to a junction (red-yellow) 10 minutes into the hike. Continue on the yellow-blazed Rocky Ridge trail that follows the shore of the pond before talking a sharp right turn and moving uphill. Notice the distinct change in footing and in the forest community; The drier soil supports a greater hardwood population of maple, birch, white pine, and red oak, and ground cover that includes Indian cucumber-root, twinflower, pipsissewa, and ground cedar clubmoss. Five minutes from the red-yellow junction you will come to the red-blazed Lee's Loop trail (left) leading back to the pond. Continue on the Rocky Ridge trail as it moves over a stony ridge. After 5 minutes you will reach another junction where Lee's Loop rejoins the trail. A right leads to Underwood Road. Turn right (west) again on Underwood Road for the 0.6-mile walk back to the parking area.

Sightseeing: Before or after your hike, you can explore Jaffrey Center, located 1.9 miles west of the town of Jaffrey. Here you will find the handsome First Congregational Church, and at the top of the green, the Old Meetinghouse, built in 1775 to serve both as town hall and church. According to one account, the huge granite doorstone of the First Church was pulled from Marlborough over Mount Monadnock by 14 oxen. The frame of the Old Meetinghouse was raised on June 17, 1775, the day of the Battle of Bunker Hill, and according to tradition, workmen could hear the sound of distant cannons. Services were discontinued in 1844, and the building is now owned by the town of Jaffrey and used as a community house. The famed Amos Fortune lectures are held here. Amos Fortune was a Black slave (born about 1710), who at age 60 purchased his and his wife's freedom. In 1781 he came to Jaffrey where he established a tannery, gaining respect for his honest work and earning a reputation as an upstanding citizen. At his death he left a fund to the town of Jaffrey, and today the bequest is used for educational purposes. The Amos Fortune Forum presents nationally-known speakers in a series of free lectures held at the Meetinghouse on Friday evenings during July and August. Visit www.amosfortune.com for more information. The Meetinghouse is also used for Monadnock Music concerts.

The Horse Sheds are located directly behind the meetinghouse.

Names of the original settlers can still be seen above the openings. Next to the Meetinghouse you will find the Little Red Schoolhouse maintained by the Jaffrey Historical Society. It is open to the public on weekends during the summer, or by request. Call 603-532-6527 for more information. Amos Fortune's gravesite is located in the old burying ground behind the Meetinghouse. His gravestone records that he "lived reputably and died hopefully." Also here are the gravestones of Willa Cather (1873–1947), the eminent American novelist who spent many summers in the Monadnock Region and wrote some of her best-known works in Jaffrey Center; and "aunt" Hannah Davis, a resourceful and beloved spinster who made, trademarked, and sold the first wooden bandboxes used for women's bonnets in the United States. Historical notes and a locator map are located at the end of the Horse Sheds. The Meetinghouse cemetery is a peaceful place to visit, with the craggy summit of Mount Monadnock serving as a backdrop. Near the First Church and Meetinghouse is Thorndike Pond Road, which leads to an outstanding view of Mount Monadnock from the eastern shore across the water of Thorndike Pond.

16

Eliza Adams Gorge

Rating: An easy hike along a section of the Monadnock-Sunapee
    Greenway that leads to a scenic spillway and gorge.
Distance: 2.4 miles
Hiking Time: 1.5 hours
Lowest Elevation: 1,200 feet
Highest Elevation: 1,378 feet
USGS Map: Marlborough
Other Map: SPNHF Monadnock-Sunapee Greenway Trail Guide
Trailhead: Marlborough, New Hampshire

This easy hike will bring you to a scenic gorge and spillway at the
Howe Reservoir in Harrisville, New Hampshire. The 1.2-mile trail is
along part of the Greenway, a 49-mile-long footpath that stretches
from Mount Monadnock to Mount Sunapee in Newbury. The Howe
Reservoir, the spillway's source, is drained in early winter, making
late spring, summer, and early fall—when the water is actively flowing—a popular time to visit the gorge.

Access: From Dublin drive west on Route 101 for 3.4 miles to the
wayside parking area (left). Continue another 0.8 mile and look for a
sign reading "Monadnock Wilderness Girl Scout Camp" on the right.
There is a parking lot on the opposite side of Route 101. The area is
protected through the cooperation of the Appalachian Mountain
Club, the Society for the Protection of New Hampshire Forests, and
local landowners.

Description: The white-blazed trail starts on a logging road and
moves uphill past the "Monadnock Wilderness Girl Scout Campsite"
sign. The walking is easy on the wide path, which moves through a
mixed forest of pine, spruce, maple, birch, and beech. After 10 minutes you will reach a double blaze, which indicates a turn, as the

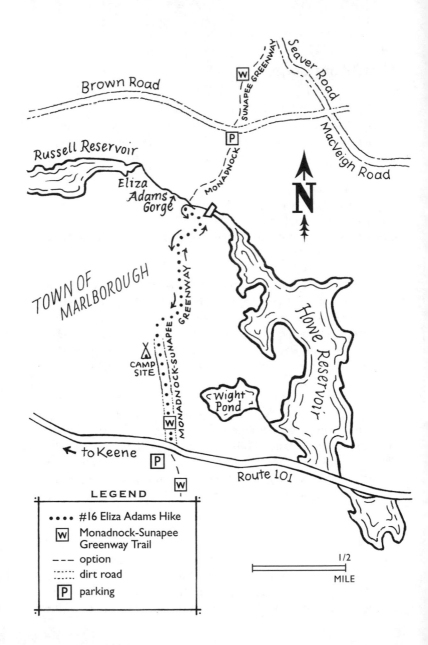

Brown Road

SUNAPEE GREENWAY

W

Seaver Road

P

MacVeigh Road

Russell Reservoir

Eliza Adams Gorge

MONADNOCK

N

TOWN OF MARLBOROUGH

GREENWAY

Howe Reservoir

CAMP SITE

MONADNOCK-SUNAPEE

Wight Pond

W

← to Keene

P

W

Route 101

1/2

MILE

LEGEND

•••• #16 Eliza Adams Hike

W Monadnock-Sunapee Greenway Trail

--- option

······ dirt road

P parking

trail turns sharply right and uphill past an area clear-cut for electrical right-of-ways. As you pass beneath a power line, you will get a glimpse of the Howe Reservoir below the power-line cut to the right. Howe is a body of water popular with canoeists and kayakers; From the low profile of a boat the view of Mount Monadnock's northern flank rising above the forest on the opposite shore of Dublin Lake is one of the best. The white-blazed trail continues on a grassy path through hardwoods. After passing an intersecting woods road to the left, the trail turns right and moves downhill past stone walls and downed logs sheathed in bright green moss.

Look for turkey tail fungus (*Trametes versicolor*), a common bracket fungus that grows on dead deciduous trees, especially oaks, in overlapping, leathery, semicircular caps that resemble miniature turkey tails. It is characterized by concentric colored bands that may include brown, auburn, green, blue, and yellow segments. Like other fungi, turkey tail is the name for the part that you see—the "flower" that grows from May to December. Most of the fungus is inside the bark of the log.

Soon you will make the transition from hardwood to hemlock woods and get another glimpse of the reservoir through the trees as you approach a shorefront area. After turning left, the trail drops on switchbacks to the gorge and a bridge that crosses the outlet brook that flows to Russell Reservoir to the northwest. Take some time to enjoy the quiet sounds of the forest and splashing water below the dam. When you are ready, cross the bridge and climb the steep bank out of the gorge. The grassy bank area near the concrete dam makes an ideal spot to sprawl out, enjoy lunch, and listen to the rush of water as it moves over the dam and spillway. After lunch, you may want to explore more of the Monadnock-Sunapee Greenway, which continues north to the town of Nelson, or conclude your walk and retrace your steps back to Route 101 and your car.

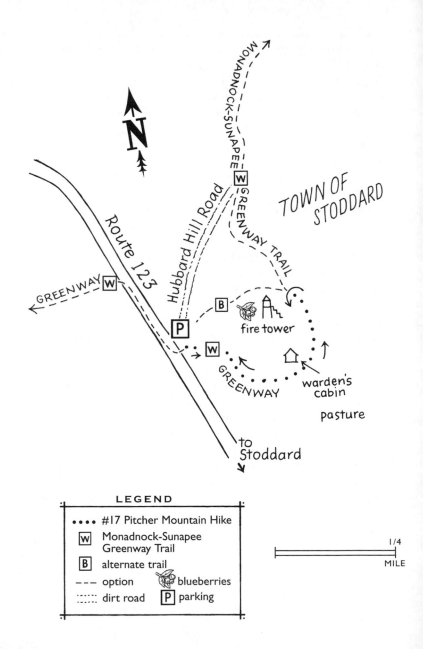

N

MONADNOCK-SUNAPEE GREENWAY TRAIL

TOWN OF STODDARD

Route 123

Hubbard Hill Road

GREENWAY Ⓦ

Ⓦ GREENWAY TRAIL

Ⓟ

Ⓑ

🫐 fire tower

Ⓦ

GREENWAY

warden's cabin

pasture

to Stoddard

LEGEND

•••• #17 Pitcher Mountain Hike

Ⓦ Monadnock-Sunapee Greenway Trail

Ⓑ alternate trail

--- option 🫐 blueberries

⋯⋯ dirt road Ⓟ parking

1/4
MILE

17
Pitcher Mountain

Rating: An easy hike on a section of the Monadnock-Sunapee
   Greenway that leads to an overgrown pasture on the summit,
   and an outstanding 360-degree view of the Monadnock
   Highlands.
Distance: 0.8 mile
Hiking Time: 30 minutes
Lowest Elevation: 2,000 feet
Highest Elevation: 2,153 feet
USGS Map: Stoddard
Other Map: SPNHF Monadnock-Sunapee Greenway Trail Guide
Trailhead: Stoddard, New Hampshire

Pitcher Mountain today is part of the Andorra Forest, a lush, 12,000-
acre SPNHF (Society for the Protection of New Hampshire Forests)
preserve, the largest one in New Hampshire protected by a private
easement, and prime habitat for the wildlife of the region. Standing
on the steps of the Pitcher Mountain observation tower and gazing
out at the gently rolling hills, it is difficult to imagine that this area
as a charred wasteland. But in April, 1941, the Great Marlow-Stoddard
forest fire turned 27,000 acres of this bucolic forest into a smoldering
ruin. The fire first broke out near a logging operation, then zigzagged
out of control, forcing the wildlife to scatter before the onrush of
smoke and flames. The spring of 1941 had been unusually dry, with
April 1941 as the driest month in 70 years; and the Hurricane of 1938
had provided many downed and damaged trees for kindling. The
Great Fire is recorded as one of the most destructive in the history of
southern New Hampshire.

The hike to Pitcher Mountain is within everyone's ability. It begins
on the Greenway, a 49-mile-long footpath that connects Mount Monadnock in Jaffrey and Mount Sunapee in Newbury. The Monadnock-
Sunapee Greenway Trail Guide is available from the Society for the

Preservation of New Hampshire Forests. The society is located at 54 Portsmouth St., Concord, New Hampshire, 03301; and can be reached by phone at 603-224-9945 or online at www.spnhf.org.

Access: From the Manchester area, take Route 101 west to Peterborough. Continue north on Route 123 to Hancock, and then 10 miles to Stoddard. One mile west of Stoddard is the Pitcher Mountain Farm, famous for its long-haired Scottish highland cattle, open daily to the public 6 A.M. to 4 P.M. The parking area and trailhead to Pitcher Mountain is 0.5 mile north of the farm.

Description: Two roads branch off from the parking area. Start your hike on the one that leads east (to the right), which is blazed in white rectangles. The road to the left is the Hubbard Hill Road, which will cross the Greenway at 0.66 mile ahead. After crossing Route 123 at the parking lot, the Greenway travels the fire warden's road 0.4 mile up the south side of Pitcher Mountain. Along the way you will get a nice view of Mount Monadnock across a pasture before reaching the fire warden's cabin just below the Pitcher Mountain fire tower. An alternate route is a shorter but steeper and rockier blue-blazed trail that enters the woods immediately after you start out on the Greenway. Either trail, white or blue, takes only about 15 minutes to complete.

The 50-foot fire tower is staffed from April to October, and hikers are welcome to visit the observation cab if the watchman is not busy spotting fires. Without trees in the immediate vicinity, the view from the top is a spectacular 360 degrees. You can see Mount Monadnock to the south, Lovewell to the north, Kearsarge to the northeast, and Crotched Mountain and the Wapack Range to the southeast.

Sunapee stands slightly beyond Lovewell to the west; the big mountain to the northwest is Mount Ascutney in Vermont; Killington is a four-peaked mountain to the left of Ascutney. As you look toward Killington and gaze southwest along the line of mountain tops, you can see all the well-known ski areas in Vermont: Okemo, Magic, and Bromley. South of Bromley you can see Stratton, Snow, Haystack,

Pitcher Mountain Tower.

and on a clear day, Hogback. To the east, Highland Lake nestles serenely in a forested pocket.

All of the distant blue hills of the region comprise the rocky divide between the Merrimack and Connecticut Rivers known as the Monadnock Highlands. Town histories report that rain falling on one side of a house located in Stoddard trickles into the Merrimack River, whereas rain from the other side makes its way into the Connecticut River.

After enjoying the view, consider following the white-blazed Greenway further before returning to your car. The Greenway continues north along the ridge of Pitcher Mountain. Be particularly careful to stay on the footpath here because there is a maze of side paths, courtesy of the blueberry-pickers.

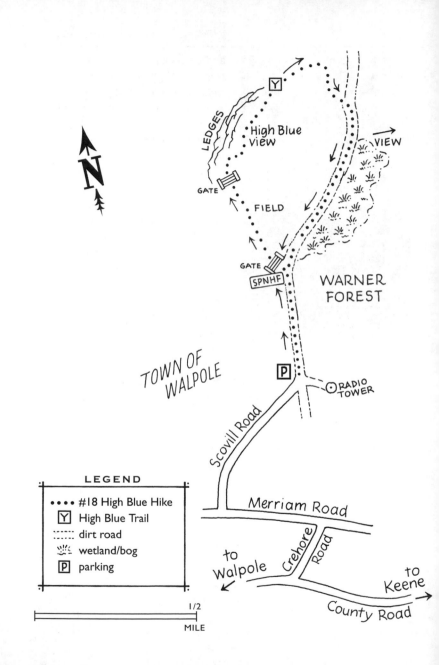

N

LEDGES

High Blue
view

VIEW

GATE

FIELD

GATE

SPNHF

WARNER
FOREST

TOWN OF
WALPOLE

P

RADIO
TOWER

Scovill Road

Merriam Road

Crehore Road

to
Walpole

to
Keene

County Road

LEGEND

•••• #18 High Blue Hike
Y High Blue Trail
‥‥ dirt road
⋇ wetland/bog
P parking

1/2

MILE

18
High Blue

Rating: A short and easy loop hike that leads to a ledge overlook with sweeping views of the Connecticut River Valley and the Green Mountains.

Distance: 1.5 miles

Hiking Time: 1 hour

Lowest Elevation: 1,489 feet

Highest Elevation: 1,588 feet

USGS Map: Walpole

Trailhead: Walpole, New Hampshire

This hike is an easy woodland walk past stone walls and fields that leads to a ledge with wide views. High Blue is part of the Warner Forest, a 165-acre preserve donated to the Society for the Protection of New Hampshire Forests (SPNHF) in 1981 by Stephen Warner of Malibu, California, who used the property for relaxation and picnics.

Access: From Keene take Route 12 north to Route 12A. Continue on 12A for 0.7 mile. At a signal light turn left onto Old Walpole Road. (After 4.6 miles the name changes to County Road.) At 5.8 miles from the junction of Route 12A and Old Walpole Road, turn right onto Crehore Road and drive 0.2 mile. Turn left onto Merriam Road (dirt) and drive 0.2 mile. Turn right onto Scovill Road and continue 0.4 mile to a junction where you will see a small turnoff for parking.

Description: A 0.2-mile walk left (north) down the unimproved dirt road past tall birch trees and a bog brings you to a SPNHF sign and green gate on the left. The trail starts at an old road that leads into the woods beyond the Forest Society sign. Shortly you will come to a field that brims with clover and wildflowers in July, and is bordered by beech woods and raspberries. As you continue along the left edge of the tall grass look behind you to the southeast for a view of Mount

High Blue Vista Loop,
Walpole.

Monadnock's silhouette in the distance. At the end of the field go around a stone wall and aluminum gate. The trail continues gradually uphill past beech, birch, ferns, and boulders covered with rock tripe. In the woods near a stone wall to the right, the remains of a tumbled-down chimney of an old foundation have been reclaimed by nature. You will soon spy a tiny pond (right), and moments later arrive at an open space at the top of a rise that shows a glimpse of the blue horizon and the reason why this hike is named High Blue. A sign, "High Blue 1,588," marks the ledge overlook. From the ledges beyond the steep hillside clearing, which is somewhat obstructed by trees, the Connecticut River Valley and majestic Green Mountains of Vermont (Stratton Mountain stands out prominently) unfold to the west. Take some time to sit in the sun on the ledges and enjoy lunch. When you are ready to continue on the trail, look for a yellow blaze. After moving through a mixed forest of hemlock, maple, birch, and beech trees, you will walk past an open area of impressive tall ferns blanketing both sides of the trail.

Ferns are the largest group of seedless vascular (duct or "pipeline" system for transporting water) plants in the world. The roughly

12,000 species of ferns play an important role in the environment by helping to form and hold soil in place. These simple but remarkable plants have been with us more than 300 million years and reproduce through the release of spores, which fly in the wind, settle onto moist soil, and then germinate. (The mysterious regeneration of ferns led to an ancient belief that the spores could confer invisibility to a person sprinkled with them.) A single fern can produce millions of spores, which are stored in clusters on the fronds or the visible part of the leaf.

After you've gained a new appreciation for these early "trees" of the first forests, continue on the trail, which is marked by double blazes, and descend to cross a crude log bridge. Ten minutes from the ledges you will reach the unimproved dirt road and "High Blue Vista Loop" sign. Turn right. A 15-minute walk past a field (left) with good upland views toward Keene to the south brings you back to the SPNHF sign.

Sightseeing: After your hike you may want to visit the historic town of Walpole, a classic New England village of quiet charm located on a plateau 0.5 mile east of the Connecticut River. Walpole reveals its distinguished past in its spacious town common, tree-shaded streets, and well-kept early period houses, some dating from the late eighteenth century. During the early to mid-nineteenth century, Walpole was a popular summer retreat, with several large inns.

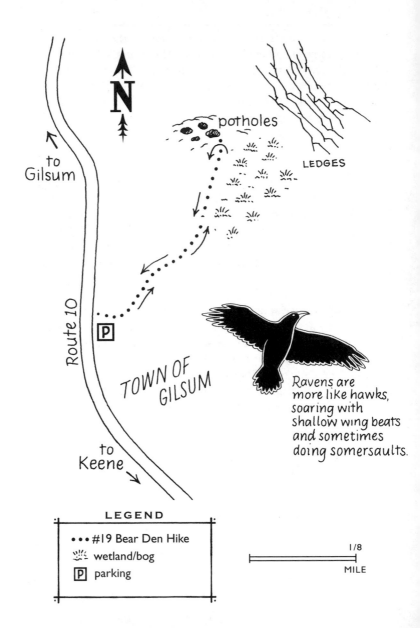

potholes

LEDGES

to
Gilsum

Route 10

P

TOWN OF
GILSUM

to
Keene

Ravens are
more like hawks,
soaring with
shallow wing beats
and sometimes
doing somersaults.

LEGEND

••• #19 Bear Den Hike
⚬⚬ wetland/bog
P parking

1/8
MILE

19

Bear Den Geological Park

Rating: A short hike to an intriguing geological area with steep
   rock outcrops, ledges, and potholes. Farther back in the woods
   are caves that may have been a bear-denning area.
Distance: 0.6 mile
Hiking Time: 45 minutes
Lowest Elevation: 941 feet
Highest Elevation: 1,161 feet
USGS Map: Gilsum
Trailhead: Gilsum, New Hampshire

The tiny town of Gilsum has a big reputation for its rocks. Every June,
hundreds of mineral collectors, dealers, and jewelers descend on the
small community 8.0 miles northeast of Keene to buy, sell, and swap
beryl, quartz crystals, and minerals of all sorts at the Gilsum Rock
Swap and Mineral Show.

   Gilsum was once a center for the mining of feldspar and mica. According to early histories, after a heavy rain the unpaved main street
once sparkled with red garnets, although the gems were too small to
be of commercial value. The town's geology and old mine sites continue to attract visitors.

   This short hike takes you to a remnant of the Ice Age that features
pot holes and huge boulders 200 million years old. The Bear Den Natural Area is a New Hampshire State Park and is open to the public (although it is not actively maintained by Park Service staff).

Access: From Keene, take Route 10 north. The parking area (dirt)
is marked by a sign on the right, 1.6 miles south of the village of
Gilsum.

Description: The trail starts at the back of the parking lot and immediately enters a forest of tall hemlock and pine. The dirt road soon

turns left and moves up a south-facing slope where oak trees grow in the drier soil to heights equaling the enormous conifers passed earlier. As you continue, keep your eyes on the ground for veins of quartzite and flakes of mica, with its thin layers that are tough enough to bounce back into shape when bent. Turn your eyes to the sky and there is a good chance you will see a raven (*Corvus corax*), although you will often hear their guttural "aulk aulk" before you see them. Although they are members of the crow family, common ravens are distinctly different from crows. Ravens are large birds, often weighing more than 2.5 pounds, with prominent beaks, wedge-shaped tails, and broad wings spanning more than 4.5 feet. Crows typically weigh less than a pound, have shorter and narrower beaks, and fan-shaped tails and wings spanning less than a yard.

Although ravens and crows regularly fly at speeds of 30 to 60 miles per hour, ravens fly more like hawks, soaring with shallow wing beats and sometimes doing somersaults. Crows flap. Ravens also have deeper, hoarser calls than the caw of crows, its voice a low-pitched, reverberating croaking or "gronk-gronk." In fact, ravens have perhaps the most complex vocabulary of any bird. They warble, scream, caw, cackle, croak, trill, yell, and make sounds like dripping water and bells.

Another bird to look for is the pileated woodpecker, a crow-sized bird with a red crest extending from the head to the nape. Look for oblong holes in the trunks of large hollow trees weakened by fungus. These are feeding cavities excavated by birds in their search for larvae from termites, ants, and wood-boring beetles. More than any other woodpecker, pileated woodpeckers feed on decaying, fallen trees and have their own special hammering note. A large pileated woodpecker gives an average of 12 strokes delivered with increasing force and frequency toward the middle of the sequence and fading off towards the end. The tattoo of the much smaller hairy woodpecker is short with loud, deliberate, well-spaced taps, while the downy woodpecker gives a softer, longer, and more rapid drumming sequence. After completing your bird study, continue on a trail that requires some picking over stones and roots as it steadily ascends.

Large boulders in the woods presage the granite outcrops and ledges you will soon encounter.

At 0.3 mile at the top of the rise in a stand of birch trees, you come to an impressive granite, moss-covered outcrop to the left, sculpted with concave openings and potholes. Take some time to explore these smooth-sided cylindrical holes that were scoured out from the rock by the abrasive force of the sand and gravel carried by melt water during the retreat of the glaciers. Natural foot and hand holes in the rock allow you to clamber to the top of the outcrop to further explore these geological marvels. After checking out the potholes, you may want to explore the ledges and huge boulders for other intriguing geological patterns before retracing your steps for the short walk back to your car.

Sightseeing: Vessel Rock, a relic of the Ice Age, is a large boulder measuring 45 feet long, 32 feet wide, and 25 feet high. Its name is derived from its resemblance to a ship under full sail. To get there from the Bear Den parking area, continue on Route 10 north for 0.9 mile and turn left onto Vessel Rock Road. The enormous boulder is 0.7 mile farther on the right. The outline of the seagoing vessel is easy to see, but it was more prominent years ago before a large chunk of rock resembling a bow and jib-boom fell from the boulder's west side.

Gilsum is also the site of the Stone Arch Bridge, which was constructed in 1863 without the use of mortar. With an arch that averages 36 feet, 6 inches above the Ashuelot River, the Gilsum Stone Arch Bridge has the highest vault of any dry stone-laid bridge in New Hampshire. The bridge is listed on the National Register of Historic Places and it is located on Surry Road 0.1 mile north from the Route 10/Vessel Rock Road junction.

MODERATE HIKES

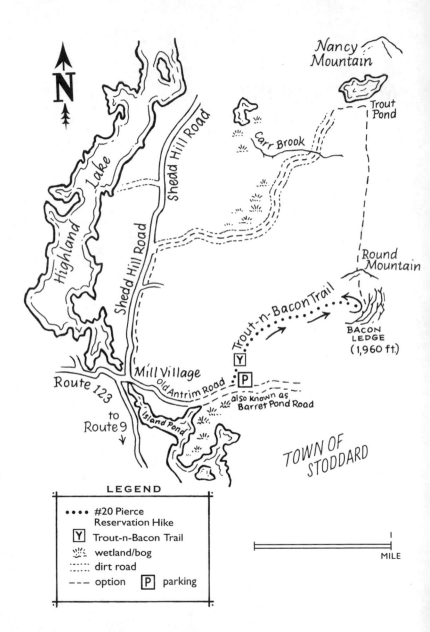

Nancy
Mountain

Trout
Pond

Carr Brook

Highland Lake

Shedd Hill Road

Shedd Hill Road

Round
Mountain

Trout-n-Bacon Trail

BACON
LEDGE
(1,960 ft.)

Mill Village

Old Antrim Road

Route 123

also known as
Barret Pond Road

to
Route 9

Island Pond

TOWN OF
STODDARD

N

LEGEND

•••• #20 Pierce
       Reservation Hike

Y Trout-n-Bacon Trail

wetland/bog

dirt road

--- option   P parking

MILE

20

Peirce Reservation

Rating: A moderate hike through unspoiled forest that leads to a ledge overlook with sweeping views. An optional longer walk takes you to a secluded pond and returns on an old logging road.
Distance: 2.2 miles
Hiking Time: 1.5 hours
Lowest Elevation: 1,356 feet
Highest Elevation: 1,960 feet
USGS Map: Stoddard
Trailhead: Stoddard, New Hampshire

The Trout-n-Bacon Trail is located within the Charles L. Peirce Wildlife and Forest Reservation, a 3,661-acre Society for the Protection of New Hampshire Forests (SPNHF) preserve that contains more than 10 miles of trails and woods roads winding through a mixed Northern hardwood forest. The name of the hike, "trout-and-bacon trail," comes from the Bacon ledge and Trout Pond that highlight this walk.

Access: To get to the trailhead from Manchester, take Route 101 west to Keene. From Keene, take Route 9 east for 17.4 miles to junction of Route 123 north. Follow Route 123 north 1.8 miles to Mill Village. (On the way to Mill Village you will drive past 158-acre Island Pond, which makes a good swimming stop after your hike. It includes a large beach area and boat landing, but swim at your own risk.) Turn right at the Stoddard fire station, cross the bridge, and immediately bear right onto Old Antrim Road (dirt), which is also called Barrett Pond Road. Continue 0.9 mile (road is rough) and park in the small cleared area (left). If the road is muddy, at 0.5-mile, park in a cleared area (right) near the "Road Closed at Own Risk" sign.

Description: The yellow-blazed Trout-n-Bacon Trail leaves Old Antrim Road just west of the parking area near a large boulder, small brook,

Trout Pond, Peirce Reservation.

and green-and-white sign that reads "Forest and Wildlife Management Area." The trail quickly turns (right) onto a woods road. The walking is easy along the leaf-strewn path, which is littered with acorns in the fall, before descending through a stand of hemlock.

The trail moves steadily uphill and past large boulders, and beech and birch trees displaying dazzling yellow canopies in the autumn, then narrows, becomes washed-out, and boulder-strewn. Twenty minutes into the hike you'll reach a fork. Stay right. The yellow-blazed trail crosses a stream and continues past an impressive area of ferns and over a surface matted with pine needles. Double blazes show the way (left) as the trail moves uphill and parallels a stone wall. After passing through an opening in the wall, the trail continues to parallel the ancient stone barrier and soon turns right. A short scramble over an outcrop covered with juniper bushes brings you to the summit at 1.1 miles. At Bacon Ledge (1,960 feet) you will be surprised at how suddenly the countryside opens up. To the west, the broad waters of 7-mile-long Highland Lake spread across the valley with the hills of the Greenway stretching toward Mount Sunapee beyond. With its fire tower, Pitcher Mountain is easy to recognize. Mt. Kearsarge and Mt. Ascutney in Vermont are further north.

Optional Extension: You can add 5.7 miles and 3 hours onto the hike by continuing on the yellow-blazed trail to Trout Pond as it moves beyond a large cairn on the summit and proceeds north over the ridges of Round Mountain. Fifteen minutes into the walk you will begin a descent. Approximately one hour from Bacon Ledge you will reach an open field and cottages, which were once owned by Elizabeth Babcock, who donated this property to the SPNHF. A side trail leads to Trout Pond where you will see Nancy Mountain (1,780 feet) reflected in the waters.

The main trail to Shedd Hill Road turns left, then left again on another woods road. Forty-five minutes of mostly uphill walking on an old tote road (look for old foundations and cellar holes on the side of the road) brings you to a gate and SPNHF sign. A 0.8-mile walk down paved Shedd Hill Road returns you to Mill Village and Old Antrim Road. Continue 0.8 mile on Old Antrim Road to your car.

Sightseeing: The Stone Arch bridge in Stoddard is a twin-arch structure built without mortar, supported solely by expert shaping of its arch stones. From the Route 123 north/Route 9 junction drive north on Route 9 for 2.3 miles. Look for the bridge on the south side of Route 9 in a roadside rest area.

Stone Arch Bridge, Stoddard.

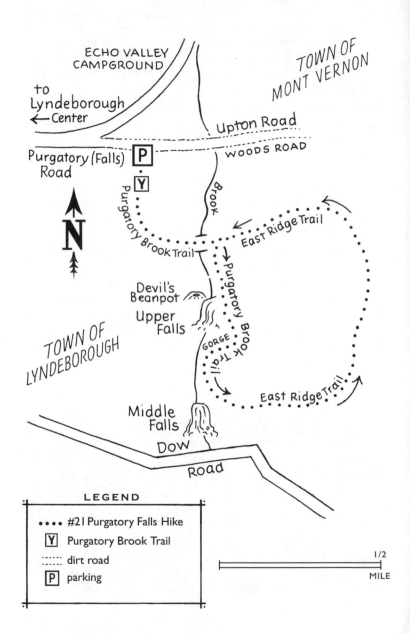

ECHO VALLEY
CAMPGROUND

TOWN OF
MONT VERNON

to
Lyndeborough
← Center

Upton Road

WOODS ROAD

Purgatory (Falls)
Road

P

Y

Brook

East Ridge Trail

Purgatory Brook Trail

Purgatory Brook Trail

N

Devil's
Beanpot

Upper
Falls

TOWN OF
LYNDEBOROUGH

GORGE

East Ridge Trail

Middle
Falls

Dow

Road

LEGEND

•••• #21 Purgatory Falls Hike

Y Purgatory Brook Trail

:::::: dirt road

P parking

1/2

MILE

21

Purgatory Falls

Rating: A moderate woodland walk to a rugged gorge and water-
falls. The return trip climbs a ridge and crosses an old woods
road. Caution: The trail can be wet and slippery in places. The
stream may be dry in late summer.
Distance: 1.2 miles
Hiking Time: 1.5 to 2 hours
Lowest Elevation: 430 feet
Highest Elevation: 775 feet
USGS Map: Milford, New Boston
Trailhead: Lyndeborough, New Hampshire

This hike will take you to a place called purgatory, but it is anything but an unpleasant experience. Straddling the Mont Vernon-
Lyndeborough border and owned jointly by the towns, the 40-acre
Purgatory Falls Conservation area is a tranquil oasis for those seeking
solitude and respite from the bustle of the everyday world. For years
this was a spot where families gathered for weekend outings, church
picnics, and Fourth of July celebrations. In the late nineteenth century, H. A. Hutchinson, the enterprising owner of the falls, parlayed
the popularity of the site into a recreation area called "Hutchinson's
Grove," which offered a viewing bridge, dancing pavilion, bowling
alley, and bandstand. According to town histories, more than 2,000
people attended a dedication ceremony in August of 1889. At one
time a hermit lived here, who used to set his whiskers on fire and
burn his beard when it grew too long. Today, all that remains of the
grove are a few foundation stones and iron rods in the rocks that
once supported bridges.

Purgatory Falls is an interesting place to visit in the early spring
when huge slabs of vertical blue ice in cauliflower, pillar, and mushroom shapes sheath the steep moss-covered rock walls rising from
the basin floor. The water thunders through the chasm like a freight

train, spouting over the lip of a 10-foot-high cliff into a wide rocky bowl.

Access: Take New Hampshire 31 north out of Wilton. At 0.5 mile beyond the South Lyndeborough village store, turn right onto Center Road. Continue 5.4 miles to Johnson Corner Road on the left. Follow Johnson Corner Road for one mile to Purgatory Road. After 0.4 mile on Purgatory Road, it turns into a dirt surface (Purgatory Falls Road). Continue another 0.8 mile to the Echo Valley Camping Area. Keep to the right of the entrance sign and continue 0.1 mile. Park in a pull-off to the right.

Description: From the parking area, the yellow-blazed trail descends immediately into a hemlock forest with beech, red oak, birch and maple mixing in, and shortly moves past the waters of Black Brook to the left. After crossing a footbridge at 0.2 mile, continue (right) on the Purgatory Brook Trail, which stays close to the ribbon of stream as it wends its way over a rocky bed into a series of pools. Take time to search for trillium, as well as Clintonia, mountain laurel, and delicate fiddlehead-shaped ferns that are usually found along riverbanks.

The root of the name "trillium," "tri," refers to the sets of three— a whorl of three leaves, three sepals, and three petals that make up this plant. There are 38 different varieties of this showy spring wildflower that grow mostly in damp, rich, wood soils all over the northern hemisphere. The season for trillium begins in April. The most common trillium, "red trillium," is also known as "wake robin" because it often appears the same time as robins return from their winter migration. Other common names include stinking Benjamin or wet dog trillium, both because of its pungent odor. Trillium is also called "birthroot," because it was used by the Native Americans and early settlers to ease childbirth pain.

Ten minutes from the start of the hike, you will arrive at a ledgy area at the top of the Upper Falls. Exercise extreme caution here as there are no handrails or safety barriers. Take time to look down at the brook as it surges and dances through a deep curving flume before tumbling over the lip of a cliff into a frothy pool.

Purgatory Falls.

Look for a large pothole known as the "Devil's Beanpot," located on the other side of the flume in the granite shelf beyond a string of iron posts in the rock that once supported bridges for viewing the falls. Legend has it that the Devil once attempted to lure the towns-people of Mont Vernon to this lonely gulf by promising to cook them a baked bean supper with "all the fixings." At first, all went according to plan, but just as the Devil reached out for the black cauldron of beans, the intense heat caused his foot to sink in the rock—resulting in a string of expletives that frightened the people away. Next to the Devil's Beanpot is an imprint of a foot embedded in the rock known as the Devil's Footprint.

From the ledgy area at the top of the falls, the trail continues to the left on the edge of the ravine then swings down to the gorge. A sign points to a spur, which leads to the bottom of the upper falls.

"Devil's Beanpot,"
Purgatory Falls.

Loll on a sun-warmed rock and feel the pulse and rumble of the waterfall as it plunges into the frothy basin. Take some time to watch the sunlight reflect off the water as it dances in firelight patterns on the curved rock face of the cliff rising steeply from the pool. You may even want to peel off your boots and socks to soothe your feet and weary spirit.

Purgatory Falls is full of devilish allusions. The rock bowl is sometimes called Hell's Kitchen. The Old Boy's Face (Giant's Head or the Indian Head) is a rock profile in a grotto on the basin floor. The pulpit, overhanging rock, and hog rock are other geological formations in the gulf that will also hold your attention for a while.

There is a real feeling of isolation as you stare down at the seething waters and steep forested banks of the ravine. Jumbles of boulders deposited by the ancient glaciers and splayed tree roots clinging tenaciously to the steep banks like long-deformed fingers only add to this eerie primordial scene. Branches and felled trees serve as landing pads for buldging-eyed green and ultramarine dragonflies.

An aura of mystery surrounds dragonflies and has captured the human imagination for centuries. In Medieval England tales were told of how "devil's darning needles" sewed up the lips, ears, and eyes of naughty children. Mule-killer, snake-feeder, mosquito-hawk and snake-doctor are some of its other nicknames. In reality, dragonflies are harmless to people, although they are a serious threat to mosquitoes and other insects.

The dragonfly and damselfly belong to one of the oldest orders in the animal kingdom, *Odonata*, which means "toothed" and refers to the needle-sharp teeth in the mouth of the insects. Both dragonflies and damselflies have long, rather narrow wings; but at rest dragonflies hold them out to the sides like the wings of an airplane, while most damselflies hold them together raised above the body, just as butterflies do. Damselflies also have a narrower body and finer features. They are seen more often than dragonflies and are the small blue creatures that will often sit on the tip of your fly rod when you are not retrieving the line.

The dragonfly is a remarkable flying machine. Because its center of gravity lies just below the base of the wings, it can hover, dart, zip, spin, or stop on a dime and turn square corners to change directions. This elegant flier enjoys a brief life on the wing—only two weeks. Upwards of two years of its existence is spent as larva in the muck beneath the moss of a riverbed or pond, preying on small insects. After shedding its exoskeleton several times to accommodate its lengthening body, the primitive insect crawls out of the mud in early spring to cling to plants, with wings tucked tightly on its back. When dragonflies finally take flight, their extraordinary eyes enable them to see as far as forty yards, and they can reach an air speed of 30 miles per hour. The Green Darner is the most common dragonfly.

After admiring the natural beauty of the falls and exploring its geological features, continue on the trail. The route swings onto higher ground in the woods slightly away from the gorge, then moves past overlooks and back down to the stream past another cascade and view of the rugged ledge cliffs rising on the opposite side of the brook. After moving uphill, at 0.7 mile the trail reaches a sign pointing to East Ridge Trail. Continue on the East Ridge Trail, which levels out after 10 minutes and crosses a woods road before arriving back at the footbridge. A 5-minute walk brings you back to the parking area.

Optional Extension: To get to Lower Purgatory Falls from the Johnson Corner-Center Road intersection, turn left onto Center Road. Continue for 3.1 miles toward Milford to North River Road (Fitch's Corner). Turn left onto Purgatory Road and continue for 0.5 mile to the parking lot and McClellan Trail sign on the left. The yellow-blazed McClellan Trail wends 0.4 mile through a canopy of scrub pine and birch. You will shortly get a view of 695-foot Federal Hill in Milford to the southeast, and then move through a hemlock forest as the trail drops into Purgatory Brook ravine. Lower Purgatory Falls spreads across a ledge and drops 20 feet into a pool. Surrounded by ferns and mountain laurel, the site is popular with photographers and artists because of the unusual natural lighting in the area.

Sightseeing: If you have time you may want to visit Mont Vernon, a charming hilltop community that was once a popular summer resort that boasted several grand hotels, a golf course, and numerous boarding houses. The most imposing of these hotels was the Grand Hotel, which was topped by a two-story cupola where guests could watch the movement of ships in Boston Harbor through telescopes. With the advent of the railroad in the mid-1800s, Mont Vernon became a three-hour trip from Boston. The arrival of summer people tripled the normal size of Mont Vernon's population. Picnics at Purgatory Gorge no doubt were a popular draw for summer visitors. Beginning in the 1920s, however, the era of the grand hotels began to decline. One by one, the big hotels burned to the ground and all that remained were several buildings used as boarding houses. On Labor Day in 1930 the Grand was struck by lightning and destroyed by the subsequent fire; It is said the flames could be seen in Boston. Today the foundations of the old hotel have been replaced by a modern residence. To get there from the center of the village, turn right onto Grand Hill Road and continue as a loop around the former site of the Grand. There are also two private residences that once were Queen Anne style caretaker "cottages" on top of Prospect Hill.

22

Granite Town Rail-Trail

Rating: An easy to moderate hike that follows an old rail bed once used to transport granite from the Milford quarries, with opportunities to see marsh and woodland habitats along the way.
Distance: 5 miles
Hiking Time: 2.5 hours
Lowest Elevation: 260 feet
Highest Elevation: 360 feet
USGS Map: Milford
Other Map: Town of Milford Conservation Commission map
Trailhead: Milford, New Hampshire

Milford began as a farming community but with the arrival of the railroad (and easier transportation of the town's native granite) in the 1850s became known the "Granite Town." More than a dozen quarries scattered through the hills employed hundreds of men who drilled and blasted blocks of stone used for paving and edging streets, and the construction of monuments and buildings, including the West Point Military Academy and U.S. Treasury Building in Washington, D.C. Today the quarries are silent but you can still experience a sense of the town's fabled industry by walking along an old rail bed that once provided a transportation route for the huge granite blocks. Along the way you will explore marsh and woodland habitats and enjoy the hushed tones of nature as the world enters a state of suspension. There are also ridge-top views, some natural oddities and an impressive boulder left by the glaciers to see. For the most part, the trail is flat and wide, except for a section that narrows as it briefly travels uphill.

Access: From the Milford oval in the center of town, drive 0.75 mile south on South Street (Route 13) to the Public Works Garage. Park in a parking area to the right.

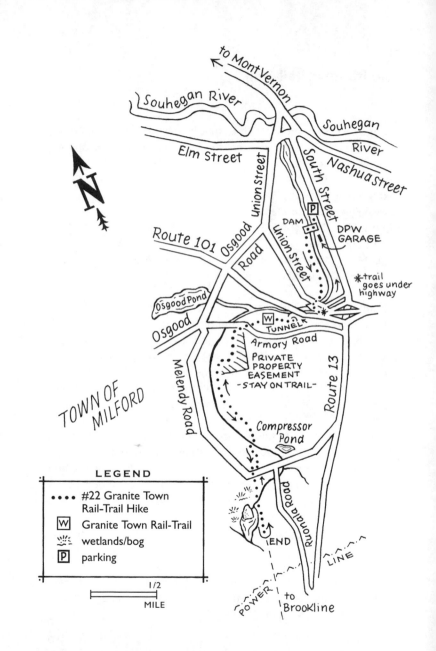

to Mont Vernon

Souhegan River

Souhegan River

Elm Street

Nashua Street

South Street

Route 101

Osgood Union Street

Road

Union Street

DAM

P

DPW GARAGE

*trail goes under highway

Osgood Pond

W TUNNEL

Osgood

Armory Road

PRIVATE PROPERTY EASEMENT
- STAY ON TRAIL -

Melendy Road

Route 13

TOWN OF MILFORD

Compressor Pond

Ruonala Road

LEGEND

•••• #22 Granite Town Rail-Trail Hike

W Granite Town Rail-Trail

🔥 wetlands/bog

P parking

1/2
MILE

END

POWER LINE

to Brookline

Description: The trail starts on a wooden footbridge behind the DPW Garage. Your path crosses Great Brook over a dam that once maintained high water for the town wells upstream, then continues under towering pines along Great Brook. In summer, the brook's edge is rife with purple loosestrife (*Lythrum salicaria*), with its tightly clustered pink-purple flowers on a long spike. The nicknames for purple loosestrife—beautiful killer, marsh monster, and exotic invader—are telling. The plant, which was introduced into this country from Europe in the early 1800s, is so aggressive that some botanists call it the "purple menace." It is a species that readily establishes in a variety of urban and rural wetlands; Once present, it has a tendency to dominate, competing with native vegetation, crowding reeds, grasses, and other wetland plants that are food for ducks and geese.

At 0.5 mile into the hike, as you reach Union Street, you can feel traffic on the Route 101 Milford bypass vibrate in contrast to the silent other world of the marsh. After crossing Union Street and continuing over a concrete span over Great Brook, the trail runs through a 110-foot long tunnel that is actually an overflow culvert protecting the state highway from possible flooding of Great Brook. On the other side of the culvert, the trail runs into the woods over a surface of knotted tree roots as white rectangular blazes show the way. You will shortly pass a field that in summer brims with Queen Anne's Lace, a member of the parsley family also known as wild carrot (*Daucus carota*). Pull up its root, and you can smell a sweet carrot aroma. The name "Queen Anne's Lace" comes from a British monarch who was adept at lacemaking and the plant's flower is lacelike, resembling an old-fashioned doily. It is also known as bird's nest because in late summer when blossoming is over and the fruits begin to ripen, the sides of the flower head curl inward, creating a deep cup that resembles the nest of a bird.

After coming to a red stop sign marking a road crossing (Armory Road) at 1.2 mile, the trail continues through private property. Respect the rights of the landowners and stay on the trail, which turns left and moves uphill. At the top of a rise, take in the view (west) of the Wapack Range, then step through a gap in a stone wall and begin a descent. Look for a globe-shaped gall on a maple tree as you walk downhill. A gall, which is like a tumor or canker, is a tree's response to a wound caused by insects. On large tree trunks, galls may reach a diameter of two to three times that of the tree at the point of occurrence. At the bottom of the hill, the trail turns left and follows the flat cinder-and-pine-needle surface for easy walking under tall pines. In 20 minutes you come to Compressor Pond (left) and then scale a steep embankment and reach Melendy Road at 2.2 miles. Trains used to pass under Melendy Road but the road-cut was filled in when rail service ceased in the 1940s. (The Granite Town Rail-Trail is the old Ayer-Milford branch of the Brookline and Milford Railroad).

After turning right and walking approximately 50 yards on Melendy Road, the trail continues into the woods. At 2.5 miles you will come to a large sprawling marsh spiked with snags and a sea of cattails (*Typha latifolia*) with their brown, cigar-shaped seedheads standing erect just below the tallest leaves. Cattails are a valuable food source for wildlife and were for the Native Americans, who ground cattails into meal. As the sausage-like head of this native plant is highly flammable, it was used as a torch before colonists arrived with kerosene. Its common name (cat-o'nine-tails or Candlewick) comes from the shape of the plant, which could remind one of a cat's tail rising up from the marshes.

In the marsh you will also see a large tooth-shaped boulder deposited by the glaciers and a "beaver baffler," or a perforated white pipe that is used to control the water's level and prevent flooding of the rail trail. This hike ends at the marsh, so turn around and retrace your steps back to your car. If you have time, continue on the trail 0.5 mile farther to the power lines and Public Service of New Hampshire (PSNH) easement. From there, the trail moves on to the 115-acre Palmer Wildlife Preserve in Brookline, New Hampshire, and then on to Massachusetts.

Sightseeing: At the 258-acre Tucker Brook Town Forest in Milford, you can explore wetlands, pine groves, glacial erratics, beaver ponds, a waterfall, and mill-dam sites. The three entrances into Tucker Brook Town Forest are located off Boulder Drive, Whitten Road, and Savage Road. You can also visit an old granite quarry operation on the Mayflower HIll Town Forest trail, which has an access in two areas: on Shady Lane and at the end of Falconer Avenue Extension.

The highlight of the Hitchiner Town Forest is 751-foot Burns Hill with open and sunny granite outcroppings, blueberry bushes, and views to the west. Trails connect the Hitchiner Town Forest to the Holland-Burns Farm. The Hitchiner Town Forest is located off Mullen Road. The Milford Conservation Commission maintains the Souhegan River Trail, which is located on property owned by the state of New Hampshire and managed by the Fish and Game Department as a fish hatchery on North River Road. Free maps are available at Milford Town Hall.

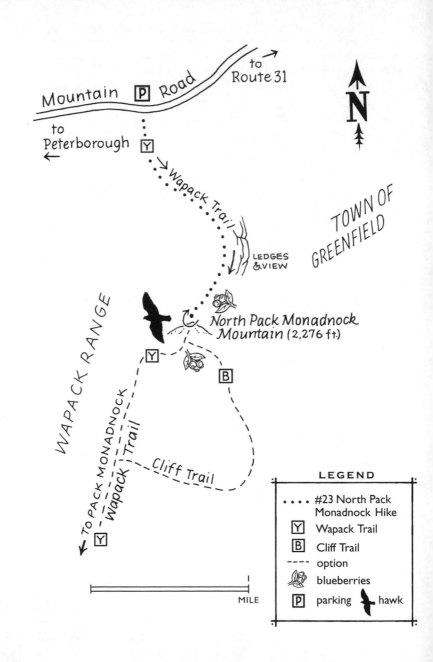

to Route 31

Mountain P Road

to Peterborough

Y

Wapack Trail

LEDGES & VIEW

TOWN OF GREENFIELD

North Pack Monadnock Mountain (2,276 ft.)

WAPACK RANGE

Y

B

Cliff Trail

TO PACK MONADNOCK

Wapack Trail

Y

MILE

LEGEND

• • • • #23 North Pack Monadnock Hike

Y Wapack Trail

B Cliff Trail

- - - option

blueberries

P parking   hawk

23
North Pack Monadnock Mountain

Rating: A moderate climb up the north face of the anchoring
mountain of the Wapack Range. Ledgy outcrops offer expansive
views along the way, and from the summit there is a sweeping
view of the Wapack Range and Mount Monadnock.

Distance: 3 miles
Hiking Time: 2 hours
Lowest Elevation: 1,314 feet
Highest Elevation: 2,276 feet
USGS Map: Greenfield
Other Maps: Wapack Trail Guide and map; New Hampshire Division
of Parks and Recreation map
Trailhead: Greenfield, New Hampshire

North Pack Monadnock Mountain is certainly not as well known as
the 3,165-foot Mt. Monadnock to the southwest. It even pales in com-
parison to its sister peak, South Pack Monadnock Mountain in Peterborough, which boasts a scenic 1.3-mile auto road leading to Miller
State Park on its windswept summit. But taking the 1.5-mile trail to
the 2,278-foot summit of North Pack Monadnock Mountain is worth
the hour's effort it takes to reach the top.

Actually, North Pack is just one of many mountains in southwestern New Hampshire that geologists call "monadnocks." These isolated hills rise above the rolling terrain as masses of durable rock
that resisted the erosion of the surrounding land. Getting to one of
these solitary peaks requires an hour's drive from the Manchester/
Nashua area. In many ways, the long sweeping views here are supe-
rior to the vistas of the more crowded summits to the north.

You will be hiking the final leg of the Wapack Trail, a 21-mile-long
string of monadnocks extending northward from Mount Watatic in
Ashburnham, Massachusetts, to its terminus at North Pack. Well-
marked by yellow triangles painted on trees and rocks, the trail will

carry you through quiet forest glens, abandoned farm pastures, and along open ledges and summits marked by cairns.

The Wapack National Wildlife Refuge (1,672 acres) occupies a major portion of North Pack. It is mostly a timbered area, containing a swamp, bog, and bare rock ledge and cliff area. A valuable habitat for upland wildlife and an important hawk migration flyway, it also provides a nesting area for tree sparrows, winter wrens, pine grosbeaks, cedar waxwings, and thrush and warbler species. Camping and open fires are prohibited. The refuge is administered by the Great Bay National Wildlife Refuge in Newington, New Hampshire.

Access: To get to the trailhead from the Manchester area, take Route 114 west to Route 13 south in Goffstown. Follow Route 13 as it wends it way along the South Branch of the Piscataquog River for 7 miles to New Boston. Then travel Route 136 west for 12 miles to Greenfield. At a blinking light, take Route 31 south for approximately 2.8 miles before turning right onto Russell Station Road. Watch for the Yankee Farmer, an outdoor farmstand, where Wapack trail maps and information are available. After turning onto Russell Station Road, drive over a set of railroad tracks and past an intersecting dirt road before coming to Mountain Road. Turn right onto Mountain Road. Continue driving uphill past an unusual house made of fieldstone. The trailhead is 0.9 mile beyond this point. Park your car on the shoulder of the road and look for a yellow triangle blaze on a maple tree and a Wapack trail sign.

Optional Access: For the south approach to North Pack Monadnock, take Route 101 west to Wilton from the Manchester area. From the center of town, continue north on Route 31 for 7.9 miles to Russell Station Road.

Description: The sign at the trailhead informs you that it is 1.5 miles to the summit of North Pack. Early on, the hiking is easy but be wary of tentacle-like roots that run tangled across the trail. You will travel through a corridor of huge white pine, many of them dead and decaying, with the eerie silhouettes of branch skeletons mixing in with the growth of young trees.

North Pack Monadnock Mountain.

After five minutes, the trail winds through a stone wall, then descends into a grove of young maples. A stream, the first of several watercourses traversing your path, splashes on the left. According to the AMC Guide, there is a spring of reliable drinking water halfway up the mountain. Shortly after crossing the stream you will walk through an impressive display of mountain laurel growing on both sides of the trail.

You will approach the trail's halfway point 30 minutes later. Climb hand-over-foot for a short stretch over a jumble of huge boulders and flat sloping rocks, then walk past several small cairns before stepping out onto a series of wide, flat, open ledges for your first open view. Directly behind you to the north, glinting in the sunlight, is the cluster of buildings that comprise the Crotched Mountain Rehabilitation Center. The village of Greenfield is in the valley below, while the rounded summits of Winn, Lyndeborough, and Rose Mountains rise gently to the east. In between, there are the Uncanoonucs in Goffstown, and beyond them the city of Manchester.

You will often see people sunning themselves on the rocks, as many hikers chose to end their walk here. But after catching your breath and perhaps refreshing yourself with a snack and drink of water, head back on the trail that continues up over a series of granite ledges worn smooth by the glaciers and flanked by spreading shrubs of juniper. There's a good chance of hearing the high-pitched explosive scream of a red-tailed hawk adrift in the summer sky. The red-tailed hawk is a high-profile bird, unlike the secretive forest-loving species like the Cooper's hawk and the goshawk. When it is soaring, the red-tailed hawk spreads its trademark chestnut-red tail into a wide, rounded fan, showing it to its advantage, especially when the bird veers and the tail glints in the sunlight.

The trail alternately travels up over granite outcrop, and then disappears into a spruce and hardwood forest. In 15 minutes, you will come to what looks like a dry stream bed to the right of the trail. Be sure to stay to the left, noting the yellow blaze on a tree and two small cairns, which will guide you back on your return trip. From this point, a 10-minute walk through a quiet spruce forest is all that separates you from the summit. A 6-foot stone cairn announces the end of your hike up the mountain. Just to the west of this marker, the Wapack Trail leaves the ledges and continues 2.2 miles south to Pack Monadnock Mountain.

From where you are standing on the summit, you can see Pack Monadnock's lookout tower, microwave dish antennae, and communications tower. Toward the southwest, Temple, Kidder, and Barrett Mountains stretch to Mount Watatic on the horizon in Massachusetts. Mount Monadnock in all its glory stands out on the horizon. According to the AMC Guide, views of the Contoocook River Valley, Mount Washington, and other White Mountain peaks are visible to the north on a clear day. A short walk to the east of the summit cairn leads to an exposed rock outlook and an unusual view of what look like two white gigantic golf balls. These are spotting towers of a United States Air Force satellite tracking station in New Boston, just southeast of Joe English Hill. Back on the summit cairn, a blue trail leads to a cliff outlook on the southeast side of North Pack. The view stretches from Pack Monadnock all the way down to the ski-scarred slopes of Mount Watatic in Massachusetts and is one of the finest of all the vistas on the Wapack Trail. Mount Wachusett also stands out on the southern horizon while Mount Monadnock and the Green

South Pack Monadnock Mountain from North Pack.

Mountains anchor the horizon on the west. When you have soaked in enough of the scenery, walk north and look for the yellow-blazed return trail entering the spruce forest.

Optional Extension: Ted's Trail is a 6.0-mile loop trail from Mountain Road to the south cliff below North Pack's 2,276-foot summit and back. Hiking time is 4.5 hours. The yellow-blazed route takes you past a waterfall, moves through hemlock, beech, and spruce forests, and offers good views to the east, northeast, and south. The trailhead is located off Mountain Road 0.5 mile from the junction of Russell Station and Mountain Road.

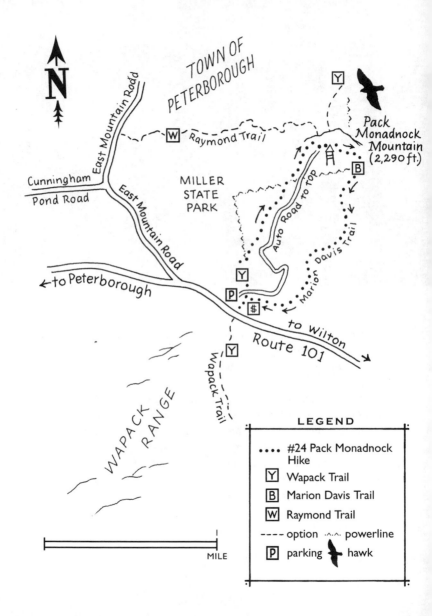

N

TOWN OF PETERBOROUGH

East Mountain Road

W Raymond Trail

Pack Monadnock Mountain (2,290 ft.)

Cunningham Pond Road

East Mountain Road

MILLER STATE PARK

Y

B

Auto Road to Top

Marion Davis Trail

←to Peterborough

Y

P

$

to Wilton

Route 101

Y

Wapack Trail

WAPACK RANGE

MILE

LEGEND

•••• #24 Pack Monadnock Hike

Y Wapack Trail

B Marion Davis Trail

W Raymond Trail

- - - option   ᴧᴧ powerline

P parking   🦅 hawk

24
Pack Monadnock Mountain

Rating: A loop hike that follows the Wapack Trail to the summit
   and returns via the Marion Davis Trail. There are ledgy uphill
   sections and good views of the Contoocook River Valley along
   the way.
Distance: 2.8 miles
Hiking Time: 2 hours
Lowest Elevation: 1,485 feet
Highest Elevation: 2,290 feet
USGS Map: Peterborough South
Other Maps: New Hampshire Division of Parks and Recreation map;
   Wapack Trail Guide and map.
Trailhead: Peterborough, New Hampshire

For more than 100 years, Miller State Park on the summit of Pack
Monadnock Mountain in Peterborough has been a popular spot to
enjoy a picnic, watch hawks wing their way along their migratory
routes, or savor the view of the Souhegan River Valley from the 37-
foot lookout tower. Along with three foot trails, there is a 1.3-mile
paved switchback road that climbs to the top. The loop hike outlined
here takes you up the 2,290-foot mountain on a yellow-blazed 1.4-
mile section of the Wapack Trail, with the return route via the blue-
blazed 1.4–mile Marion Davis Trail. The first interstate hiking trail in
the United States, the Wapack Trail is a 21-mile-long footpath that
runs from Mount Watatic in Ashburnham, Massachusetts, to North
Pack Monadnock Mountain in Greenfield, New Hampshire.

The park is New Hampshire's first state park, deeded in 1891 by
Charles F. Melendy and Andrew A. Spofford, and was dedicated in
memory of General James Miller for his heroism in the Battle of
Lundy's Lane during the War of 1812. Miller State Park is an especially
busy place in the fall on weekends. It is not uncommon for cars to be
backed up for a half hour's wait to drive to the top. Dogs are allowed,

Miller State Park, Peterborough.

but must be leashed, and the park is staffed until November. For more information, contact the New Hampshire Division of Parks and Recreation, P.O. Box 1856, Concord, New Hampshire, 03302-1856.

According to the park brochure, the name "Pack" comes from a Native-American word meaning little. Others believe the "pack" was a misspelling by a draftsman or engraver of an early map, perhaps for a family named "Packer" who owned and farmed land on the mountain. Still another reason for "pack" stems from the fact that the Pack Monadnock Range resembles a "pack" of wolves.

Access: To get to Miller State Park on Pack Monadnock from the Manchester area, take Route 101 west to Milford. From Milford, continue west on Route 101. Miller State Park is approximately 14 miles farther. The foot trails area is located a short distance east of a large information sign and toll station in the parking lot. The park is open weekends from mid-April to mid-May, then from late October until snowfall, and daily from mid-May to late October. Admission is $3 for adults; $1 for children aged 6 to 11. Children aged 5 and under and

New Hampshire residents aged 65 and over are admitted free. Restrooms are available at the park's base. The yellow Wapack Trail starts to the left (northeast) of a glassed-in bulletin board displaying a map of the entire Wapack Range. For information, call the toll station at 603-924-3672.

Optional Access: The 1.6-mile white-blazed Raymond Trail travels up the west side of Pack Monadnock with a good view of Mount Monadnock along the way. There is no fee to use the trail. To get to the Raymond Trailhead from the Miller State Park entrance, continue on Route 101 west for 0.3 mile to East Mountain Road. After 0.7 mile turn right. The parking area is 0.2 mile farther.

Description: The trail begins in a mixed forest of maple, spruce, and oak, where you will see Canada mayflower (the wild lily-of-the-valley), the first bitter green to appear on the forest floor in spring. Canada mayflower grows in masses that cover the ground with shining leaves, heart-shaped at the base. A spike of white flowers is borne erect on a single stem followed by a cluster of berries. In late summer the green berries of Canada mayflower turn to pinkish-beige, and in fall change again to red. Shortly the trail crosses the auto road, then re-enters the woods to ascend a steep ridge with difficult footing over rough slabs of schist. In late summer, notice the acorns that have dropped from leafy oaks, and the scallop-like cliffs of fractured ledge provide an interesting natural sculpture. Although this stretch may not demand the physical exertion of some of the White Mountain hikes, it is nonetheless a knee-lifter, which explains why the contour lines are bunched together on a topographical map of the area.

After you pass beneath a power line, some fine views of Temple Mountain begin to show to the southwest. Twisted birch trees literally sprout from the rocky ledge like weeds pushing up between flagstone walkways, making the maximum use of the limited soil at their base. A few minutes later a great view of Mount Monadnock will stop you dead in your tracks. Take time to walk a few steps off the trail for an even better view—to a flat rock overlook marked by several semi-circular, balcony-like rock walls, many of them pushed over. The ledgy footing alternates with scrub woods and brush as you continue to climb. Far below to the left, Route 101 winds its way westward through the forested valley and past Cunningham Pond.

As you continue, you can see the trail work done by the Friends of the Wapack, a volunteer group that clears brush, tree limbs, and blow-downs, helping to preserve the well-blazed path. About 30 minutes into the hike will bring you to an old pasture overtaken by juniper. Like many hills and mountains of the Monadnock region, the slopes of Pack were once open fields and pastures where cattle, driven up from farms in Massachusetts, grazed during the summer. After passing several misshapen beech trees, the trail descends into a gully where in late summer and early fall bright clusters of daisy-like wood aster grow alongside the dry stream bed. As you enter the 2000-foot elevation zone, you will notice more spruce trees, as well as bright red bunchberry, clintonia, and wood sorrel, its pink-tinged blossom and shamrock-like leaves making it easy to identify.

Ten minutes later, step through an opening in a stone wall to enter a dense spruce forest with broken and dying lower tree limbs. You might hear the sound of cars off to the right, and then you will continue for 15 minutes to a small intermittent brook crossing. After a few minutes the trail intersects the (red circles) Summit Trail. Continue right for the short walk to the summit. At the top you will find an air quality monitoring station, parking lot (40 spaces), communication and observation towers, picnic tables, water bubbler (from a 300-foot-deep spring-fed well), fireplaces, pit toilets, and a three-sided stone shelter. The Wapack Trail continues from the summit 2.3 miles to North Pack Monadnock.

The summit is a popular place to picnic, and is the site of an occasional wedding and meeting place for ham radio operators. The view from the 37-foot tower is a spectacular 360 degrees. Visitors are welcomed by the watchman who will explain how the fire-finder works and what the Forest Protection Bureau does to ensure forests are watched over when he is not spotting fires. (New Hampshire maintains 15 towers, and a staff of 15 full-time seasonal watchers. The town of Moultonborough operates its own tower and employs a watchman).

Pack Monadnock Fire Tower.

Chances are that you had lots of company at the top because Pack Monadnock has always been a mecca for humans. At the turn of the century, many families in nearby Temple profited from the boarding house and hotel trade when "summer people" nearly doubled the town's population. After morning chores, the farm-owner would drive his guests to Pack Monadnock and Miller State Park where they would enjoy lunches packed in round wooden cheese boxes, gallon jugs, and two-gallon milk cans, returning in the afternoon in time for the owner to begin his evening chores.

The summer people also enjoyed one of Temple's most acclaimed spots—the Pack Monadnock Lithia Springs owned by Sidney Scammon. Scammon bottled and sold the water, claiming that it was the most wonderful natural spring water known in the world. For 20 years people from miles around came to seek out the curative powers of the spring as a remedy for kidney trouble, rheumatism,

Bright's disease, eczema, indigestion, and dyspepsia. The site also gained renown as a popular recreation and picnic grove. In 1911, however, Scammon was caught mixing a batch of lithium into the spring. When news of the deception got out, the crafty entrepreneur beat a hasty retreat to Malden, Massachusetts. Shortly afterwards, a portable lumber sawmill company bought the property and removed the grove of great pines. Temple's most acclaimed landmark was no more.

Pack Monadnock once even had its own hotel—the Pioneer House—a rambling two-story structure built on the southwest shoulder with a reputation for its uncluttered vista and healthy mountain air. Unfortunately, it burned to the ground in 1896. A new structure replaced it and was used as a hunting lodge, but was later abandoned and fell into disrepair; it was then leveled by fire in 1924.

The mountains that are easily distinguishable include Temple to the south; the Wapack Range to the southwest; Mount Monadnock (12 miles away), Gap Mountain, Little Monadnock Mountain, Stratton Mountain in Vermont to the west and Killington farther north. North Pack (directly in the foreground), Crotched, and Kearsarge (behind Crotched) can be seen to the north. To the northeast lie the Lyndeborough Mountains, Joe English Hill, and the radome of the U.S. Air Force satellite tracking station in New Boston, which looks like two giant white golf balls. To the right of the tracking station you can see the brick buildings of the city of Manchester sprawling in the valley. On a good day the Manchester airport and its control tower are visible to the east. To the east southeast you can see with binoculars the Seabrook New Hampshire Nuclear Power Plant on the horizon, 60 miles north of Boston.

To the distant northeast lie Saddleback Mountain and the double-bumped Pawtuckaway Mountains in Nottingham, New Hampshire. Cardigan Mountain lies northwest, with Mount Ascutney in Vermont a little more to the west of Cardigan. The large body of water to the southeast is the Greenville Reservoir, and to the west are Cranberry Meadow and Cunningham Ponds in Peterborough.

On a clear day in fall or late spring, you can see white-capped Mount Washington in the distant north, 100 miles away. It is visible on the horizon just off the left shoulder of North Pack Monadnock Mountain in the foreground. Follow the left shoulder of North Pack about one third of the way down until you see a notch in the tree line. Look through the notch and you will see Mount Washington looking like a white cloud. Have patience, for it takes a steady eye to see it. The city of Boston is visible 55 miles away to the southeast. The Prudential and Hancock buildings stand by themselves to the right of the cluster of buildings comprising the Boston skyline. A different perspective of the same view may be obtained by following the less than 0.5-mile long Summit Loop Trail (red circles), which leads to several good outlooks. The trail begins to the north (left) of the air quality monitoring station. There is also a path marked "Boston viewing area" that leads to a ledge where you will get views to the south of Mount Watatic and Mount Wachusett in Massachusetts and southeast to the Boston skyline.

Take some time to enjoy lunch and the show put on by nature. In July dragonflies buzz around the summit like squadrons of miniature helicopters. Slate-colored dark-eyed juncos show white along sides of their tails in flight. Towhees and white-throated sparrows are some of the other common mountain birds you will see and hear. The white-throated sparrow is also known as the "Peabody bird." Its song sounds like a clear, whistled "poor Sam Peabody, Peabody, Peabody."

In mid-September you are apt to catch the Audubon Society of New Hampshire monitoring the fall hawk migration. A Raptor Migration Observatory is located on the north-facing ledges, a short distance from the summit parking lot.

When you go hawk-watching, take warm clothing, food and drink, binoculars, a compass, spotting scope, notebook, and some field guides. The Wapack Range is a leading line for hawks seeking wind currents to ride. Hawks fly by day, riding the rising heat columns (thermals) or the currents along the ridgeline. Thermals form over areas that absorb the sun's energy, such as the slopes of mountains, plowed fields and large expanses of pavement. ("Kettle" is the term for a group of hawks rising up in swirling communal eddies, wings and tails spread to catch maximum lift). The prime conditions for watching are the first day after a passing cold front with north-west winds and mostly sunny skies.

The hawks seen most often are of the genus *Buteo*, a group of large, soaring hawks with broad, rounded wings and short tails spread out like a fan, a design well-suited for exploiting the lifting power of winds and thermals. It is possible to see Peregrine falcons or duck hawks, probably the rarest of North American hawks. You might also spot robin-sized kestrels, or sparrow hawks that fly low and get blown around by the wind as they flap by; Northern Harriers with their telltale white rump-patch, ravens, and turkey vultures (easily recognizable because their wings tip upward in a "V" shape). Other possible sightings are Sharp-shinned hawks, about the size of a blue jay, with their hallmark quick flaps and longer glide, Ospreys, Bald Eagles, Cooper's, Red-tailed, Red-shouldered, Northern Goshawks, and crow-sized Broad-wings, with their conspicuous white and brown banded tails, the first to leave for the warmer climes and who make up the greater numbers.

After you have enjoyed the sights, look for the sign and blue trail blazes for the Marion Davis Trail. Marion Davis was a rugged outdoorswoman and champion rail-splitter, who helped to establish and maintain the Wapack Trail during its early years. Davis and her husband later built the Wapack Lodge in 1925, a two-story structure that accommodated up to 25 overnight guests, on New Hampshire Route 123/124 in New Ipswich (see Hike 28, Stony Top, p. 168). Davis herself provided the hikers with hearty home-cooked meals. The lodge closed in 1958, fell into disrepair, and in July of 1993, was struck by lightning and burned.

Although strewn with boulders, the Marion Davis Trail traverses less strenuous terrain than the Wapack Trail. On the 1.4-mile route back to the parking lot, you will pass airy, wooded dells and soft-spoken streams along the way.

25
Temple Mountain (North)

Rating: A moderate walk up a former ski trail leading to an outlook with panoramic views of the Souhegan and Contoocook River Valleys.
Distance: 2.8 miles
Hiking Time: 2 hours
Lowest Elevation: 1,485 feet
Highest Elevation: 1,987 feet
USGS Map: Peterborough South
Other Map: Wapack Trail Guide and map
Trailhead: Peterborough, New Hampshire

A section of the 21-mile-long Wapack Trail stretches over Temple Mountain, making it an ideal hiking destination within an hour's drive of the more populated areas of southern New Hampshire. A long north-to-south axis of monadnocks, resembling a serpent's back and following the path of the ancient glaciers, the Temple Mountain ridgeline is comprised of five separate summits. Many of these peaks offer solitude and breathtaking panoramic views for those willing to lace up a pair of hiking boots. Of these vantage points, the one that offers the best views is known as Temple Mountain Ledges, a 1,987-foot outcrop straddling the Temple-Sharon town line that can easily be reached in an hour's walking time.

Access: To get to the Temple Mountain Ledges from Manchester, follow Route 101 west to the Miller State Park, 14 miles west of Milford. You may be charged a parking fee, especially during the busy fall season. A trailhead sign is on the south side of the highway across from the Miller State Park lot. Use caution approaching the trailhead as this is a busy stretch of highway.

Description: The 1.4-mile trail, with yellow triangle blazes (Wapack Trail) painted on trees and rocks, follows a southeasterly direction,

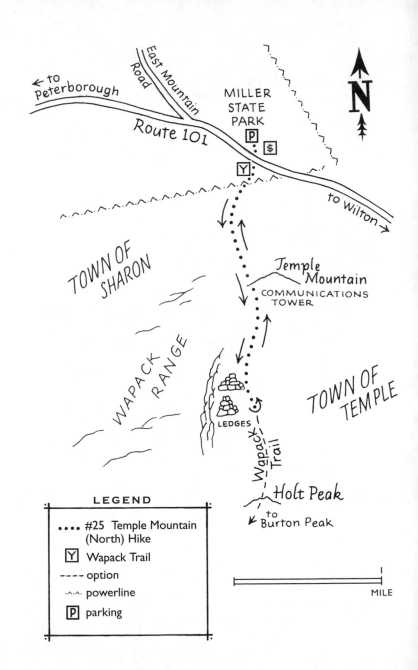

to Peterborough

East Mountain Road

Route 101

MILLER STATE PARK

P

$

Y

to Wilton

TOWN OF SHARON

Temple Mountain
COMMUNICATIONS TOWER

WAPACK RANGE

TOWN OF TEMPLE

LEDGES

Wapack Trail

Holt Peak

to Burton Peak

LEGEND

•••• #25 Temple Mountain (North) Hike

Y Wapack Trail

---- option

.^.^. powerline

P parking

MILE

and begins opposite the entranceway to Miller State Park. The trail-head sign directs you into the woods, but within seconds you will emerge at two large gravel lots that in August are overgrown with goldenrod. The trail continues on a narrow path and in a few minutes a sign directs you right onto a wide, grassy former ski trail now over-grown with birch trees and in late summer spiked with a wildflower cornucopia of wood aster, meadowsweet, clover, goldenrod, and bot-tle gentians. The gentian (*Gentiana andrewsii*) is one of the wildflow-ers that signal autumn's approach. The bottled or closed gentian is so named because its flower, which generally remains shut like a bud, looks like a bottle.

As you walk uphill, turn around for a good view of Pack Monad-nock Mountain and the blue hills of south central New Hampshire rising beyond. The whisper of automobiles traveling Route 101 below can be heard, but you will feel many miles removed from civilization. After zigzagging across the old ski trail, the path continues uphill on a dirt and gravel road used as an access road for a communica-tions tower. You will soon leave the dirt road, which turns to the left. Continue walking up the old ski trail and watch for a Wapack Trail sign and yellow blaze. The hiking trail continues (left) down a grassy path and rejoins the dirt road, which then moves uphill and becomes ledge-filled. In August, grasshoppers clack at your heels with a raspy buzz, spreading their paper-thin wings to leapfrog ahead of you, and colorful clusters of goldenrod grow in the dry, sandy soil on the side of the road and in clearings. After climbing over a stretch of wide, jagged rock ledge, the trail turns right into a spruce and birch woods to the west of a communications tower. This signals the end of the steepest portion of the hike. From here the trail is an easy jaunt over a needle-padded path that carries you past stone walls, ledge out-crops, waving ferns and cairns. In 10 minutes you'll come to a tall sin-gular cairn marking a ledge area. Continue walking on the trail five more minutes past several smaller cairns. You will know for certain that you have arrived at the Temple Mountain Ledges when you come to a grassy ledge area and see several small piles of rock formations and a monument-like 6-foot cairn. The surprise of these unusual fig-ures looming on the expansive ledges above you may make you feel as though you have stumbled upon an ancient sacrificial altar. The views from the top are no less magical. Directly to the south looms the wooded dome of Holt Peak and Burton Peak beyond. Holt Peak (2,084 feet) is the main summit of the Temple Mountain ridgeline. The undulating green countryside of the Souhegan Valley unfolds to the southeast. The Uncanoonuc Mountains and whalebacked Joe English Hill capture your attention to the northeast. Grand Monadnock appears on the horizon to the west. The breezy ledges are an inviting place to have lunch or test a pair of binoculars on fluffy cloud formations drifting overhead. If you have the urge to explore, take a three-minute walk south on the trail to another cairn-topped ledge area with good views west.

26
Temple Mountain (South)

Rating: An out-and-back hike that follows the Wapack Trail past stone walls, abandoned pastures, and sunny ledges that offer good views of the Souhegan River Valley along the way to Burton Peak. An optional longer walk carries you over the ridge line of the Temple Mountain system.

Distance: 2.8 miles
Hiking Time: 3 hours
Lowest Elevation: 1,297 feet
Highest Elevation: 2,020-foot Burton Peak
USGS Map: Peterborough South
Other Map: Wapack Trail Guide and map
Trailhead: Sharon, New Hampshire

Hiking the south end of Temple Mountain is like taking a walk on the wild side. There are panoramic views of the Souhegan Valley from several bare outlooks along the less-civilized south end of the system as it gradually curves northeastward toward Holt Peak, which is Temple Mountain's 2,084-foot main summit. If you are up to the challenge of exploring long-forgotten stone walls, abandoned pastures, and clusters of bluebead lilies and other woodland plants, you can hike the nearly 5-mile-long ridge line. This will require a friend and two cars; leave one vehicle in the Miller State Park base parking lot off Route 101 in Peterborough Gap; Leave the other car at the south foot of Temple Mountain, and hike between the two parked cars. If you are looking for a half-day outing with a real sense of serenity, then there are plenty of good outlooks only 0.5 mile into this lightly-hiked section of the Wapack Trail.

Access: The trailhead can be reached by taking Route 101 from Milford. Three miles west of Miller State Park, turn left onto Route 123 (Elm Hill Road). Drive 4 miles south and turn left again (just beyond

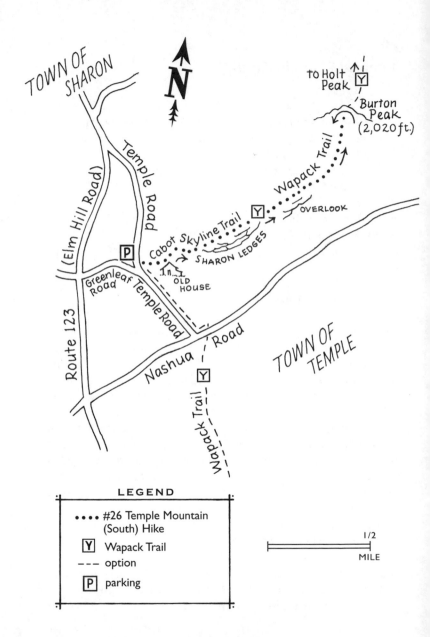

TOWN OF SHARON

N

to Holt Peak [Y]

Burton Peak (2,020 ft.)

Wapack Trail

Temple Road

(Elm Hill Road)

Cabot Skyline Trail [Y] OVERLOOK

SHARON LEDGES

[P]

OLD HOUSE

Greenleaf Temple Road

Road

Nashua Road

Route 123

TOWN OF TEMPLE

[Y]

Wapack Trail

LEGEND

•••• #26 Temple Mountain (South) Hike

[Y] Wapack Trail

--- option

[P] parking

1/2 MILE

Sharon Arts Center) onto Temple Road, which climbs uphill and then narrows. After 0.7 mile look for a small parking area on the right.

Optional Access: Leave one car in the Miller Park base lot. During the busy fall season you may be charged $3 per person; $1 children aged 6 to 11; no charge for children aged 5 or under, nor for New Hampshire residents aged 65 or over. Leave a second car in the parking area at the south foot of Temple Mountain. Hike from car to car.

Description: The Wapack Trail starts off steeply on a wide, rocky path that climbs past maple, hemlock, birch, and several gigantic red pines. Immediately to the left is a mapboard for the entire Wapack Trail and a sign indicating that the next 2.2 miles of trail are the Cabot Skyline. A few moments later, you will come to an abandoned two-story cabin, its wooden shingles weathered black by the years. Beyond the cabin, the path narrows as it continues uphill over the rocky, tree-root-filled surface. Soon you will notice running uphill a long stone wall that will appear again and again on the trail. The wall, carefully constructed of flat rocks, forms part of the border between the towns of Temple and Sharon. Indeed, on some old maps the Temple Mountains are referred to as the Boundary Mountains. After 10 minutes look for an opening near the wall on the right that offers a good view south toward Barrett Mountain. From here the trail continues over a sunny ledge area known as the Sharon Ledges. To the northwest is an eye-stretching view of Mount Monadnock, Gap and Little Monadnock Mountains, giving way to the rolling countryside as it ambles toward Massachusetts. Continue on the trail several minutes more to bring you to a sign that points to an overlook. For a fine view to the south, take a few steps to your right off the path. You will spy 1,832-foot Mount Watatic in Ashburnham, Massachusetts, 11 miles away, and behind it 2,006-foot Mount Wachusett just south of Fitchburg, Massachusetts. If you have them, look through a pair of binoculars to see Wachusett crowned by its observation tower. As you continue, young maple, birch, oak, juniper, and low bush blueberry fill in the ledgy trailside, along with a few spruce trees. You will walk past another outlook and a stretch of woods dominated by slender white

Along the Wapack Trail, Temple Mountain.

birch trees before coming to a sun-warmed boulder on the left. This rock "seat" provides an excellent rest spot and another great view. In the foreground, slightly southeast to south, lie Kidder Mountain, Wildcat and Conant Hills. Watatic Mountain anchors the view in the distance while the long multisummited ridge of Barrett Mountain in New Ipswich stretches off to the southwest. To the southeast, Boston can be seen on the horizon. There is also a good chance of seeing a hawk soaring the thermals. From the boulder outlook, a 10-minute walk past several more cairns takes you back into the woods, but this time the path will be needle-covered and evergreen-shaded, reminding you of the conifers up north. From this point the view will be limited, but this stretch is rewarding nevertheless. There is a real sense of isolation here; The still quiet is broken only by the squeaky tick of a bird, the high-pitched kissing sound of chipmunks, or the scurrying of a small animal in the woods. A highlight of this wooded walk is the clusters of bluebead-lily plants (also called Clintonia; named after DeWitt Clinton, governor of New York from 1769 to 1818). Other common names for *Clintonia borealis* are Clinton's Lily, corn lily, cow's tongue, yellow beadily, and yellow bluebeadily. The fruits of this plant are extraordinarily blue. After walking past a stone wall that parallels the trail to the right, you will reach a sign (left) that points the way to the Berry Pasture Trail—a blue-blazed 1.7-mile side trail that leads to Mountain Road in Sharon. Three hundred yards beyond the Blueberry Pasture Trail turnoff, another sign informs you that you have reached Burton Peak (2,020 feet), which is wooded with no view. Holt Peak, also wooded with no view, is a 30-minute walk from here, with a few good views along the way of Mount Monadnock and Peterborough to the west.

Optional Extension: If you've left another car in the Miller State Park parking lot (see Optional Access, p. 157), it will take 2 hours of hiking time from here to reach it, a 3-mile trip, from Burton Peak. From Burton Peak, the Wapack trail continues to Holt Peak, which is also wooded with no view, but along the way there are good views of Mount Monadnock and Peterborough to the west. An hour and a half more of hiking from Holt Peak brings you to the Miller State Park parking lot.

Sightseeing: If there is time, you may want to visit the Wales Preserve off Spring Hill Road in Sharon. This 48-acre Nature Conservancy property features a boreal bog, majestic softwoods, ferns, wildflowers, and a series of small cascades along the Gridley River. To get there, return to the Junction of Temple Road/Route 123. Drive south on Route 123 for 0.6 mile. Turn right on Jarmany Hill Road and continue for 2.7 miles where you will make a left turn onto Mill Road. Follow Mill Road 0.7 mile, make a right onto Spring Hill Road, and park near a one-lane bridge. The trail begins 125 feet farther up Spring Hill Road on the left. Dogs are not allowed on the trail.

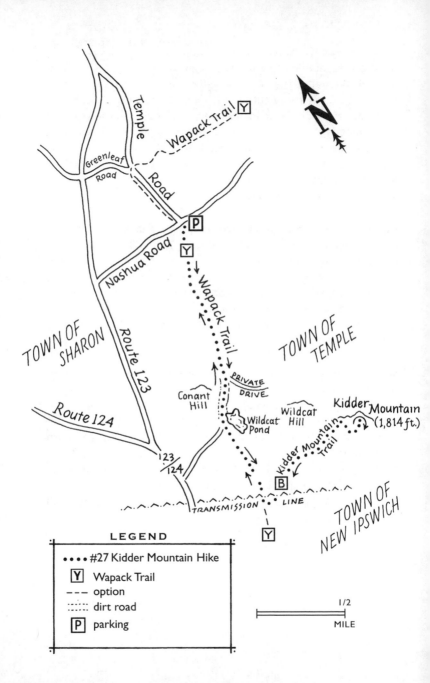

LEGEND

•••• #27 Kidder Mountain Hike

Y Wapack Trail

- - - option

⋮⋮⋮ dirt road

P parking

27
Kidder Mountain

Rating: A moderate walk following old woods and dirt roads before continuing through spruce woods to an abandoned blueberry pasture and wide views of southwestern New Hampshire on the summit. There are two possible access points, from the north and from the south.

Distance: 5 miles
Hiking Time: 2.5 hours
Lowest Elevation: 1,228 feet
Highest Elevation: 1,814 feet
USGS Map: Peterborough South
Other Map: Wapack Trail Guide and map
Trailhead: Sharon, New Hampshire

This hike to the summit of Kidder Mountain in New Ipswich is slightly off the Wapack Trail, but offers expansive views of southern New Hampshire that makes the detour worth the effort.

Access: For the north approach, take Route 101 west from the Manchester area to Milford. Continue on Route 101 west to Wilton and 2 miles past the Route 31 south junction, turn left onto Temple (West End) Road. Continue 3.3 miles to Temple. At the southeast corner of the town common, turn right onto the West (Sharon) Road, also known as Nashua Road. Go 3.2 miles further to the intersection of Temple Road, where the trailhead is marked by a Wapack Trail sign on the left. Park off the shoulder. A small horse barn sits in a field behind a split-rail fence to the right.

Optional Access: At the trailhead for the north approach (Temple Road junction), continue west on Nashua Road for 0.6 mile to Route 123. Turn left onto Route 123 south. After 1 mile you will reach the 123/124 junction. Continue south on Route 123/124 for 0.6 mile to Old

Rindge Road (left). Park in a dirt lot and look for a Wapack Trail sign, indicating distances to Nashua Road, Temple Mountain Ledges, and Route 101.

The trail starts out on a dirt road but immediately enters the woods on the left. Several minutes later it descends into a clearing near a residence on the right, and continues up a hill to re-enter the woods. After five minutes, the trail turns left and north. Soon you will emerge at the power lines and Kidder Mountain trailhead. From Route 123/124 this is 0.6 mile, about a 15-minute walk.

Description: The first leg of the hike follows the Wapack Trail (blazed in yellow triangles) on an old woods road for approximately 1.6 miles. The Wapack Trail sign informs you that the road is closed to vehicles and Route 124 is 2.3 miles distant. Shortly after starting out, you will step over boulders to cross a small stream, then immediately detour onto a path to the right that circumvents the muddy and eroded woods road. Pine needles and leaves soften your step as you walk past a variety of ground cover that includes partridgeberry, bunchberry, wild lily-of the-valley, prince's pine and wintergreen, which is also known as "teaberry" in reference to the tea made from the leaves, as well as the chewing gum originally flavored by wintergreen oil.

Soon the trail briefly rejoins the woods road, then re-enters the woods to the left. The trail alternates between the detours and woods road, and then, 15 minutes into the hike, comes to a sign showing the direction to Todd Road. Continue straight ahead and south on the woods road, past a swampy area and brook. You will move uphill through more hemlock and mixed hardwood, and past towering red oaks with an understory of striped maple, which you can distinguish by its double-toothed leaf margin, and green and white vertical stripes in the bark of young trees. Striped maple is sometimes called "goosefoot maple" because the three shallow lobes at the apex of the wide leaves resemble a webbed foot. It is also known as whistlewood, as well as moosewood or moosemaple because the green shoots are browsed by moose.

Just beyond the oaks you will come to a dirt town road. A driveway on the left leads to a private residence. Continuing on, you will reach a pond with the sign "Wildcat Partnership: No Trespassing." Beyond the pond, the trail continues southeast into the woods on a wide, grassy path. In 15 minutes you will come to a area cleared for powerlines overhead. At this point you leave the Wapack Trail (which continues south for 0.6 mile to Routes 123/124), and follow the sign onto the blue-blazed Kidder Mountain Trail.

The almost 1-mile-long Kidder Mountain Trail starts east on a rocky path that follows the power line. Meadowsweet, steeplebush, goldenrod, sheep laurel, and wood aster grow along the trail, as do raspberry and blueberry bushes. You will shortly cross a small stream next to mountain holly shrubs. More commonly found in northern latitudes, this tall, colorful shrub will capture your attention with its elliptical-shaped leaves and dull red velvet berries. Wildlife value this tall wetlands plant because its berries survive through the winter after the leaves fall off.

After passing beneath the power line, the trail continues into the woods. A 5-minute walk brings you to an area that was clear-cut in 1998 (young evergreens now grow amid the stumps in the logged area); 5 more minutes and you are back into a spruce woods, with ledges, juniper and blueberry bushes. The trail continues through another clear-cut before reaching the summit, which is marked by a blue triangle on a big boulder. Stone walls and exposed bedrock ledge indicate that you are standing on what was once a pasture. Scrub oak, gray birch, and red spruce poke up through a blanket of blueberry bushes that ripen in August. Kidder Mountain itself descends somewhat, then expands into a tableland or plateau known as Flat Mountain (a ski area operated on Kidder Mountain in the 1960s). There is an expansive view to the south and southeast of ponds, farms, gleaming metal roofs, and open fields among wooded hills. To the southwest, multisummited Barrett Mountain stretches in a continuous ridge toward Mount Watatic just over the New Hampshire border to Ashburnham, Massachusetts, 3.5 miles away.

Sightseeing: If you have time, you may want to drive to New Ipswich to explore the Barrett House, located on Main Street (Route 123A). This stately mansion built in 1800 by Charles Barrett, Sr., was a

Barrett House, New Ipswich.

wedding gift for his son. Barrett was instrumental in promoting the textile industry in New Ipswich, the site of the first cotton factory in New Hampshire. The Barrett House is a fine example of Federalist architecture. It is operated by Historic New England (formerly the Society for the Preservation of New England Antiquities). Guided tours are offered on the first Saturday of the month from June 1 through October 15, every hour from 11 A.M. to 4 P.M. For more information, call 860-928-4074, or go to www.historicnewengland.org.

If you are still in the mood for the outdoors, the Williams Property offers a 2-mile hike through wetlands, majestic pines, and former pastureland. The trailhead is located at the Old Schoolhouse (c. 1842) on Main Street (Route 123A), 0.2 mile south of the Barrett House.

Nearby, the town of Temple is full of history and also worth investigating. Temple is the site of the first glass works in New Hampshire; it was established in 1780 by Robert Hewes, a soap and tallow chandler from Boston. At this time, the British had blockaded northern ports and prevented window glass and bottles from entering the colonies. Because the colonists were prevented by the British from manufacturing glassware for themselves, Hewes chose a remote location to establish his glass factory—on the north slope of Kidder Mountain. Hewes is credited with producing bulls-eye glass, a brilliantly-hued high-quality optical glass with a thickened center ("bulls-eye") left by the glassworker's rod.

Temple is one of the few towns in New Hampshire where the cultural, religious, and civic activities are still centered in buildings standing on the common. The village cemetery and a row of classic white New England structures are nearby—an old store, post office, Congregational Church, town hall, and the 1842 Miller Grange Hall, formerly the Universalist Church. At the end of the row is the Solon Mansfield Memorial Library (built in 1890).

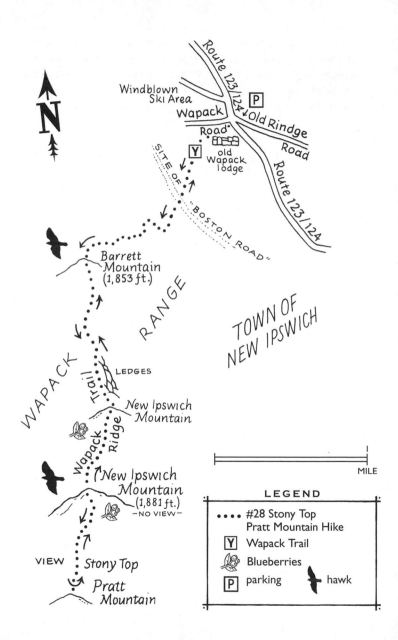

N

Windblown
Ski Area

Route 123/124

P

Wapack
Road

Old Rindge
Road

Route 123/124

Y old
Wapack
lodge

SITE OF

"BOSTON ROAD"

TOWN OF
NEW IPSWICH

Barrett
Mountain
(1,853 ft.)

WAPACK

RANGE

Trail

LEDGES

New Ipswich
Mountain

Wapack Ridge

New Ipswich
Mountain
(1,881 ft.)
—NO VIEW—

VIEW

Stony Top

Pratt
Mountain

MILE

LEGEND

•••• #28 Stony Top
Pratt Mountain Hike

Y Wapack Trail

Blueberries

P parking   hawk

28

Stony Top, Pratt Mountain

Rating: Moderate with short, difficult stretches, this ridgeline trail travels over the spine of Barrett and New Ipswich Mountains, past stone walls, old fields, overgrown clearings, and a thick forest of spruce to Stony Top, a ledge outcrop with wide views.

Distance: 7.2 miles

Hiking Time: 3.5 hours

Lowest Elevation: 1,440 feet

Highest Elevation: 1,881 feet

USGS Map: Ashburnham, Peterborough South

Other Map: Wapack Trail Guide and Map

Trailhead: New Ipswich, New Hampshire

The yellow-blazed 21-mile-long Wapack Trail follows a chain of monadnocks running from Mount Watatic in Ashburnham on the Massachusetts border to North Pack Monadnock Mountain in Greenfield, New Hampshire. This moderate hike, with its short difficult stretches, leads to Stony Top, a ledge outcrop on the northern shoulder of Pratt Mountain, just south of New Ipswich Mountain. Opportunities for blueberry-picking abound, and there is a good chance you will flush a ruffed grouse, startle a deer, or see turkey vultures soaring the thermals. This is one of the more heavily-wooded sections (with great fall colors) along the Wapack Trail, but there are also numerous lookout points. An optional longer hike carries you further south to the terminus of the Wapack Trail at the Massachusetts Route 119 parking lot in Ashburnham, but this requires spotting two cars.

Access: Starting at the junction of Routes 101 and 202 in Peterborough, follow Route 202 west to Jaffrey, then Route 124 east for 6.6 miles to the junction of Routes 123/124 (Turnpike Road). Continue south on 123/124 for 0.6 mile. Look for a sign that says "Wapack Road (dead end)," a private dirt drive on the right. Park on the road

Wapack Trail.

shoulder or at a dirt parking lot off Old Rindge Road opposite the Wapack Road sign. The trail begins off Wapack Road near a sign on a tree where the driveway turns left past a stone foundation from the old Wapack Lodge site. The Wapack Lodge was struck by lightning and burned in the summer of 1993.

Optional Access: Leave one vehicle at the Mass 119 parking lot in Ashburnham, Massachusetts, and a second car off Route 123/124 near the old Wapack Lodge in New Ipswich. Follow the trail directions outlined below until you reach Stony Top, where the Wapack Trail offers spectacular views in all directions.

To reach the trailhead from the Manchester area, take Route 101 west to Milford, then Route 101 west to Route 31 south in Wilton.

Continue on Route 31 to Route 123 north in Greenville. Continue on 123 north to Route 124. (Route 123 joins Route 124 to become Route 123/124). Continue on Route 123N/124W for 4.4 miles to Wapack Road.

Description: The yellow-blazed trail begins by climbing an embankment, then moving through a mixture of oak, maple, spruce, birch, and pine. Near the top of an incline, look for a bulletin board displaying a map of the entire Wapack Trail. After passing a residence on the right and moving through a gap in the stone wall, the trail widens as it continues downhill. Use caution as the trail crosses, and in several cases briefly follows, several ski trails for more than a mile through the Windblown Ski Touring Center. Shortly, a Wapack Trail sign directs you to the left. Climb uphill past ferns to a ledge outcrop looking south to Watatic Mountain. Barrett and New Ipswich Mountains are also visible.

After you work your way down the ledge and step through a gap in a stone wall, the trail levels out, then turns left again. Continue past several more ski trails, turning left two more times, then descend into a ravine, a site that became a route for the "Boston Road" in the mid-1700s.

After crossing the ravine, the trail climbs the rugged eastern slope of Barrett Mountain (1,853 feet) for the first steep portion of the hike. Notice a seasonal brook that parallels the trail here, and boulders, stout birch, and beech trees that are rooted in the mountainside. The trail continues uphill, and after crossing a woods road, continues its steep ascent before leveling out on Barrett's north shoulder at an old pasture marked with juniper, birch, steeplebush, and meadowsweet.

Catch your breath here before looking for a sign, "To Mt. Watatic—Wapack," that directs you to the right. There are limited views as the trail passes over Barrett Mountain and enters a dense spruce forest. Notice how the bark of many of the older spruce trees resembles potato chips, for it becomes more scalloped and pronounced as the trees age. You will appreciate the cathedral-like hush and solitude of this quiet stretch.

In the next 0.7 mile, you will cross stone walls, descend into shaded hollows, and climb two minor knobs. Eventually you reach a ledge affording a good view north of Temple and Pack Monadnock Mountain with its tower, as well as Kidder Mountain to your right and Mount Monadnock to the west (left).

As you follow the trail back into the woods, several ledges offer views to the west of Mount Monadnock, Little Monadnock, and Gap Mountains. After 15 minutes you will reach another ledge with a wider prospect of the same mountains. Three more minutes of walking leads to the actual summit of New Ipswich Mountain, which is wooded with no view. Another 15 minutes walking south brings you to Stony Top, a major clearing with wide views toward Mount Monadnock.

To get to Stony Top from the summit of New Ipswich Mountain, continue on the trail, which descends into quiet woods and crosses two stone walls before emerging at a ledge area overgrown with juniper, blueberries and oak. Here you will get a good view of Pratt, Watatic, and Wachusett Mountains. From the ledge area, the trail then drops into a gap, moves past the Pratt Pond Trail (orange-blazed on the left), and a brook (which in late summer may be a line of dry rocks) before rising to Stony Top. Enjoy the views here before making your return trip. To the west, you can see the white steeple of the Second Rindge Meeting House in Rindge Center, one of the largest buildings of its kind in northern New England, with Mount Monadnock dominating the horizon. Mount Grace in Warwick, Massachusetts, is farther to the southwest.

Optional Extension: From Stony Top, follow the Wapack Trail over the top of wooded Pratt Mountain (1,817 feet). The trail descends to move past the western edge of Binney Pond, then turns left to follow Binney Hill Road. It then turns right (south) to follow a logging road to the Massachusetts state line, passes over Nutting Hill (1,620 feet), and moves on to the summit of Mount Watatic. From Watatic's summit, the Wapack Trail heads southwest and descends to the Mass 119 parking lot. If you wish to avoid the summit of Mount Watatic, just after you cross the Massachusetts border, take a connector that branches right to the State Line Trail, which continues 1.2 miles to the Mass 119 parking lot. The distance from Stony Top to the Mass 119 parking lot is approximately 5.5 miles.

Sightseeing: After you complete your hike, you may wish to visit the Nussdorfer Nature Area, a 60-acre nature preserve located in New Ipswich off Route 124, 2.2 miles from the junction of Routes 31 and 124, and 0.5 east of Mascenic Regional High School. The 2-mile trail is marked with yellow blazes. Look for the good picnic site near Hoar Pond. Call 603-878-2772 for more information.

The Rhoads Easement, also located off of Route 124, offers 4 miles of loop trails in the yellow-blazed Furnace Brook and Island Trails on the Souhegan River and Furnace Brook. It includes forests, wetland, old fields, and wildflowers in the spring. At the start of the trail, look for a waterfall known as Furnace Brook Falls, the site of an old tin mill. The trailhead is on Route 124 just east of the Souhegan Valley Ambulance Service building and Old Tenney Road where Furnace Brook crosses the highway. The other end is on Mill Street behind Warwick Mills. Mill Street is located 0.1 mile south of the junction of Routes 123 and 124. Parking is available for several cars.

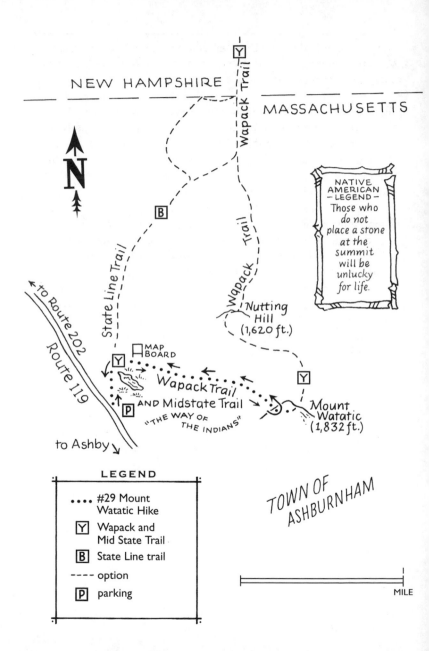

NEW HAMPSHIRE

MASSACHUSETTS

N

Wapack Trail

Y

B

State Line Trail

Wapack Trail

NATIVE
AMERICAN
— LEGEND —
Those who
do not
place a stone
at the
summit
will be
unlucky
for life.

to Route 202

Route 119

Nutting
Hill
(1,620 ft.)

MAP
BOARD

Y

Wapack Trail

AND Midstate Trail

P

"THE WAY OF
THE INDIANS"

Y

Mount
Watatic
(1,832 ft.)

to Ashby

TOWN OF
ASHBURNHAM

LEGEND

•••• #29 Mount
Watatic Hike

Y Wapack and
Mid State Trail

B State Line trail

---- option

P parking

MILE

29
Mount Watatic

Rating: A moderate climb through a hemlock forest to open ledges and an outstanding view of the mountains to the north and the Boston skyline on the horizon to the southwest.

Distance: 2.4 miles

Hiking Time: 2 hours

Lowest Elevation: 1,200 feet

Highest Elevation: 1,832 feet

USGS Map: Ashburnham (Massachusetts)

Other Maps: Wapack Trail Guide and map; Midstate Trail Guide

Trailhead: Ashburnham, Massachusetts

Rising in Ashburnham, Massachusetts, and marking the beginning of the 21-mile-long Wapack Trail, Mount Watatic makes the perfect outing for new or experienced hikers. In the fall, the craggy southeast summit provides an excellent outlook to watch the annual hawk migration.

Access: To reach the trailhead from the Manchester area, take Route 101 west to Route 31 south in Wilton. Continue south on Route 31. After 4.1 miles you will reach Greenville and notice a stone pillar (left) that once supported the highest railroad trestle in New Hampshire. The trestle, six hundred feet long and rising 100 feet above the Souhegan River, was taken down for safety reasons. After driving 13 miles on Route 31 you will reach Route 119. Turn right and follow Route 119 for 1.5 miles to the small town of Ashby, Massachusetts. Continue for 5 miles more and look for a small parking area to the right (north), enclosed by a chain-link fence. The Wapack Trail starts at the north end of the parking lot, on an old cart path beyond a metal gate.

Description: The Wapack Trail is blazed with yellow triangles and begins heading north in conjunction with the Midstate Trail, "the Way of the Indians," a 93-mile-long Massachusetts footpath that begins at the Rhode Island border and terminates at the New Hampshire/Massachusetts border. For more information about the Midstate Trail, call 617-727-3180. Shortly you will cross a brook that flows through a culvert under the road, and then you will pass a small pond to the right. After a brief rocky upgrade and 0.2 mile, the Wapack and Midstate trails turn right and east into the woods for the 1.0-mile journey to the summit. A signboard with a map details the entire route of the Wapack Trail. (The blue-blazed State Line Trail continues 0.9 mile north to the Massachusetts/New Hampshire border.)

For the first few minutes as you continue on the hike, you will cross a stream and pass tall white pines, hardwoods with odd-shaped burls, and an enormous split boulder. For the next 10 minutes you will climb steadily uphill through a quiet hemlock forest, over boulders and tree roots, before coming to a fine view of Mount Monadnock to the northwest. The trail continues along a stone wall and leads to a ledge area where scaly flecks of mica shimmer in the sunlight. Little Watatic Mountain rises to the southwest; to the south is 2,006-foot Wachusett Mountain, the highest point in Massachusetts east of the Berkshires. The trail now turns left. After stepping through an opening in a stone wall, you will move uphill and south through another grove of hemlocks and shortly reach the summit. Turn right to walk out to the open ledges.

The view from the top is spectacular, especially to the north where the entire Wapack Range unfolds before you like a sea of green waves. The early settlers used Watatic as a resort for observation in their travels from the seacoast to the Connecticut River. The view to the northeast of the Wapack Range includes the Lyndeborough Mountains, Joe English Hill, and the Uncanoonucs in Goffstown, New Hampshire. Further east lie Saddleback Mountain and the Pawtuckaway Mountains marching toward the New Hampshire coast. To the northeast, you can see the blue silhouettes of the Belknaps near Lake Winnipesaukee, and on a clear day, the White Mountains. Mount Monadnock is clearly distinguishable to the northwest, with Stratton Mountain further to the west in Vermont. A labyrinth of lakes with Native American names (such as Naukeag and Wapanoag) glis-

View from Mount Watatic.

tens like jewels behind you to the southwest. To the west-southwest, Mount Greylock is visible in the far corner of Massachusetts.

From the main summit make your way down to Watatic's lower, southeastern summit 450 feet away. The bare knob makes an excellent perch to take in the annual fall hawk migration, which takes place from mid-August into November. You will also get a good view southwest to the buildings of the Boston skyline. After enjoying the views and lunch on the open ledge, you may want to search the summit rocks for the geodetic marker, as well as initials and dates of those who have passed this way before you. A granite monument commemorates the purchase of the mountain by the Ashburnham and Ashby land trusts and the Commonwealth of Massachusetts to keep it as an open space. If you are superstitious, find a rock and place it on the summit ledges. Although there is no longer a large cairn on the summit, there once was, and according to Native-American legend, those who did not add a stone to the large pile of rocks before leaving the mountain would be unlucky for life.

Sightseeing: After you complete your hike, you may want to explore Ashby Center on Route 119. Perched above the town common is the

First Parish Church that was built in 1809 as a meetinghouse and church. The octagonal steeple holds a 1,280-pound church bell cast at the Paul Revere Foundry in Boston. A clock-keeper, who is appointed on an annual basis by the town, climbs the rickety stairs every week and winds the clock with a hand crank. The position of town clock winder came into being in 1846 when Louis Gould presented the "Howard" clock made by the Stephenson, Howard and Davis Company of Boston to the town. The gift came with the stipulation that the cock always be maintained at the expense of the town of Ashby. (The church owns the building and the bell tower; the clock and the bell belong to the townspeople.) The view from the tower includes the Boston skyline off to the east; Mount Watatic to the west; and the fields and forests of New Hampshire to the north.

In the old burial ground behind the church you will find the small gravestone for Prince Estabrook, a slave who became the first black soldier in the American Revolution and who was wounded in the first battle at Lexington on April 19, 1775. Estabrook served in the army until 1783 and became a free man. The gravestone is located in the northwest corner of the cemetery. Next to the church is a restored carriage shed. Inside are panels describing the history of the town common, which has been the scene of community events since the early 1770s. Also west of the First Parish Church is a restored Revolutionary-era home (the Abijah Wyman House) with a barn-like addition that houses the Ashby Post Office.

Nearby 2,828-acre Willard Brook State Forest offers camping, hiking, swimming, fishing, bicycling, horseback riding, birding, and winter trail sports. Pets are allowed but must be leashed, and there are areas posted off-limit to them. To get to Willard Brook State Forest from Ashby Center, drive 1.8 miles east on Route 119 to the Damon Pond (camping) entrance in Ashby. The main park Headquarters is located 1.3 miles farther east of the Damon Pond site off Route 119 in West Townsend. For more information on Willard Brook State Forest, call 978-597-8802. A trail map of the state forest is available at headquarters. The Friends' Trail, a 4-mile hiking trail, connects the Damon Pond campground and Willard Brook State Forest to Pearl Hill State Park in West Townsend, Massassachusetts.

30

Skatutakee Mountain

Rating: An easy-to-moderate steep climb to the summit of a
2,002-foot mountain with a striking view of Mount Monadnock
and the Contoocook River Valley.
Distance: 3 miles
Hiking Time: 2 hours
Lowest Elevation: 1,342 feet
Highest Elevation: 2,002 feet
USGS Map: Marlborough
Other Map: Harris Center Trail map
Trailhead: Hancock, New Hampshire

You do not have to journey to the White Mountains to get spectacular views of the New Hampshire countryside. Less than an hour's
drive from the Manchester/Nashua area stands Mount Skatutakee,
a little-known mountain in Hancock with a big-time view. Some believe the 1.5-mile Harriskat Trail leading to the summit of Skatutakee
might be the most gradual climb a hiker can make to a two-thousand
footer. Every switchback was laid out with precision to construct a
low-impact route to the top. With its open views to the south, southeast, and southwest, Skatutakee also makes an excellent spot to
watch for migrating hawks. Make sure to pack a lunch as you will
want to spend more time on the 2,002-foot summit, and remember
to bring a canteen of water, as it is not available on the trail.

Part of a 12,500-acre "supersanctuary" block of land protected
from development and open to the public's enjoyment, Mount
Skatutakee is a gift of Eleanor Briggs who founded the Harris Center for Conservation Education in 1970. A nonprofit organization
dedicated to promoting the understanding and enjoyment of the
outdoors, the Harris Center coordinates hikes and walks throughout
the region and is respected for its conservation and wildlife management programs. The Harris Center's headquarters is a former

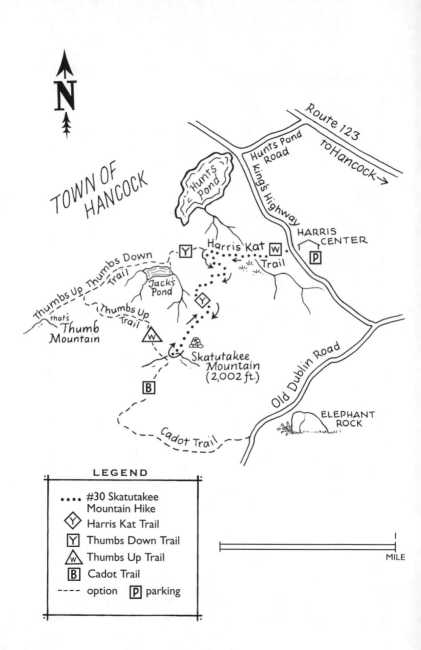

N

Route 123

TOWN OF HANCOCK

Hunts Pond Road

to Hancock →

Hunts Pond

kings Highway

HARRIS CENTER

Y Harris Kat W Trail

P

Thumbs Up Thumbs Down Trail

Jack's Pond

Thumbs Up Trail

that's Thumb Mountain

Y

W

Skatutakee Mountain (2,002 ft.)

B

Old Dublin Road

ELEPHANT ROCK

Cadot Trail

LEGEND

•••• #30 Skatutakee Mountain Hike

Y Harris Kat Trail

Y Thumbs Down Trail

W Thumbs Up Trail

B Cadot Trail

---- option   P parking

MILE

Harris Center for Conservation Education, Hancock.

summer house built in the 1920s that has been remodeled according to environmentally-responsible, green-design guidelines. Weekend educational programs range from mushroom-identification and bird-counts to forestry management and trail construction. Short interpretative trails are available on the property site. The Center's environmental education curriculum, which includes such programs as air- and water-quality-monitoring projects, reaches 1,500 adults and more than 3,500 students in 23 private and public schools in southwestern New Hampshire each year.

Mount Skatutakee is located in Hancock, a classic New England town named for the man who was first to place his signature on the Declaration of Independence. Although he owned nearly 2,000 acres of town land, John Hancock never set foot in this town. Across from the town green you will find the First Congregational Church/Meeting House (built in 1820), which is reputed to be the most photographed church in New England. This handsome white building has a pedimented main portal and a large Palladian window flanked by ionic pilasters. In 1851 the building was moved to its present site from across the road and divided into two stories for church and town use. In the belfry is a Paul Revere Bell, which rings on the hour, all day and all night. Other local points of interest include the Hancock Inn (built in 1789), an old cemetery, and the peaceful waters of Norway Pond across the town common.

Access: To get to Skatutakee, take Route 123 north from the center of Hancock. After 2.2 miles, a sign will direct you left onto Hunt's Pond Road and the Harris Center. Go uphill for 0.4 mile, and then turn left onto the King's Highway. The parking areas are located adjacent to the Harris Center.

Description: Start at the sign on King's Highway, across from the center, that reads "Briggs Preserve." An adjacent sign indicates the Harriskat Trail, which starts climbing rather steeply through a wooded rock-strewn hillside, but soon levels off. The first part of the trail is a pleasant walk through the woods of slender maples poking through a green blanket of Canada Mayflower. There's a good chance you will see Pink Lady's Slipper (*Cypripedium acaule*), members of the orchid family that are on the endangered species list. With nearly 20,000 species, the orchids probably form the largest plant family. Other names for Pink Lady's Slipper are moccasin flower, camel's foot, old goose, Noah's ark, and whippoorwill's shoe. The several allusions to foot, shoe, slipper, and moccasin refer to the round, inflated sac of the blossom called the lip. Lady Slippers bloom in May and June. You will also see fragile white starflowers in the moist woods. The name "starflower" (*Trientalis borealis*) comes from the white flower against the background of green leaves that accentuates the allusion to a star.

At about 15 minutes into your hike, you will maneuver through huge boulders amid a boggy area. The trail rises gradually past a spur on the right. (This is the yellow-blazed Thumbs Down Trail). Keep left as indicated by the white blazes and yellow diamond-shaped markers carrying a Harris Center bobcat logo. You will step through the first of several stone walls on the way to the summit 5 minutes later. After walking over a "train" of boulders left behind by the glaciers, walk a few more minutes uphill to a wooden Harris Center sign pointing the opposite way. Here the trail takes a sharp right turn and continues past towering spruce and white pine. After 50 minutes

Elephant Rock, Hancock.

on the trail, you will come to a sunny open ledge. A short scramble over an outcrop covered with blueberry bushes and juniper lands you on the summit. At the top, the countryside suddenly opens up. The highlight of the vista is the broad, dark shoulders of Mount Monadnock, ruling the horizon across a wide valley to the west. This 3,165-foot giant never fails to inspire and the view from Skatutakee is one of the best. Crotched Mountain provides its own inspiration to the east. In between, the scenic 21-mile-long Wapack Range runs along a ridgeline of mountains from North Pack Monadnock Mountain in Greenfield to Mount Watatic in Ashburnham, Massachusetts.

Sightseeing: If you have some extra time after enjoying lunch on the open ledges, you may want to explore Mount Thumb to the west of Skatutakee. For years it was inaccessible to hikers except by bushwhacking, but Mount Thumb can be reached by using the Thumbs Up Trail (built in 1987). Blazed with white triangles, the trail descends Mount Skatutakee's upper slopes and across a saddle before ascending the 1,920-foot Thumb Mountain. From the summit of Skatutakee, which is marked by a large cairn, descend on the Cadot Trail (formerly Beeline Trail) for 40 yards then turn right on the Thumbs Up Trail.

   There are many other opportunities for hiking at the Harris Center. Children will enjoy the 1-mile-long (0.5 mile each way) Dandelyon

Trail that leads to a glacial boulder field. Pick up *Dandelyon Detectives: A Trailside Companion* (interpretative guide about the landscape) for kids at the Harris Center's office. Children will also enjoy seeing a boulder that resembles a sleeping elephant. To get there from the Harris Center parking lot, continue on the King's Highway for 1.6 miles to Old Dublin Road. Turn right and continue for 1 mile. The "Elephant Rock" is on your left.

31
Bald Mountain

Rating: A moderate hike along the edge of a wilderness pond to
the ledgy summit of a 2,083-foot mountain with good views
of the Wapack Range and Mount Monadnock, and options for
extended hiking.

Distance: 3.3 miles

Hiking Time: 2.5 hours

Lowest Elevation: 1,158 feet (Willard Pond)

Highest Elevation: 2,083 feet

USGS Map: Stoddard

Other Map: Audubon Society of New Hampshire Field Guide map

Trailhead: Antrim, New Hampshire

Bald Mountain in Antrim is the highest point of the dePierrefeu-
Willard Pond Wildlife Sanctuary, a preserve protected by the Audubon Society of New Hampshire. The undeveloped tract is contiguous
to other protected lands and part of more than 2,000 acres that include hills, pristine ponds, and a mixture of woodlands that are home
to coyotes, fox, porcupine, snowshoe hare, bobcat, deer, moose, and
an occasional black bear. Fishers, large members of the Mustellid
family (mink, weasel) who feed on squirrels, hares, and porcupines,
also live here. This is a prime birding location and nesting area for
both the turkey vulture and raven. Because the area is a protected
wildlife sanctuary, dogs are not allowed. Be sure to bring plenty of
water, as it is not available on the trail.

Access: To reach the trailhead from the Manchester area, take Route
101 west to Peterborough. Continue north on Route 123 to Hancock.
From the village center, follow 123 north until you see a Harris Center sign. At 0.9 mile beyond the sign, turn right onto Davenport Road
(dirt), which goes immediately downhill. Stay to the right of a triangle intersection with Willard Pond Road. About 0.2 mile beyond the

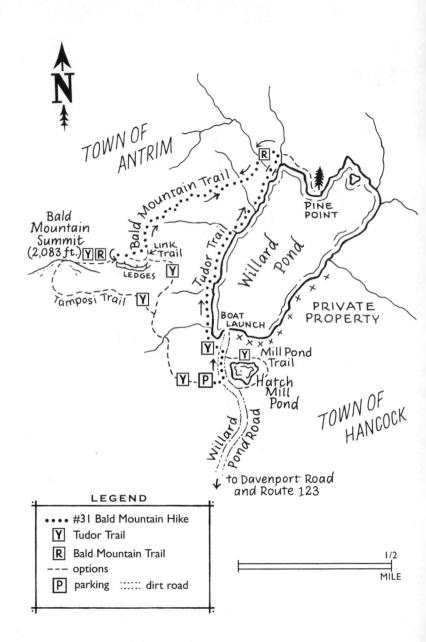

N

TOWN OF
ANTRIM

R

PINE
POINT

Bald
Mountain
Summit
(2,083 ft.) Y R

Link
Trail

Bald Mountain Trail

Tudor Trail

Willard
Pond

LEDGES

Tamposi Trail Y

Y

BOAT
LAUNCH

PRIVATE
PROPERTY

Y

Mill Pond
Trail

Y

Y - P

Hatch
Mill
Pond

TOWN OF
HANCOCK

Willard Pond Road

to Davenport Road
and Route 123

LEGEND

•••• #31 Bald Mountain Hike

Y Tudor Trail

R Bald Mountain Trail

- - - options

P parking ⋯⋯ dirt road

1/2

MILE

Bald Mountain from across Hatch Mill Pond.

intersection, you will reach a small brown wooden shed sheltering a cluster of mailboxes. Stay left to follow Willard Pond Road. The parking lot is 1 mile beyond this point.

Description: From the parking area, walk north up the dirt road that leads to Willard Pond. The trailhead (yellow-blazed Tudor Trail) is located to the left in the woods about 100 yards beyond a caretaker's cottage. The first stretch of the hike is a pleasant 25-minute walk that skirts the western shoreline of Willard Pond to avoid the steep eastern flank of the mountain. Named for an old hunter who fished its waters and trapped on its shores, the 96-acre Willard Pond somewhat similar to a high country lake in that it is Is cold and deep (80 feet in some places). Swimming is allowed, but at your own risk. Willard Pond is also a popular spot for canoeists and fishermen (fly-fishing only). Public access is provided for boats—petroleum-powered motors, however, are prohibited. A mill pond at the outlet of Willard Pond was once the site of a saw and shingle mill that was later converted to a factory that produced bobbins, washboards, and clothespins.

As you walk along the shoreline, you cannot help but notice the abundance of large boulders strewn about the woods—evidence of the glaciers' work 13,000 years ago. Beech, birch, maple, and some huge white pines are a counterpoint to the soft blanket of ferns, evergreen yew, clintonia, and a variety of mosses. A granite bench facing a tree-shrouded cove studded with boulders will tempt you to sit for a while and contemplate the lake. Look for waterfowl who visit here, including wood ducks, common loons, and hooded mergansers; the males having a white, fan-shaped, black-bordered crest.

Ten minutes into the hike, you will see a series of enormous boulders that seem to have tumbled out of the steeply-sloped woods to the left. Huge beech and birch trees dominate this section of the hike, and the gnawed trunks on the shoreline show evidence of beavers' work. You are likely to see coyote or raccoon scat, or porcupine teeth markings on a beech tree. Bald Mountain was once a foraging ground for moose that abounded here. After crossing a plank bridge, the trail passes by more boulders, some the size of small houses, their flat surfaces cloaked in green lichen, and reaches a junction. Turn left to follow the red-blazed Bald Mountain Trail. The Tudor Trail continues right to a pond overlook. This section of the Bald Mountain Trail is moderately strenuous and steep. After 10 minutes, step through a gap in a stone wall and continue past a grove of bushy striped maples. Soon you will reach the Link Trail junction (left), which leads to a large ledge overlooking Willard Pond. The summit is 0.5 mile further from this point. Continue on the red-blazed Bald Mountain Trail as it climbs past towering hardwoods and a red spruce forest before joining the yellow-blazed Tamposi Trail for the final stretch to the top. As with many other peaks with the same name, the "baldness" of Bald Mountain is the result of a forest fire.

At the summit, impressive Mount Monadnock dominates the horizon to the southwest. The expansive sheet of water in the foreground, three miles to the southwest, is Lake Nubanusit, which is connected to Spoonwood Pond. Skatutakee and Thumb Mountains rise behind Lake Nubanusit. Directly south, ribbons of marsh curve like silver snakes against the backdrop of the Wapack Range. Further east lie the Lyndeborough Mountains and Crotched Mountain. The

Uncanoonuc Mountains in Goffstown are visible in the distance behind Crotched. Willard Pond sparkles like an emerald jewel directly below you, with Goodhue Hill rising behind it.

The blueberry- and juniper-covered ledges invite you to sit, have lunch, and soak in the solitude. When you are ready to return, walk eastward and follow the same route back to the parking lot.

For an alternate route down, take the yellow-blazed Tamposi Trail. From the summit, follow the red-yellow markings that lead to the singular yellow-blazed Tamposi Trail that descends the south side of the mountain to the parking lot.

If you have time, you may want to follow yellow markers to the Mill Pond Trail. This 30-minute, 0.8-mile-round-trip loop around 2.7-acre Hatch Mill Pond begins opposite the Tudor Trail sign and leads past a beaver lodge, an old dam site, and an interesting stone sluiceway and foundation. Hatch Mill Pond was created when Willard Pond was dammed for a sawmill.

Optional Extension: The yellow-blazed Tamposi Trail leaves from the back corner of the parking lot. Walking time for the 2-mile moderate loop is two hours. Switchbacks in the steep sections help to maintain a moderate slope. The trail starts uphill through a forest of beech and red oak. Soon you will walk past a field of large boulders broken off from the top of Bald Mountain as ice moved southeast during the last Ice Age. Many of the giant rocks lie scattered in tunnel and cave formations that kids and adults will want to explore. Look for polypod fern and rock tripe lichen here, attached to the rocky surfaces like leathery dark lettuce leaves. Rock tripe forms large patches with curling edges, and the top of the plant is usually black.

After squeezing through a narrow opening between two boulders, the trail continues uphill past a stone wall to the right. At 0.5 mile, you will reach a junction—stay right. Shortly you will glimpse Willard Pond 600 feet below. Twenty minutes from the start of the hike, you will reach an expansive ledge-outcrop area with ample room for stretching out. This is the highlight of the hike, so spend some time taking in the spectacular view of Willard Pond and surrounding mountains from the top of the ledges.

From the ledge area, the trail runs uphill and shortly intersects with the (red) Bald Mountain Trail. Walk a few more minutes following the red-yellow blazes to get to the summit. From there, follow the red-yellow markings that lead to the singule, yellow-blazed Tamposi Trail that descends the south side of the mountain, past a meadow, turning right to move past the boulders back to the parking lot.

32
Crotched Mountain

Rating: A moderate hike with a few steep sections, which leads to a promontory with an outstanding view of the Contoocook River Valley to the west.
Distance: 2.4 miles
Hiking Time: 2 hours
Lowest Elevation: 990 feet
Highest Elevation: 2,066 feet
USGS Maps: Peterborough North, Greenfield
Trailhead: Bennington, New Hampshire

Rising like a fortress from the south-central upland, Crotched Mountain offers sweeping views from its 2,006-foot summit of Mount Monadnock and the Contoocook River Valley. In the late 1800s and for many years afterward, Crotched Mountain was home to a thriving blueberry enterprise. Local shopkeepers employed entire families to pick the fruit. The freshly-picked berries were transported in crates by train to the Boston market. Depending on the time of year you hike and your schedule, you may elect to pick a bucketful for yourself. They are small, deep blue, and sweeter than the high bush variety.

Access: To get to the trailhead from the Manchester area, take Route 114 west to Route 13 south in Goffstown. Follow Route 13 for 7 miles to New Boston, and then travel Route 136 west for 12 miles to Greenfield. From Greenfield take Route 31 north (Sawmill Road) for 0.9 mile to a large blue sign saying "Crotched Mountain Rehabilitation Center" and Crotched Mountain Road (right). Continue on Route 31 for 2.5 miles to Mountain Road (right). After 0.4 mile, Mountain Road turns into a dirt surface. Continue right for 0.2 mile to a pull-off.

Description: The Bennington Trail is blazed in orange but initially the trail markings are scarce. You will immediately come to a fork.

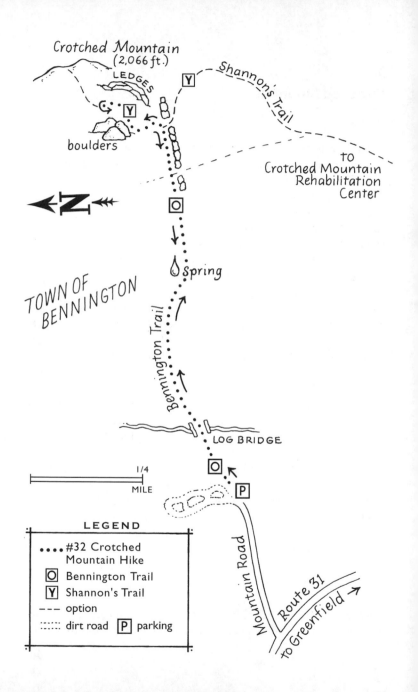

Crotched Mountain
(2,066 ft.)

LEDGES

Y

Shannon's Trail

boulders

Y

to
Crotched Mountain
Rehabilitation
Center

N

TOWN OF
BENNINGTON

O

Spring

Bennington Trail

LOG BRIDGE

O

P

Mountain Road

Route 31

to Greenfield

1/4
MILE

LEGEND

•••• #32 Crotched
Mountain Hike

O Bennington Trail

Y Shannon's Trail

--- option

:::::: dirt road   P parking

Crotched Mountain.

Continue left. A few steps more brings you to another fork. Take either the right or left path. After 100 yards, the trail continues left and uphill on a boulder-strewn path that steepens and moves through a mixed hemlock forest, then levels out briefly before crossing a crude log bridge. On the left, near a large boulder that resembles a canine tooth, the Bennington Trail continues uphill and moves past a huge pine tree. The trail turns right and rises through a gap in a stone wall, and then turns left to follow the wall. This section of the trail is a pleasant woodland walk. There is a good chance you will be startled by the explosive whir of wings underfoot as a Ruffed Grouse suddenly flies from cover.

The Ruffed Grouse (*Bonasa umbellus*) gets its name from the "ruff" of greenish-black feathers sprouting from the base of the neck and draped over the shoulders of the bird. The bird's tail, significantly larger on males, varies in color from a reddish brown to steel gray and all the various tweedy shades in between. The tail feathers are tipped in black, which shows as a terminal band when the tail is spread in flight. Native Americans called the Ruffed Grouse "the carpenter bird" because they believed that it beat upon a log with its wings to produce the drumming sound. This sound is actually made by the male bird cupping his wings and rapidly beating them against the air to attract females and scare off other males.

After reaching a spring 0.5 mile into the hike, the trail turns right and climbs up a steep section through a birch forest. Catch your breath and look for bluebead lily, starflower, Canada Lily, partridgeberry, and other woodland plants. After moving past an open area of impressive ferns, the Bennington Trail reaches a junction near a stone wall at 0.8 mile. Continue straight on a spur to join Shannon's Trail (yellow-blazed). The trail turns left and moves uphill past ledge and giant boulders. One large rock balancing precariously on the left looks as if it is about to tumble onto the trail at any moment. Shortly you will emerge at a ledge with an expansive view looking to the Contoocook River Valley with Mount Monadnock rising beyond. Continue on Shannon's Trail (left) uphill into the woods and over more ledges before reaching a promontory a few minutes later. Here the broad valley spreads before you in a patchwork of lakes, steepled churches, and ribbon roads. The buildings comprising the Crotched Mountain Rehabilitation Center nestle on a lower ridge to the south with North and South Pack Monadnock Mountains and the rest of the Wapack Range marching off behind. In the foreground, to the right of the Crotched Mountain Center, lie Greenfield State Park and Otter Lake. Mount Monadnock anchors the horizon to the southwest. In the foreground the broad waters of Powder Mill Pond, part of the Contoocook River, expand into what looks like the body of a goose and its beak, with the Powder Mill Dam crossing the "beak." The prominent mountains rising beyond Powder Mill Pond are Skatutakee and Thumb Mountains in Hancock. Farther in the foreground, close to the base of Crotched Mountain, is Lake Whittemore. To the right of Powder Mill Pond lies the town of Bennington, and if you continue to gaze in that direction you can see a gray plume of smoke rising from the smokestack of the Monadnock Paper Mill in Bennington. Antrim, with its white, steepled churches, sprawls in the valley 3 miles farther north, with Bald Mountain anchoring the ridge on the western edge of the town to the south. Stratton Mountain in Vermont is visible on the western horizon.

Optional Extension: Shannon's Trail is a 3.5-mile round-trip trail that begins near the Crotched Mountain Rehabilitation Center in Greenfield and rises to a rocky promontory below the summit. Average hiking time is 2.5 hours. To get to the trailhead for Shannon's Trail, from the "Crotched Mountain Rehabilitation Center" sign on Route 31 north, turn right onto Crotched Mountain Road. Continue uphill for 1.4 miles until you see the main entrance sign for the Crotched Mountain Rehabilitation Center. Drive 0.2 mile farther and park off the right shoulder opposite a metal gate and the trailhead sign. The yellow-blazed trail turns right into the woods and shortly comes to a meadow where there is a nice view to the north of Crotched Mountain—a three-peaked mountain with heights in Bennington, Francestown, and Greenfield—and to the east of the twin-peaked Uncanoonuc Mountains and whale-back-shaped Joe English Hill. Look for quaking aspen growing on the south-facing slope. Quaking aspen (*Populus tremuloides*) have fine-toothed, rounded leaves anchored by flattened stalks, causing them to tremble in the slightest breeze. The quaking aspen's leaves are shiny green and pale below; in the fall they turn clear golden.

The trail climbs uphill along the edge of the meadow, re-enters a birch-maple woods, and then emerges at a gravel road. It continues on the other side of the road and moves uphill to "the Knoll," an open plateau and hawk-viewing area (the Knoll can also be reached by the gravel road). There is a good view here of Mount Monadnock to the west and the Pack Monadnocks to the south. The trail drops and continues through spruce woods where you will see a good display of bunchberry and Pink Lady's Slipper in the spring. It then rises uphill where wild blueberries grow on both sides of path on the exposed ridge in late summer. At 0.8 mile you'll come to Nancy's Trail (right). Turn left (northeast) as the trial descends into a cool spruce woods, and then slender maple and birch trees stretch overhead. If you are hiking with kids along this stretch, ask them to keep an eye out in the woods to the right for an unusually-shaped boulder that resembles a giant clam. At 1.2 miles you will reach a small stream that may be dry in late summer. The trail moves uphill and reaches a junction that points the way to the Bennington Trail. Turn right and continue on Shannon's Trail, which passes through a gap in a stone wall, then turns left past large boulders and onto open ledge with expansive views.

Sightseeing: Nearby Greenfield State Park, with 401 acres located on the shores of 61-acre Otter Lake, offers swimming, hiking, fishing, boating, picnicking and camping, 257 tent sites, restrooms, and showers. For more information on Greenfield State Park, call 603-547-3497, or go to www.nhstateparks.org. Pets are permitted in the designated area of the campground only, not in the day-use area.

33
Little Monadnock Mountain

Rating: A moderate hike with some steep sections, through a state
park with showy thickets of rhododendron, leading to a rocky
promontory with fine views across a valley to Mount Monadnock
and the Wapack Range.

Distance: 2.2 miles
Hiking Time: 2 hours
Lowest Elevation: 1,200 feet
Highest Elevation: 1,883 feet
USGS Map: Monadnock
Other Map: AMC Metacomet-Monadnock Trail Guide
Trailhead: Fitzwilliam, New Hampshire

Standing at slightly more than half the elevation of Mount Monadnock, and with only two trails leading to its 1,883-foot summit, Little
Monadnock Mountain in Fitzwilliam does not come close to measuring up to the Grand Monadnock in size or reputation. But don't let
this peak's lower elevation discourage you from seeking it out. Little
Monadnock Mountain is a gem in its own right, waiting to step out
of the shadow of her big sister and show off some of her own sparkle:
open ledge overlooks, a mind-boggling botanical display, and a mod-
erately-paced 2-mile hike you will more than likely have to yourself.

Designated a National Natural landmark in 1992, Rhododendron
State Park features a 16-acre grove of *Rhododendron maximum* that
is the northernmost native stand of wild Rhododendrons in New
England. Members of the heath family, rhododendrons are cousins
to mountain laurel, sheep laurel, azaleas, wintergreen, blueberry,
and trailing arbutus. These magnificent leathery-leafed plants are in
full bloom in mid-July, but more than 40 different varieties of wildflowers can be viewed along the loop trails that skirt the natural bog
area. Self-guided tour brochures are available at the park. A 0.6-mile
long, universally-accessible trail encircles the grove. A day-use fee is

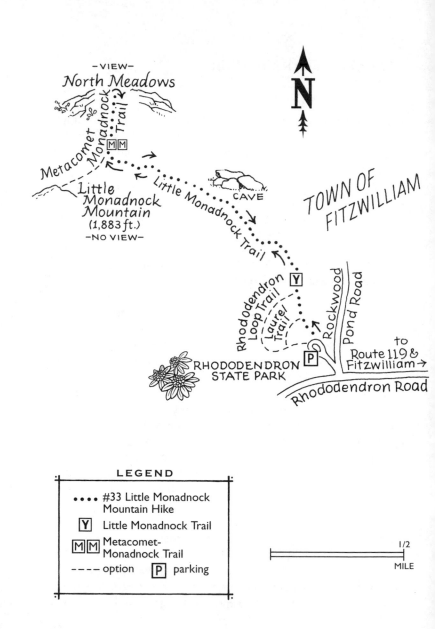

-VIEW-
North Meadows

Metacomet Monadnock Trail

M M

Little
Monadnock
Mountain
(1,883 ft.)
-NO VIEW-

Little Monadnock Trail

CAVE

TOWN OF
FITZWILLIAM

Y

Rhododendron Loop Trail

Laurel Trail

Rockwood Pond Road

P

to
Route 119 &
Fitzwilliam →

RHODODENDRON
STATE PARK

Rhododendron Road

N

LEGEND

•••• #33 Little Monadnock
Mountain Hike

Y Little Monadnock Trail

M M Metacomet-
Monadnock Trail

---- option   P parking

1/2
MILE

charged when the park is staffed. Senior citizens and children aged 11 and under are free. Pets are permitted only on the trail to Little Monadnock. For more information, call 603-532-8862.

Access: From Keene, travel on Route 12 south to the Route 119 junction. Continue west on Route 119 to Fitzwilliam, a small community with a well-kept town common. One-half mile beyond the common, turn right onto Rhododendron Road and proceed to the parking area and trailhead.

Description: The trail to Little Monadnock starts at the north end of the circular parking area, to the left of a wood bulletin board. After stepping between two rectangular stone pillars, you will walk past a picnic area in a shaded grove presided over by old-growth white pines taller than three-story apartment buildings. Neck-craning is required to fully appreciate the beauty and stature of these giants. A few moments later, you will walk past a dazzling display of rhododendron bushes. The Laurel Trail branches left. Continue on the Rhododendron Loop Trail. Soon you will come (right) to the yellow-blazed Little Monadnock Trail, which meanders through a mixed forest of hemlock, beech, maple, and pine. This section of the hike is a pleasant woodland walk where you are likely to hear the tapping of a woodpecker digging its lunch from a decaying pine, or the sudden flutter of wings of a startled ruffed grouse. The trail will ascend gradually in a northern direction.

After stepping between a gap in a stone wall, climb over a rocky outcrop before encountering the most difficult stretch of the hike: an uphill climb over a boulder-strewn path that will test your lungs and legs for five minutes. But before you start, children will enjoy squeezing through a boulder cave to the right of the trail here. The trail skirts the edge of the woods on a ledge of granite outcrop, and then levels out. At this point, a long stone wall parallels the trail to the right for several minutes as you walk uphill. After turning right and stepping between the stone wall, the path steepens again, but by the time you have had a chance to work up a sweat, you will be near the top, standing on the northeast end of the summit ridge.

Little Monadnock's summit is a short distance above you to the left, but it is wooded with no view. Although the view from the ridge is good, take time to locate a large "MM" painted in white with an arrow pointing northeast. This is the Metacomet-Monadnock Trail, which originates in southern Massachusetts near the Connecticut state line and ends at the summit of Mount Monadnock.

Follow the M-M Trail down the backbone of the ridge and into the woods for a few minutes to an open ledge area known as the North Meadows. Here the view opens up as if you were looking at a vast ocean of land. Nestled in the valley to the north is the quiet village of Troy, with its white, steepled town hall, Congregational church and landmark red brick smokestack chimney of the Troy Mills; Mount Monadnock's treeless summit and the notched ridgeline of Gap Mountain stand out prominently to the northeast; and like a long black fan, the Wapack Range unfolds to the southeast. The view to the Connecticut River Valley and Vermont is no less impressive, stretching like a rumpled blanket, with copper green, jade, and cobalt bumps dotting the glacially-carved landscape as far as the eye can see. Take some time to enjoy sounds you do not normally hear: the wind rustling in the trees and the shrill notes of mountain birds. When you are ready to return, re-enter the woods for the short walk back to Little Monadnock's summit ridge and descend to the park by retracing your route.

Sightseeing: The nearby town of Fitzwilliam is well worth investigating. The white-spired town hall (which is on the National Register of Historic Places) is the centerpiece of the village common. The handsome building, originally a Congregational Church, burned in 1816 shortly after its dedicatin, but was rebuilt in 1817. The bell survived the fire, but was later cracked in sounding an alarm. When it was later recast, 300 silver dollars were added to its metal in the belief that the bell's tone would be improved. A pedimented portico supported at each end by two pairs of Ionic columns frames the main entrance of the two-story building, which is crowned by a four-storied steeple consisting of a square clock tower, belfry, and two octagonal lanterns topped by a short spire and weathervane.

In the second story is a Palladian window. The Fitzwilliam Museum at the Amos J. Blake House is located on the village common and is open year-round on Thursdays, 9 to 11 A.M. and, from late May through mid-October on Saturdays, 1 to 4 P.M. For information, call 603-585-7742. Exhibits include a law office, an old-time schoolroom, military room, and an antique 1779 fire engine.

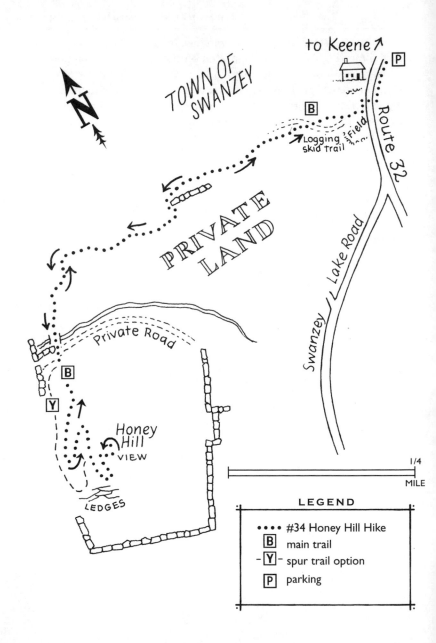

to Keene

TOWN OF SWANZEY

PRIVATE LAND

Route 32

Swanzey / Lake Road

B
Logging skid Trail
Field

Private Road

B

Y

Honey Hill
VIEW

LEDGES

P

1/4
MILE

LEGEND

•••• #34 Honey Hill Hike

B main trail

-Y- spur trail option

P parking

34
Honey Hill

Rating: Easy to moderate woodland walk past stone walls, wild-flowers, and thickets of mountain laurel, toward a bald-faced ledge with good views of hills around the Keene Valley and Mount Monadnock.
Distance: 2.25 miles
Hiking Time: 1.5 hours
Lowest Elevation: 480 feet
Highest Elevation: 860 feet
USGS Map: Winchester
Other Map: Swanzey Conservation Commission map
Trailhead: Swanzey, New Hampshire

Take an ideal family outing along the trail leading to the top of Honey Hill, where you will enjoy bursts of fall color and views of Mount Monadnock rising beyond the shoreline of Dublin Lake. Located in Swanzey, Honey Hill is a property protected through conservation easements of the Land Conservation Investment Program (LCIP) and monitored by the Swanzey Conservation Commission. Although it remains private land, the public is invited to use the blue-blazed trail that leads from Route 32 to the summit.

Access: To reach the trailhead from Manchester, take Route 101 to Route 12 in Keene. Continue on Route 12 south for 0.9 mile to Route 32 (Old Homestead Highway). Continue 4.9 miles on Route 32 south, past Swanzey Center, to a metal gate on the east side of the road near a pasture. Park on the shoulder of the road opposite a white farmhouse. Do not block the gate. Walk south for 0.15 mile on Route 32, using caution. Look for the entrance to a field on the right. Continue walking across the field for 175 yards.

Description: Two paths enter the woods. Stay right—the "path" to the left is a skid trail from logging activity that crosses the trail several times during the first 0.4 mile. There are no blue blazes at this point as the trail moves over a wet section and then climbs steadily uphill through a mixed forest of oak, pine, hemlock, beech, birch, and maple. Look for clubmosses, ferns, wild sarsaparilla, and wintergreen along the path. In early spring you will find violets, bluets, starflowers, and wood anemone. After moving over a grassy section and past an intersecting skid trail (left), the trail enters a hemlock forest and shortly turns left at the end of a stone wall. At this point follow the blue blazes downhill as you continue through the hemlock forest.

After another five minutes, you will cross two wooden plank bridges. After crossing a private woods road, you will come to a blue-yellow trail junction. Bear left and continue following blue blazes. As the trail levels out, you will see an impressive display of mountain laurel, and then on the right, a smooth ledge offering a view to the west of Franklin Mountain (1,422 feet). Further to the south are Bullard Mountain, Rattlesnake Mountain, and the sugarloaf-shaped Gunn Mountain.

Just beyond this outlook, the trail begins to switchback up the hill. After passing a yellow-blazed spur trail on the right, you will come to a good view of Swanzey Lake to the west, with Stratton Mountain (Vermont) in the distance. It's a short scramble from here to the summit, where there is a 180-degree view. To the north is Mount Caesar (See Mt. Caesar Option below), and the hills around the Keene valley. The village of East Swanzey and a large gravel pit fill in the valley floor to the east. Beyond these are the Marlborough-Richmond ridge and Mount Monadnock. Retrace your steps to return to your vehicle.

Optional Extension: You can view the rocky ledges of 962-foot-high Mt. Caesar looming over Swanzey as you drive north on Route 32 back toward the village. The mountain was named for Caesar Freeman, a freed Black slave, and Native Americans once used it as a lookout. It is about a 30-minute walk to the top. To get to Mt. Caesar, look for the white entrance gate to the Mt. Caesar Cemetery opposite the Swanzey Town Hall. Drive through the entranceway between the stone posts and bear to the right. After 0.1 mile, park near the huge white pine trees. The trail, a woods road bordered on both sides by a stone wall, begins beyond a stone wall in the far corner of the cemetery 200 feet to the right. After passing over a ledgy section, the trail descends and comes to a woodsy area of stag horn sumac. Just beyond this you will come to a woods road (left). Continue on the rutted road that gradually climbs uphill. After ten minutes (or 0.3 mile) the road forks to the left, near a residence in the woods to the right. Continue uphill through a hardwood forest. Ten minutes more of walking brings you to the south-facing ledges topped by a red beacon light on a 50-foot metal pole. Just before reaching the top, look to the left to see an interesting glacial erratic. From the ledges, below you to the east lies the village of Swanzey Center. Honey Hill is directly south. The biggest mountain to the west is Franklin Mountain, with sugarloaf-shaped Gunn Mountain to its left.

Sightseeing: After your walk, consider a visit to Swanzey, which boasts one of the densest concentrations of covered bridges in the country. A map and directions to the bridges are available at the Swanzey Historical Museum located on Route 10, West Swanzey. Visitors to the museum have access to a playground for children and a picnic grove. The museum is open on weekdays from 1 to 4:30 P.M. and on Saturdays and Sundays from 10 A.M. to 4:30 P.M. through Columbus Day. For more information, call 603-352-4579.

Swanzey actually comprises several village centers, including Westport, East Swanzey, West Swanzey, and Swanzey Center. The Potash Bowl, an open-air natural arena, is located in Swanzey Center where "The Old Homestead," a play based on the lives of nineteenth-century townspeople, is performed annually in July. For more information, call 603-352-3251.

You might also wish to visit the Old Holbrook Farm, which is believed to be where Joyce Kilmer (1886–1918) composed his famous poem, "Trees." Kilmer was looking out from the porch of the farmhouse at a panorama of majestic maples and scribbled the verse for "Trees" on a brown paper bag. To get to the site of his inspiration from the trailhead parking area, drive south for 0.3 mile on Route 32 to Swanzey Lake Road. Continue 2.4 miles and turn onto Pebble Hill Road (dirt). Go 0.3 mile to Winch Hill Road. The Holbrook Farm is located 0.4 mile farther down Winch Hill Road.

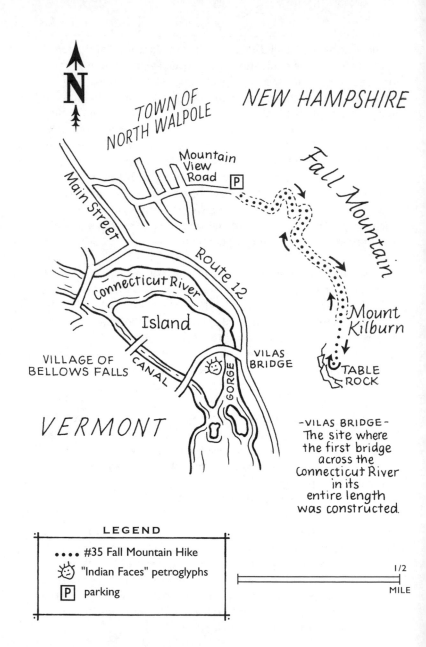

N

TOWN OF
NORTH WALPOLE

NEW HAMPSHIRE

Fall Mountain

Mountain
View
Road
P

Main Street

Route 12

Connecticut River

Island

VILLAGE OF
BELLOWS FALLS

CANAL

GORGE

VILAS
BRIDGE

Mount
Kilburn

TABLE
ROCK

VERMONT

-VILAS BRIDGE-
The site where
the first bridge
across the
Connecticut River
in its
entire length
was constructed.

LEGEND

•••• #35 Fall Mountain Hike

☼ "Indian Faces" petroglyphs

P parking

1/2

MILE

35
Fall Mountain

Rating: An easy to moderate switchback climb to a flat-topped rock and bird's-eye view of Bellows Falls, Vermont.
Distance: 1.5 miles
Hiking Time: 1.5 to 2 hours
Lowest Elevation: 492 feet
Highest Elevation: 1,060 feet
USGS Map: Bellows Falls
Trailhead: North Walpole, New Hampshire

A brooding mass of rock, Fall Mountain rises abruptly from the east bank of the Connecticut River, and offers a bird's-eye view of Bellows Falls, Vermont, and the Green Mountains beyond. After you take in the view, there is an old canal system, "Indian Faces," and historic bridges to see in Bellows Falls.

Access: From Keene: Take Route 12 to North Walpole. The road winds around Fall Mountain and barecliffed Mt. Kilburn—the highest peak on Fall Mountain—rising sharply above the railroad tracks that parallel the highway. Go 0.5 mile past the Route 5 intersection to Main Street. Continue 0.2 mile and turn right onto Mountain View Road, which is a dead end. There is a small parking area on the left.

Description: The trail begins (south) on a dirt-and-gravel road just beyond a metal gate (no motorized vehicles) and shortly moves under a power line. In late summer, wood aster, goldenrod, and sweet fern grow in the sterile soil along the trail. Sweet fern, sometimes called "small boy's tobacco," is a low, fragrant bush with fern-like foliage. A member of the wax-myrtle or bayberry family, its leaves are very aromatic when crushed. A small nut is enclosed in a burr-like husk.

The rutted road continues (east) uphill past a section of birch trees then turns right near a pond and stone culvert. Soon hemlock begins to mix into the forest community as your route switchbacks up the mountain. Twenty-five minutes into the hike you will reach a fork. Continue right (south) under the power lines; you will get a peek of Bellows Falls below the power line cut.

The trail continues south-southwest along the ridge past huge boulders (left) matted with papery-looking rock tripe—large lichen resembling a leathery, curled-up lettuce leaf attached at its lower middle to the rocks. Unless the day is wet, rock tripe is apt to be rather dry and brown.

Ten minutes from the fork you will reach some big boulders. Cautiously make your way down the narrow path to Table Rock, a flat outcrop where you will get a bird's-eye view of Bellow Falls. Sit for a while and take in the panorama of bridges, railroad yards, train station, round house, canal locks, hydroelectric powerhouse, the brick buildings, and clock tower of the Rockingham Town Hall that dominates the Square.

Directly below the cliff is the river gorge where Native Americans once congregated at the Great Falls—the largest natural falls on the Connecticut River—to harvest migrating Atlantic salmon and shad. (Fall Mountain was formerly known as Falls Mountain). Over the years at least a dozen persons have gone over the falls and lived. The first recorded incident was an Abnaki squaw who mistakenly allowed her canoe to be drawn to a point where she could not paddle against the current. Faced with the grim prospect of not surviving the plunge, the story recounts how she lay down in the canoe and drank the contents of a bottle of rum she was taking to her brave, then awaited her fate. Later she was fished out below the falls quite safe and quite inebriated. Others have taken the plunge in a more resolute manner. In 1879 Captain Paul Boyton passed over the Falls in a rubber suit as a crowd of 2,000 gathered to watch.

High above the river you might see hawks or turkey vultures soaring in the updrafts, hear the sound of train whistles penetrating the air, or simply appreciate the view as Henry David Thoreau did from this spot on September 10, 1856. In the mid-1800s, a carriage road was built up the mountain to allow guests from the Island House (a hotel in Bellows Falls) to travel to Table Rock to picnic and enjoy the views. Table Rock was also the site of the Mountain House, a pavilion built in the style of a Greek temple, which blew down during a gale on New Year's night in 1864 and was never rebuilt.

Sightseeing: The Bellows Falls Downtown Historic District (on the National Register of Historic Places) is worth a visit before or after your hike. Start at the Bellows Falls Waypoint Interpretative Center, which stands in an old railroad yard and has historic photos, a gallery, and a nature museum. Look for the timeline that depicts natural, cultural, and industrial history of the communities along the Connecticut River. The center is open from 10 A.M. until 4 P.M., seven days a week.

Pay a visit to the Bellows Falls Visitor Center and Fish Ladder at the dam, 17 Bridge Street, located just above the brick hydroelectric powerhouse, for information about local history. You will also want to check out the viewing window on the fish ladder. Open May 27 to September 3, on Saturday, 10 A.M. to 4 P.M. and Sunday, 12 P.M. to 4 P.M.

You will also see a canal system, which was among the first in America and is now dammed to generate electricity at the hydroelectric station. Just east of the canals and visitor center on Bridge Street is the historic stone Fitchburg railroad bridge. For years, Bellows Falls was a major rail center with three commercial railroad lines running through the village. The 275-foot Boston and Maine Railroad stone arch tunnel, which was constructed in 1851, passes beneath the village's downtown square. There is also the concrete Vilas Bridge, directly above the place where, in 1785, Colonel Enoch Hale constructed an open wooden bridge, the first structure across the Connecticut River at any location along the entire length of the waterway. In the rocky gorge 50 feet south of the Vilas Bridge on the west side of the river, you will find the "Indian Faces" or petroglyphs cut by the Pennacook tribe in the rocks. The story is that the carvings, discovered in 1807, might commemorate a successful fish catch or skirmish with settlers. The petroglyphs, which are listed on the National Register of Historic places, were altered in the twentieth century by recarving and by painting them in bright yellow paint in an attempt to make

The "Indian Faces" petroglyphs, Fall Mountain. Photograph by Curtis Carroll.

them more visible. Park in a large lot near the Vilas Bridge and walk a short distance down a dirt road that skirts the gorge. The carvings are 50 feet south of the Vilas Bridge just over a bank on the rock surface below. A good time to explore the potholes and other natural wonders in the gorge is in summer, when most of the water is diverted through the old canal to the power dam.

After exploring the gorge, you may want to visit the Adams Grist Mill & Museum (on the National Register of Historic places) on Mill Street, at the southern end of the village square. Located in an 1831 gristmill, the Bellows Falls Historical Society museum contains the original gristmill machinery, tools, and equipment, including all the grain elevators and storage bins. that were used to grind grain from 1831 to 1961. Open Saturday and Sunday, July to August, 1 to 4 P.M. For more information, call 802-463-9415.

Not far away is the Rockingham Meeting House (designated a National Historic Landmark in 2000), Vermont's oldest public building in nearly its original condition. The town-owned Federal-style building, built between 1787 and 1801, with its high pulpit, pigpen pews, and authentic sounding board, is open every day, 10 A.M. to 4 P.M., from Memorial Day to Columbus Day. For more information, call 802-464-3964. The Rockingham Meeting House cemetery dates back to the 1700s and includes many examples of funerary art. To get there from Bellows Falls, drive 2.8 miles north on Route 5 then continue 1.5 miles north on Route 103. Turn left on Meetinghouse TH 78 Road and continue 0.3 mile.

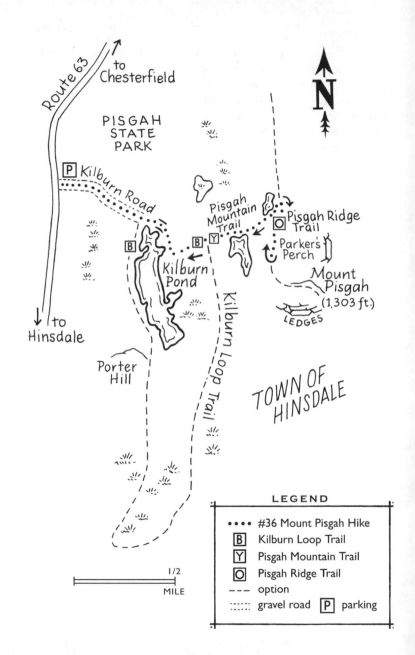

Route 63

to
Chesterfield

PISGAH
STATE
PARK

P Kilburn Road

Pisgah
Mountain
Trail

Pisgah Ridge
Trail

O

Parker's
Perch

B Y

B

Kilburn
Pond

Mount
Pisgah
(1,303 ft.)

LEDGES

to
Hinsdale

Kilburn Loop Trail

Porter
Hill

TOWN OF
HINSDALE

N

1/2
MILE

LEGEND

•••• #36 Mount Pisgah Hike

B Kilburn Loop Trail

Y Pisgah Mountain Trail

O Pisgah Ridge Trail

- - - option

⋮⋮⋮ gravel road   P parking

36
Mount Pisgah

Rating: An easy-to-moderate forested walk to a rocky outcrop with an outstanding view of Mount Monadnock and an opportunity to see lots of migrating birds along the way.
Distance: 3.6 miles
Hiking Time: 2 to 3 hours
Lowest Elevation: 1,030 feet
Highest Elevation: 1,303 feet
USGS Map: Winchester
Other Map: Road and trails map, Pisgah State Park
Trailhead: Hinsdale, New Hampshire

Pisgah State Park is the largest property in the New Hampshire park system and the second largest state park in New England. Located in the southwestern corner of New Hampshire near the Connecticut River, there are six trailheads leading into more than 13,500 acres of rugged wilderness, ponds, streams, wetlands, and second-growth forests, including northern hardwood, oak-hickory, and hemlock. At one time much of this land was privately owned and logging was a prominent industry. Today, the only clues to this logging past can be found in the old skid roads and ramps, mill sites, cemeteries, cellar holes, and abandoned settlements that dot the landscape. Pisgah's 50 miles of trails give outdoor enthusiasts ample opportunities for hiking, bird-watching, mountain biking, cross-country skiing, picnicking, and fishing. Leashed pets are permitted in park. For informatino, call 603-239-8153.

Access: From Keene, follow Route 9 west to Route 63. Turn left and continue one mile to the town of Chesterfield. The trailhead is 3.5 miles farther on the left. Park in the lot and begin your walk on Kilburn Road beyond a bulletin board and mailbox.

Description: The gravel road immediately leads you east, past beech, birch, maple, and oaks—a riot of yellows, reds and oranges by early October. The fruit (mast) of the beech trees makes for good eating as each small prickly burr contains two or three small, triangular nuts, which are highly prized by bear, deer, and many birds, including wild turkey and wood duck. Beechnuts have a rich, delicate flavor that offsets their disadvantages (small size, some barely larger than peas, and difficult-to-open thin but leathery shells). Another distinctive feature of this hardy tree is its smooth bark, which hugs the trunk and branches of the tree even in old age. A smoky, dark tone is frequently noticeable on one side of the trunk, with still darker, cracked areas around the base.

The trail descends immediately into a grove of hemlocks, and then begins a gradual ascent. Tall, white pines are rooted firmly among ledge and chaotic jumbles of glacially-scattered boulders in the woods. You will continue through thickets of mountain laurel. The shiny leaves of this hardy shrub remain green throughout the winter, long after its showy pink to white flowers have died. Look for an interesting cleft boulder on the side of the trail to the left. A triangular-shaped hole in the large rock makes an ideal hideaway for chipmunks and other small wildlife. The path darkens again as you move through another grove of hemlock and approach the first real uphill section of the hike. Awaiting you at the top of the rise are slabs of granite, matted with rock tripe lichen, on which deer graze. Rock tripe (genus *umbilicaria*) resembles a leathery dark lettuce leaf of up to three inches wide that is attached to rocky surfaces. The trail levels out, swings right and left, and then begins a descent.

In five minutes you connect to the (blue) Kilburn Loop Trail, which continues to the right and south, a 5-mile hike that returns east of the pond. A blue-marked ski trail, the return loop for the Kilburn trail, leads to the left. Take a minute to walk down to Kilburn Pond past an impressive display of hobblebush. Sedges, rushes, blueberry bushes, and sphagnum moss grow along the edge of the water, and tall white pine and hemlock ring the shoreline. In early summer look for yellow bullhead lilies and squadrons of water bugs. Children will enjoy the gyrations of the speedy water striders and whirligigs (also known

*Kilburn Pond, Pisgah
State Park.*

as lucky bugs, submarine chasers, and write-my-names). Crimson-tailed dragonflies put on their own impressive aerial show.

Return to the ski trail and Kilburn loop junction where you continue to the left. You will pass two marshy areas studded with snags—large standing dead trees. Snags are used by many members of the forest community. Woodpeckers peck holes in search of insects and also live in snags in nest cavities. Chickadees and white-breasted nuthatches excavate cavities to raise their young. At 0.8 mile you will reach a wooden footbridge with handrails. The trail continues (right) over the bridge and rolls up and down through an oak, hemlock, birch, and beech forest, in many places requiring some picking over tree roots and boulders. Take time to appreciate the subtle beauty of nature along the way: the delicate ruffles of fungi lining a decaying log; gnarled and twisted tree roots clinging to boulders;

tiny toads threading their way through the leaf litter; and the mosses and variegated greens blanketing the forest floor.

At 1.2 miles you will come to the Pisgah Mountain Trail (yellow) junction (left). Continue on the Pisgah Mountain trail, which crosses several wooden bridges as it continues past marshes, bogs with the bleached gray skeletons of solitary snags, and an impressive thicket of mountain laurel. The footing becomes tangled with tree roots and boulder studded as the path narrows and moves past a marshy area to the left. Pine needles soften the path as you move uphill and reach the Pisgah Ridge Trail junction at 1.6 miles. Continue right (south) for 0.2 mile on the orange blazed trail uphill to a lookout ledge (Parker's Perch).

The ledges offer a good view of Mount Monadnock to the east. In the foreground, across the forested valley, the rounded summit of Franklin Mountain (1,422 feet) and a chain of smaller summits that look like the backs of sleeping cats, snake southward toward the Massachusetts border. A few steps across the ledgy outcrop brings you to a good view of the ski mountains and other Vermont peaks to the west. Blueberry bushes cover the ledges here. Look for pitch pine growing alongside white pine. Pitch pine is the only native pine in New England with three needles. The common name refers to the high resin content of the knotty wood. Early Americans often would ignite pitch pine knots for torches, and used old-growth pitch pine for flooring, sills, window and door frames, and structural beams. The decay-resistant wood was also popular for ship-building, mine props, railroad ties, and fencing. Pitch pine seeds are an important food source for nuthatches, pine grosbeak, and black-capped chickadee.

From Parker's Perch, the Pisgah Ridge trail descends and climbs two more knolls before reaching the wooded peak of Mount Pisgah 0.5 mile farther. An open ledge here provides another good view of Monadnock rising beyond the valley and marshes to the east. The Pisgah Reservoir can be seen to the south.

Sightseeing: You can explore the nearby village of Ashuelot after finishing your hike. From the trailhead, drive south on Route 63 for 4 miles to Hinsdale and turn left onto Route 119 East. Continue past old brick mills and houses crowding the narrow riverbank and hills of the forested valley. From the mid-to-late-1800s, the Ashuelot River, a tributary of the Connecticut River, was an active manufacturing location, boasting numerous textile and paper mills. The wooden container industry in Winchester at one time employed hundreds of workers who produced kegs, buckets, pails, and barrels. The New England Box Company ran six stationary sawmills and as many as 53 portable sawmills—the largest mill was located on Round Pond in Pisgah State Park.

In the hamlet of Ashuelot, 3.5 miles from the junction of Routes 63/119, you can walk on the 169-foot two-span Winchester-Ashuelot Covered Bridge. Built in 1864, it is a town lattice truss-type bridge with a pedestrian walkway whose original purpose was to transport wood across the river for the Ashuelot Railroad. Or visit the Thayer Public Library, which is housed in a white colonial home that was a tenement house for the workers of the Sheridan Woolen Mill in the late 1800s. Its hours are Tuesday and Friday from 1:30 to 7 P.M.

The 209-acre Friedsam Town Forest, with hiking loops of more than three miles and large trees, cataract, potholes, and an old family cemetery, is located in Chesterfield. From the junction of Route 9 and Route 63, drive south on 63 for 0.9 mile. Turn right onto Twin Brook Road. The lower parking area is 0.8 mile farther. Maps are available there, or go online to www.chesterfieldoutdoors.com.

Consider a trip to the Chesterfield Gorge Area, which features a 0.7-mile loop trail leading to the falls and cascades through Chesterfield Gorge. Cliffs rise steeply on the west side and a few profiles, one suggesting the Minuteman, are traceable. Picnic tables, grills, rest rooms, and information center are also available for visitors. From the junction of Routes 9/63, go 3.2 miles east on Route 9. The gorge is open weekends from Memorial Day through November; daily from June to mid-October. For more information, call 603-547-3373. Pets are allowed in the designated dog walk area and must be leashed at all times.

to Route 9

Madame
Sherri
"Castle"
-ruins-

P Gulf Road

pond

to
Route
63
and
Hinsdale

TOWN OF
WEST CHESTERFIELD

Hemlock

Ann Stokes Loop

to Mount
Wantastiquet
and Mine
Ledge

Indian
Pond

*Ann Stokes
~ Loop Trail ~*

East
Hill

LEDGES

LEGEND

•••• # 37 Madame Sherri Hike

--- option

P parking

1/8

MILE

37
Madame Sherri Forest

Rating: An easy-to-moderate loop hike to the ruins of a "castle" and along the edge of a mountain pond.
Distance: 2.5 miles
Hiking Time: 1.5 to 2 hours
Lowest Elevation: 634 feet
Highest Elevation: 1,122 feet
USGS Map: Brattleboro
Trailhead: West Chesterfield, New Hampshire

Everybody loves a little mystery. On this hike you can satisfy your desire for the unknown and visit a remote woods pond at the same time. The 513-acre Madame Sherri Forest is located on the eastern slope of Wantastiquet Mountain in Chesterfield, New Hampshire. A short walk will bring you to the "castle" ruins that once belonged to the mysterious Madame Antoinette Sherri. After you visit the former summer home, continue on the 2.5-mile Ann Stokes loop trail to Indian Pond with a good view from East Hill along the way.

Madame Sherri (1878–1965) was a Paris-born theatrical costume designer who entertained her Ziegfeld Follies friends from New York City at her castle with lavish summer parties that sometimes lasted for days. She first came to Chesterfield to visit a friend, Jack Henderson, a Broadway actor who summered there.

In 1931, she purchased property on the back side of Rattlesnake (Wantastiquet) Mountain where she built a 15-room residence resembling a French chateau made of stone, with carved Roman arch windows and a chalet roof. The interior housed hundreds of figurines collected from around the world, ancient Chinese porcelain, Italian pottery, ornate, elaborately-carved furniture, gold and alabaster Buddhas, and a carved cobra-backed throne chair. Outside the house was a swimming pool with a marble statue of the Greek goddess Aphrodite.

Madame Sherri quickly developed a reputation as an exotic and mysterious figure among the locals, and her story has taken on the aspect of legend. Often accompanied by much younger male friends, she would visit nearby Brattleboro in her chauffeur-driven 1927 Packard convertible to pick up supplies, and shock the townspeople by wearing just a fur coat and pulling a wad of cash from between her breasts or a purse strapped to her thigh, her red hair tied up in a turban. Some speculate that the elaborate entertaining at her summer home involved the operation of a brothel. But the fortunes of Madame Sherri and the summer parties faded as the height of the era of Broadway musical productions declined.

In 1959, upon returning to her summer home, she discovered the interior in ruins. Heartbroken that vandals had destroyed art work, tapestries, and furnishings, she left her castle and never returned. On October 18, 1962, the castle burned to the ground in a suspicious fire. Madame Sherri spent her final years living on welfare in the Brattleboro home of her court-appointed guardians. She died in a Brattleboro nursing home at 87.

Access: From Keene take Route 9 west toward Brattleboro, Vermont. Just before the green, arched bridges that cross the Connecticut River into Vermont, turn left onto Mountain Road. Go 0.1 mile, then bear left at a fork onto Gulf Road. Continue about 2.2 miles to the property entrance, across from Egypt Road.

Description: After crossing a wooden footbridge that leads past a marshy pond enclosed by a stone wall, the trail comes to a junction. The ruins of castle are located 100 feet up on the hill to the right. An arched stone staircase—the "stairway to heaven" made up of 29 steps that rest on three arches that once led to an outdoor verandah—towering chimney, main steps carved into a rock ledge, and crumbling foundation sit eerily in silence surrounded by a forest that is slowly reclaiming it.

After exploring the castle ruins and grounds of the former estate, return to the junction and follow the trail, which parallels a beaver pond before coming to a sign for the Ann Stokes loop. Continue left

"Stairway to heaven," Madame Sherri Castle.

on the trail toward Indian Pond and Daniels Mountain. (To the right is a 0.5-mile easy walk to Indian Pond, a 30-minute round trip). At first the path is wide and rocky but it narrows as it passes through a mixed hardwood forest. Soon you will enter a section of dark hemlock forest as the white diamond-blazed trail gradually moves uphill and gets rockier. At a log bridge, the trail turns right and steepens before leveling off and descending. You will continue through a young forest of maple, beech, and birch and, 15 minutes from the start of the hike, reach a trail sign. The trail to Indian Pond continues right (Daniels Mountain, 1,225 feet, is left) and shortly turns right again before moving over a steep ledgy section. After descending into a hemlock forest you will briefly continue through open woods of oak and maple before encountering more hemlock and ledge. At 35 minutes into the hike, you will reach East Hill where there is a good view of the town of Chesterfield. After taking in the view, continue on the trail, which shortly reaches an outcrop with an excellent view of Indian Pond below against the backdrop of Mount Wantastiquet. The trail descends steeply (use caution) past thickets of mountain laurel to Indian Pond, which is surrounded by rugged hills giving it a sense of remoteness. (A connecting trail from Indian Pond leads to Mine Ledge and Mount Wantastiquet.) Take time to enjoy lunch and the solitude of the pond. When you are ready to continue, return to the trail as it descends for the 10-minute walk back to the Ann Stokes Loop trailhead sign. A short walk brings you back to the parking lot.

Sightseeing: Madame Sherri's gravesite is in Brattleboro's Meeting House Cemetery where an unpretentious one-by-two foot stone reads "Antoinette Sherri, 1878–1965." The Meeting House Cemetery is located off Orchard Street. From Exit 2 (Interstate 91) go 0.2 mile west on Route 9 (Western Avenue) to Orchard Street and continue 1 mile. Madame Sherri's gravestone is located in the western part of the cemetery toward the bottom of the hill, near a dirt loop road. A more prominent gravestone reading "Omasta" is nearby.

38
Mount Wantastiquet

Rating: A moderate switchback climb to an open ledge with a
   sweeping view of Brattleboro, Vermont, and the Connecticut
   River.
Distance: 3.5 miles
Hiking Time: 2 to 3 hours
Lowest Elevation: 276 feet
Highest Elevation: 1,335 feet
USGS Map: Brattleboro
Trailhead: Hinsdale, New Hampshire

Rising abruptly from the Connecticut River's New Hampshire shore,
Mount Wantastiquet looms over Brattleboro, Vermont, like a cresting,
green wave. But there is nothing intimidating about this 1,335-foot
peak. At one time, timber rattlers sunned themselves on the mountain's ledges, but the poisonous snakes have not been seen for years.
An hour-long walk up a wide gravel road, which was constructed in
1890 for quarrying on the mountain, winds back and forth in nine
switchbacks and brings you to the top of Wantastiquet. Many years
ago, iron ore was discovered on Wantastiquet, which is also called
Mine Mountain on old maps. From Wantastiquet's high, open ledges,
views of Brattleboro and distant Green Mountain ski peaks unfold to
the west. A short walk from the summit brings you to Mine Ledge
and even wider views.

Access: To get to Wantastiquet from Hinsdale, drive west on Route
119 for 6.6 miles. Turn right at Mountain Road (dirt). Continue 0.2
mile to the parking lot (right) marked by two granite posts. (A level
and easy, 1.5-mile river walk from Hinsdale to Chesterfield parallels
the Connecticut River.)

Description: An (orange) iron gate marks the trailhead. (To the right,
note a nice view of a seasonal waterfall). The trail climbs immediately

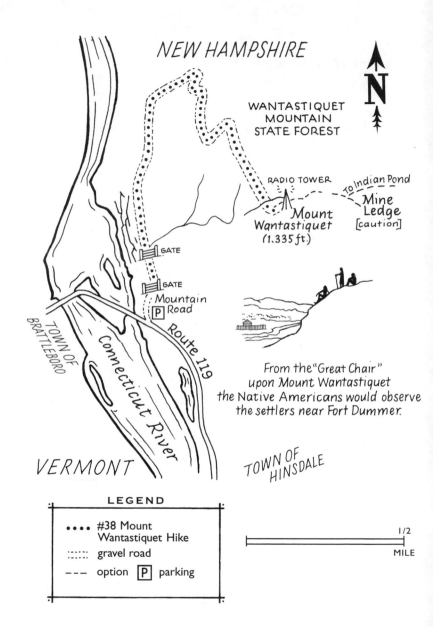

NEW HAMPSHIRE

WANTASTIQUET
MOUNTAIN
STATE FOREST

N

RADIO TOWER

To Indian Pond

Mine
Ledge
[caution]

Mount
Wantastiquet
(1,335 ft.)

GATE

GATE

Mountain
P Road

Route 119

TOWN OF
BRATTLEBORO

Connecticut River

VERMONT

TOWN OF
HINSDALE

From the "Great Chair"
upon Mount Wantastiquet
the Native Americans would observe
the settlers near Fort Dummer.

LEGEND

•••• #38 Mount
     Wantastiquet Hike
:::::: gravel road
− − − option P parking

1/2

MILE

*On the trail, Mount
Wantastiquet.*

uphill for 20 yards before you reach a fork. Bear left to follow the
gravel road. The path is a shortcut between switchbacks. Early on,
the forest is oak, pine, and maple, but along the way you will notice a
real diversity in the natural community. That's because the property
straddles an "invisible line" separating a spruce-fir forest from deciduous woods to the south. On Wantastiquet, white, red, and pitch
pine grow within yards of each other along with sassafras, red oak,
shagbark hickory, and mountain laurel. In five minutes, you will come
to another iron gate and culvert that channels a brook under the
road. Just beyond the gate, side trails (left) lead to rock promontories,
which offer views of Brattleboro's redbrick Victorian buildings, church
steeples, and the 65-foot-high cylindrical gothic tower of the Brattleboro Retreat. As you continue, hemlock shades the trail. Look for interesting terraces of gray schist and boulders to see which become
more prominent as you approach the top. After walking over a rocky
stretch—slippery and wet in the spring from runoff on streams—in
20 minutes you will reach a rock carved with initials and dates from
the 1800s. Dense thickets of mountain laurel, a broad-leaved evergreen with clusters of bell-shaped pink and white flowers looking
like mounds of snow, bloom profusely in the woods in early summer.

Rhodora also shows off its own impressive pink bloom in late May. The trail continues to switchback uphill. Fifty minutes into the hike, turn right to climb a rocky uphill stretch. At the top of the rise there is a view (north) of the Putney Road commercial area of Brattleboro. From here the trail turns right for the final 10-minute climb. Just before the road starts downhill again, a path to the right climbs up to some ledges to an open summit, where you will find a monument to Walter H. Childs from his friends, erected in the early 1800s. The cliff face offers wide views of Brattleboro and Green Mountain ski peaks to the west, including Haystack, Mount Snow, Stratton, and Bromley. At the base of the mountain, the West River joins the Connecticut River and the Retreat Meadows Lake (a flooded meadow area that was created when the Vernon dam was built in 1908) at their confluence is clearly visible. Route I-91 stretches toward Massachusetts in the distance. The Native Americans used Wantastiquet's promontories to observe the settlers in the vicinity of Fort Dummer. Dummer was the first English settlement (1724) in Vermont built to protect Massachusetts from attacks from Native Americans. The waters of the dammed Connecticut River now cover all evidence of the fort. One such promontory on the mountain was known as the "Indian's Great Chair." Sit and watch turkey vultures and hawks soar the thermals or observe the many other species of birds that the Connecticut River attracts, including eagles. The area is also a nesting site for Peregrine falcons and ravens.

When you are finished taking in the sounds and sights, continue on the trail to Mine Ledge. To get to Mine Ledge from the summit return to the road. Turn right and continue to the radio tower. As you face the tower, to your left, just beyond a clearing near a rock outcrop, pick up a rough path that heads east into the woods.

The trail immediately leads down to a hollow and continues up and down through dense thickets of mountain laurel. As you walk along the ridge, notice how some trees display burn scars resulting from the forest fires that burned here in the 1940s and again in the 1950s. Look for basal burn scars at the base of tree trunks. A basal scar looks somewhat like the dome shape of a Native American adobe oven.

Mine Ledge, Mount Wantastiquet.

In 10 minutes, you will reach a tree marked with orange directional signs. Continue east toward Madame Sherri Forest. (The summit of Wantastiquet and its northeast slopes are part of the 513-acre Madame Sherri Forest in Chesterfield, whereas 1,011-acre Wantastiquet State Forest comprises the western side of the mountain). From the directional signs, the trail climbs steeply and after several minutes will reach a fork. Left continues to Indian Pond and Madame Sherri Forest. Turn right for the two-minute walk to Mine Ledge. Use extreme caution. The sheer ledge requires close attention to the true path. At Mine Ledge, the display of mountain laurel in early summer is stunning and the views are breathtaking. To the southwest, the broad Connecticut River Valley spreads out before you; ice-blue silhouettes of the Berkshires fill the western end of Massachusetts. Equally impressive is the talus slope (or pile of broken rocks), large boulders, and little caves at the base of the cliffs. After admiring the views, continue your walk along the ridge for a view of Mount Monadnock rising above the rolling countryside of Cheshire County to the east.

Sightseeing: After your hike you may want to cross the Connecticut River into Brattleboro to check out the Retreat Tower and an old burying ground. The Brattleboro Retreat Hospital (today Retreat Healthcare, a psychiatric and addictions treatment center) was founded in 1834 as the Vermont Asylum for the Insane. It was later used as a military hospital during the Civil War. A cluster of nine red-brick and slate-roofed buildings set in the quiet seclusion of spacious landscaped grounds located on the east side of Route 30 (Linden Street) comprises the core of the institution. The tower is located on the west side of Linden Street on a hill that overlooks the Retreat and the town of Brattleboro.

Retreat Healthcare is located off Route 30 a short distance from the town common. Park on the east side of Route 30 by Linden Lodge. The 0.3-mile-long narrow dirt trail to the tower starts to the right (north) of Linden Lodge next to a fire hydrant. After moving uphill for 250 feet, the trail turns left and continues 60 yards. At this point you will continue (straight) toward an old Springhouse—but before you do, take a short detour of 50 yards (left) that will bring you to the old burying ground. The cemetery, which originally contained a vault, provided graves for patients whose remains were unclaimed. After exploring the old burying ground, continue to the Springhouse, an interesting brick and concrete structure that is covered by a pressed metal hip roof that sweeps down nearly to ground level and is topped by two square, louvered cupolas. The trail moves briefly to the right and then turns left and moves steeply uphill and over stone steps for the climb to the tower. The cylindrical gothic tower with a crenellated, granite projecting parapet was built by staff members and patients of the Retreat. (Legend has it that some of the patients hurled themselves to their deaths off the 65-foot-high structure.) The arched entrance is surmounted by a rectangular stone, carved "1887" in relief. The tower door is kept locked but there are nice views across to Mount Wantastiquet, especially in late fall when the leaves are off the trees.

Situated on the banks of the Connecticut River, Brattleboro is a town with lots of vitality and a slew of shops, art galleries, coffeehouses, and book stores to explore. The town also features interesting his-

The Brattleboro Retreat tower has a brick core faced with rough-hewn stones of all shapes and sizes.

toric buildings, including the 1930s Art Deco Latchis Hotel and the-atre (www.latchis.com) and Second-Empire-style Brooks House that dominates Main Street with its imposing Gothic cupola.

Nearby is 217-acre Fort Dummer State Park, which includes areas for camping, sheltered picnicing, and hiking trails. The Sunrise Trail, a 1-mile loop, has an outstanding view of the Connecticut River. From Exit one (Interstate 91) head north into Brattleboro. Take a right at the first light (Fairground Road) past Brattleboro Union High School and follow signs to the park which offers 51 tent/trailer sites and 10 lean-to sites. Open mid-May to Labor Day. For information, call 802-254-2610 (in summer) or 888-409-7579 or go to www.vtstateparks .com (from October to May).

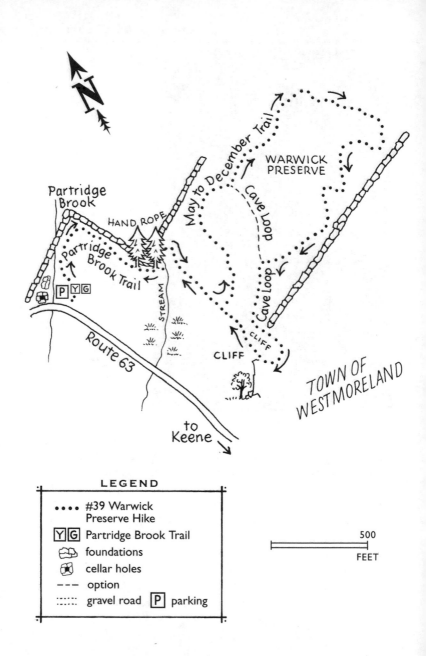

Partridge
Brook

HAND ROPE

Partridge
Brook Trail

STREAM

May to December Trail

WARWICK
PRESERVE

Cave Loop

Cave Loop

CLIFF

CLIFF

Route 63

to
Keene

TOWN OF
WESTMORELAND

LEGEND

•••• #39 Warwick
Preserve Hike

Y G Partridge Brook Trail

foundations

cellar holes

– – – option

:::::: gravel road   P parking

500

FEET

39
Warwick Preserve

Rating: A moderate hike through a rich, diversified forest with high
  rock outcrops and a wealth of wildflowers in the spring.
Distance: 1.75 miles
Hiking Time: 1.5 hours
Lowest Elevation: 480 feet
Highest Elevation: 900 feet
USGS Map: Keene
Other Map: The Nature Conservancy map
Trailhead: Westmoreland, New Hampshire

The Warwick Preserve is a 36-acre tract in Westmoreland near the
Connecticut River that has steep slopes, ravines, and cliffs. The Nature Conservancy's first preserve in New Hampshire also has enormous trees and an unusual diversity of plants and flowers because
of the residual limestone materials in the bedrock that have enriched the soil. In the spring, wildflowers abound and include maid-
enhair spleenwort, showy orchids, bloodroot, foamflower, trailing
arbutus, spring beauty, hepatica, wild ginger, purple trilliums, columbine, wood and trout lily, squawroot, and Dutchman's breeches. You
will also find a mixed deciduous and coniferous forest of hemlock,
white pine, beech, red and white oak, aspen, alder, and butternut, all
of which is especially worth a visit in the fall for its bold riot of reds,
maroons, yellows, oranges, bronzes and golds.

Access: To get to the trailhead from Keene, take Route 9 to Route 12
north and continue for 6.2 miles to East Westmoreland. Turn left onto
South Village Road and drive 3.7 miles to Westmoreland. At the road's
end, turn right onto Route 63. The Warwick Preserve is 0.9 mile farther.
Look for a small parking area on the right at the bottom of a hill.

Description: Before you start on the Partridgeberry Brook Trail
(which is well marked with yellow-and-green Nature Conservancy

Warwick Preserve.

arrows), walk a short distance to the left to examine a cellar hole surrounded by a blanket of periwinkle. This ground plant, with its deep-green leaves and pink or purple flowers, grows in extensive patches in woods, and covers the ground in many old graveyards and around old home sites.

After examining the old foundation, start on the trail that weaves its way uphill through tall pines and hemlock, maple, beech, and over a needle-softened surface. You will soon notice that this is an up-and-down route with very little level ground. In places the sloping terrain can be rugged. Soon a stone wall meanders on the left and 10 minutes into hike reach you will come to the top of a ridge where a heavy rope has been stretched between trees to form a handrail. As the trail moves downhill and crosses a stream, you will see outcroppings of quartz embedded in the hillside to the left. Five minutes from the rope handrail brings you to the Cave Loop Trail: this will be your return route. Stay left on the Partridgeberry Trail.

As you continue uphill, keep an eye out for the shagbark hickory tree (*Carya ovata*) with its light-gray bark separating into narrow, curved strips loosely attached at the middle. Shagbark has three large leaflets at the end of the leaf, and the leaves turn a golden yellow in the fall. Native Americans often used the thin-shelled sweet nuts of the shagbark hickory for food.

Five minutes from the Cave Loop junction you will reach (left) the May-December Trail, which will carry you up the southwest shoulder of Butterfield Hill and to the northern most corner of the preserve. This is a quiet stretch where you are likely to hear a variety of birdsong or see chipmunks scurrying for cover. After a rain shower on a warm summer day, you may have to share the trail with red efts so be careful where your step.

The red eft is the juvenile terrestrial stage of the red-spotted newt (*Notophthalmus viridescen*) and is found in forest habitats. Efts spend four to five years wandering before reaching sexual maturity and seeking a wetland to permanently reside in. As the red eft matures, its beautiful orange color will fade to a dull brown. After a while you will notice a distinct change in the forest as hemlock and white pine give way to sugar maples, beech, basswood, and sun-loving white and red oak. Shortly you will turn (left) onto the Cave Loop Trail. After 75 yards a sign points to an easier alternate route that avoids the steep drop of the main trail (Cave Loop) which passes a sheer chute-like rock ledge that drops precipitously to the right before coming to an outcrop that offers a good view (southwest) of the distant blue hills of the Connecticut River Valley. After taking in the vista, continue on the Cave Loop Trail, which moves over a stone wall. Look for a misshapen oak tree here that resembles a swordfish, kingfisher, or crane, depending on your imagination. The trail moves downhill past impressive boulders and high rock outcrops with talus slopes at their bases. Fifteen minutes from the Cave Loop junction you will reach the Partridge Brook Trail. Retrace you steps for the 10-minute walk downhill to the trailhead.

Sightseeing: The Park Hill Meetinghouse (on the National Register of Historic Places) is one of the most beautiful churches in New England. It was built in 1762 and moved twice before occupying its present location on Park Hill. The structure has a Greek-Revival exterior with temple facade, Palladian windows, arches, classical columns, pilasters, and a bell cast by the Paul Revere Foundry hanging in its steeple. To get to the Park Hill Meetinghouse from the Warwick Preserve, continue on Route 63 for 0.3 mile.

40

Monte Rosa, Mount Monadnock

Rating: A moderate hike that follows the Old Toll Road to the
Halfway House clearing and continues to a subpeak of Mount
Monadnock with dazzling views to the south.
Distance: 3.5 miles
Hiking Time: 1.5 to 2.0 hours
Lowest Elevation: 1,500 feet
Highest Elevation: 2,450 feet
USGS Map: Monadnock
Other Maps: New Hampshire Division of Parks and Recreation map
Trailhead: Jaffrey, New Hampshire

Monadnock is one of the most climbed mountains in the world—
and with good reason. There are 40 miles of maintained foot trails,
many leading to the bare rock summit with its spectacular 100-mile
views to points in all six New England states. While most people hike
the White Dot/White Cross Trails to explore the summit, a vast network of side trails in the vicinity of the Halfway House clearing offers
a different opportunity for adventure. Following these side trails, it
is possible to get In many hours of rewarding hiking to explore parts
of Monadnock few people see. The route outlined here brings you
to one such treasure: Monte Rosa, a subpeak where the views to the
south are dazzling.

Access: From Manchester, take Route 101 west on to Route 202 in
Peterborough. Continue to Jaffrey, and then take Route 124 west for
5.3 miles to the Old Toll Road entrance. Monadnock State Park has an
entry fee of $3 per person. For children aged 6 to 11, the fee is $1; and
there is no fee for children aged 5 or under, nor for New Hampshire
residents aged 65 or over.

Description: The trail starts out on a wide, gravel road. (A woodsier
alternative—the Old Halfway House Trail—parallels the Old Toll

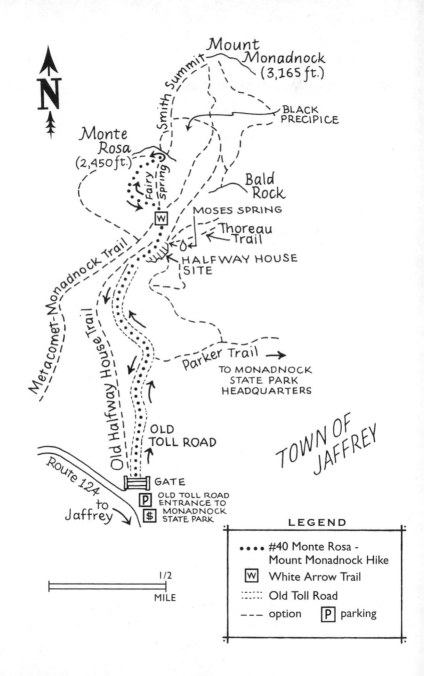

Hikers start out on Old Toll Road, Mount Monadnock.

Road and they both end in the vicinity of the Halfway House clearing). The major means of access to the south side of the mountain since the late 1770s—the Old Toll Road—was closed to public auto use in the late 1960s and is open only to foot traffic. By and large the hike is an easy walk on a road with a gentle grade. At 0.7 mile you'll see a sign (right) for the Parker Trail, which connects the Old Toll Road and Monadnock State Park headquarters, and 1 mile into the hike a private residence appears in the woods to the right. At the driveway entrance to the house, turn left and continue on the rocky path for a short distance to the Halfway House clearing with the massive, rocky bald summit of Mount Monadnock looming ahead of you.

For nearly a century, the spot on which you are standing was home to a series of hotels that were the focus of thriving activity on Monadnock. Many guests were enthusiastic outdoor lovers who demanded and often constructed walking paths leading to every interesting vista and natural feature. Maps today note many of these trails and places on the mountain with whimsical names such as Doric Temple, Do-Drop Trail, Hello Rock, Point Surprise, Black Precipice, and, this hike, Monte Rosa—a low peak that looked pink to guests at the Halfway House Hotel on clear evenings at sundown.

Monte Rosa is topped by a weathervane.

The hotel remained in operation until it burned in 1954. Today, except for a few foundation blocks to the side and a carved-out seat on a rock slab, virtually nothing remains of the Halfway House Hotel complex. On a rock face in the rear right corner of the Halfway House clearing (where the Thoreau Trail begins) an inscription reads: "Site of the Hotel known as the Mountain House and later the Halfway House, 1886–1954." Moses Spring still flows from a hole in the rock below the inscription.

After checking out the site of the once-proud and popular hotel, continue on the White Arrow Trail, which starts where the Old Toll Road Trail ends. The White Arrow Trail, laid out in 1706, is the oldest trail on the mountain. It quickly becomes quite steep, and is filled with uneven rocks and protruding roots. A little less than 0.25 mile past the Halfway House Site, look for the trail to Monte Rosa (left). You will descend to cross a brook, and soon the path becomes rockier and steeper as it loops west up through scrubby woods. Fifteen minutes of walking brings you to the Fairy Spring Trail junction. After turning left at the junction, a two-minute scramble over the rocks brings you to the top of (2,450 feet) Monte Rosa, which is crowned by an arrow-shaped weathervane.

Although the peak is a little more than a bump on Monadnock, its views are dazzling because you are 1,000 feet above the surrounding countryside—high enough to take in the eye-popping scenery. Directly to the south lie Gap and Little Monadnock Mountains, with Killington and other Vermont ski peaks to the west. To the east lies a prominent ledge on Monadnock's southeast ridge, Bald Rock, looking like a monk's tonsure surrounded by a sea of green, and Mount Wachusett in Massachusetts 30 miles to the southeast. Though the Monadnock summit blocks much of the view to the northeast, the mountain itself is an impressive sight. From Monte Rosa, take the white-blazed Smith Summit Trail, one of the finest geological trails on Monadnock, which features folded layers of quartz. The trail runs northeast across scrub spruce and open ledges, and leads to the summit, 0.7 mile farther.

If you are still in the mood for exploration, take a short walk on the Smith Summit Trail to the Amphitheatre Trail, which passes over numerous outcrops and skirts the top of the Black Precipice (2,550 feet), a dauntingly high overhanging cliff named for its dark colored rock, lichens, and shadows caused by an overhanging rock. The tooth, a large pointed boulder, is located on the Smith Summit Trail between Monte Rosa and the Black Precipice.

DIFFICULT HIKES

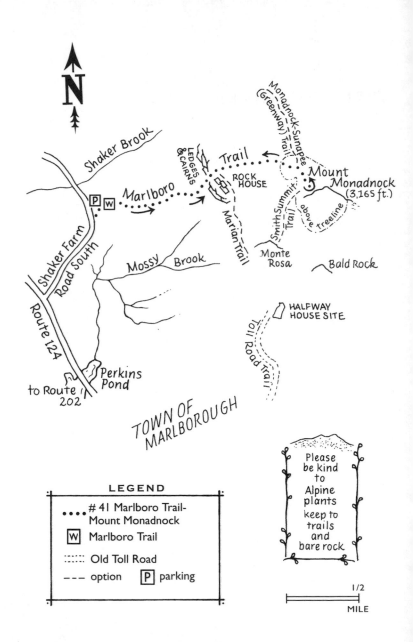

N

Shaker Brook

LEDGES & CAIRNS

Trail

Monadnock-Sunapee (Greenway) Trail

Mount Monadnock (3,165 ft.)

ROCK HOUSE

Marlboro

P W

Smith Summit Trail

above treeline

Marian Trail

Shaker Farm Road South

Mossy Brook

Monte Rosa

Bald Rock

Route 124

HALFWAY HOUSE SITE

Toll Road Trail

to Route 202

Perkins Pond

TOWN OF MARLBOROUGH

Please be kind to Alpine plants keep to trails and bare rock

LEGEND

•••• #41 Marlboro Trail-
Mount Monadnock

W Marlboro Trail

:::::: Old Toll Road

- - - option   P parking

1/2
MILE

41
Marlboro Trail, Mount Monadnock

Rating: Strenuous. The trail climbs the western slope of Mount
Monadnock over open ledges with numerous overlooks. Some
stretches of ledge will be too steep for younger children.
Distance: 4.2 miles
Hiking Time: 3 to 4 hours
Lowest Elevation: 1,325 feet
Highest Elevation: 3,165 feet
USGS Map: Monadnock
Other Maps: New Hampshire Division of Parks and Recreation map;
AMC Guidebook map; SPNHF Monadnock-Sunapee Greenway
Trail Guide; AMC Metacomet-Monadnock Trail Guide
Trailhead: Marlborough, New Hampshire

One of the oldest trails on Monadnock, the Marlboro Trail offers good
views and geological sights along the way, as well as alpine flowers
and a rock house for children to explore. This route climbs steadily
and gets you to high altitude quickly, so be prepared for a workout.
The trail traverses the western slope of Mount Monadnock over open
ledges to the stark alpine beauty of the summit cone.

Access: From the Manchester area, take Route 101 west to Milford
and on to Route 202 in Peterborough. Continue for 6.3 miles, then take
Route 124 west for 7.4 miles to Shaker Farm Road South (2.1 miles beyond the Old Toll Road entrance to Monadnock). Follow Shaker Farm
Road South (dirt) for 0.7 mile and park near an old cellar hole and
clearing to the left. The trailhead begins opposite the parking area
on land owned by the Society for the Protection of New Hampshire
Forests. Shaker Farm Road is named after the Shaker colony in Shir-
ley, Massachusetts, which owned this property in the late nineteenth
century and annually drove their sheep to summer pasture here. The
cellar holes of the Shaker community buildings are still visible.

At the summit of Mount Monadnock.

Description: The white-blazed trail goes through a northern hardwood forest of sugar maple, birch, oak, beech, white pine, and hemlock. The rocky path climbs steadily uphill and crosses a stone wall after 15 minutes of hiking. Ten minutes of rugged climbing puts you on an open ledge with good views to the south and west of Troy, Perkins Pond, and Gap and Little Monadnock Mountains. Just ahead on the trail is another open ledge with even wider views, where you will see Monte Rosa, a minor peak (2,440 feet) on Monadnock's southwest shoulder, and the prominent false summit of Dublin Peak (3,060 feet).

For the next ten minutes, the trail moves through hardwood, spruce, and over ledge outcrops. It is possible to experience several different ecological zones on Monadnock, changes which are due to the mountain's exposure to weather. As the trail rises, the maples and beech disappear, the woods become wetter, and you will notice more weather-stunted spruce, which become shorter and more gnarled, their tops bent from the prevailing northwest winds. At 1 mile into the hike, you will emerge at a wide-open ledge to see several cairns and white markers. This outcrop makes an ideal spot to rest and explore the rock house. Good views of Stratton Mountain and other Vermont ski peaks appear to the northwest. The Marian Trail leads to the south (right) from here.

As you continue on the trail, you see Mount Ascutney in Vermont to the northwest, a mountain almost exactly as high (3,168 feet) as Monadnock (3,165 feet). The trail runs through alternating ledges and woods for another 20 minutes and then reaches the treeline. A final scramble brings you to the ledges just below the summit.

Above the treeline it is easy to see the seven quartzite folds in the mountain. A good deal of Monadnock consists of metamorphic rock called schist, which is interlayered with light gray quartzite. Continue along the trail as it meets the Dublin Trail entering from the left (north). The Dublin Trail is the Monadnock-Sunapee (Greenway) Trail. From here the joint trail continues another 0.3 mile to the summit and Mount Monadnock's famous six-state view.

The alpine vegetation at the top includes sandwort and three-leafed cinquefoil, delicate plants that form mats and have five-petaled white flowers that bloom from June to August. These hardy little plants thrive in the harshest and most wind-blown terrain, and they are usually found only on the higher peaks of the White Mountains. Lichens are the best adapted organisms in the alpine zone; They require no soil to grow, and need only light, air, and minerals (which produce acids that break down the rock and cause cracks). Bits of rocks and dead lichens fill in the cracks, making soil that other organisms can grow on. Lichens are actually two plants in one: alga and fungus. The fungus provides the alga with the housing, anchorage, water, and minerals. The green or blue-green alga makes food by photosynthesis, which it shares with the fungus. Stunted red spruce and balsam fir also grow in the bare soil of the exposed summit. You will also find sheep laurel, mountain cranberry (lingonberry), mountain holly, chokeberry, and withe bushes growing in sheltered areas. These mountain flora are fragile and cannot survive trampling, so be sure to stay on marked trails or bare rock above treeline. After you have enjoyed exploring the summit, retrace your path to return to your vehicle. Use caution navigating steep and rocky stretches on your way down the mountain.

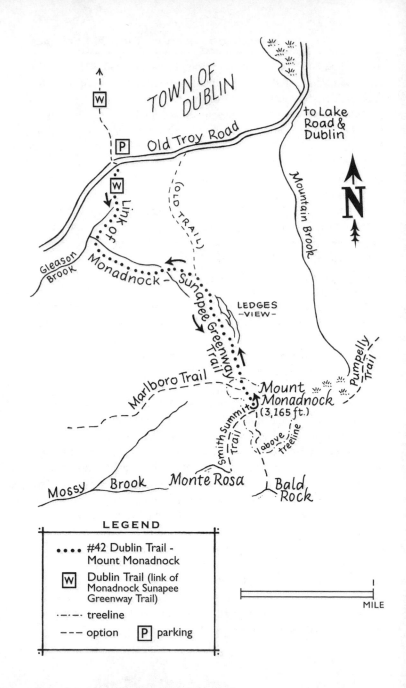

TOWN OF DUBLIN

to Lake
Road &
Dublin

Old Troy Road

W

P

W

N

Link of

Gleason
Brook

(OLD TRAIL)

Monadnock -

Mountain Brook

Sunapee

LEDGES
–VIEW–

Greenway

Pumpelly Trail

Trail

Marlboro Trail

Mount
Monadnock
(3,165 ft.)

Smith Summit Trail

above treeline

Mossy   Brook   Monte Rosa

Bald
Rock

LEGEND

•••• #42 Dublin Trail -
Mount Monadnock

W   Dublin Trail (link of
Monadnock Sunapee
Greenway Trail)

–·– treeline

––– option   P parking

MILE

Dublin Trail, Mount Monadnock

Rating: Moderately difficult. The trail climbs the north side of
Mount Monadnock over open ledges and offers far-reaching
views. The second half of the trail rises twice as high in altitude
as the first.
Distance: 4.8 miles
Hiking Time: 4 hours
Lowest Elevation: 1,486 feet
Highest Elevation: 3,165 feet
USGS Maps: Monadnock, Marlborough
Other Maps: New Hampshire Division of Parks and Recreation map;
AMC Guidebook map; SPNHF Monadnock-Sunapee Greenway
Trail guide; AMC Metacomet-Monadnock Trail Guide
Trailhead: Dublin, New Hampshire

Although only 3,165 feet in elevation, with its alpine plants, sweeping views, and breezy upper ledges, Mount Monadnock has the feel
of a White-Mountain hike. Many consider the views along the Dublin Trail the best of any on the mountain. There are some rocky slabs
but In general the trail has a moderate grade as it climbs the north
side of the mountain over open ledges. An added bonus is that the
Dublin Trail gets far less traffic than the trails up Monadnock from
the Jaffrey side.

Access: From Manchester drive on Route 101 west to Dublin. From
the flagpole in Dublin village continue 0.4 mile to Lake Road (left).
Continue on Lake Road, which becomes Old Marlboro Road, for 2
miles. Turn left onto Old Troy Road. The parking area is 1.8 miles farther. The trail is marked with a white "D" and cairns.

Description: The 2.4-mile Dublin Trail, formerly known as the Farmer's Trail and a link in the Monadnock-Sunapee Greenway, enters the

forest on the south side of Old Troy Road. The first part of the trail, which has been relocated, crosses several streams, then begins a moderate climb on the edge of a ravine. You will continue climbing a low wooded ridge before moving past a wet area and joining the old (original) trail at 0.8 mile. The pace and gradient of the trail becomes more difficult as ledgy outcrops fill in the path. One mile into the hike a rocky ledge will require a hand and toehold. The trail alternately climbs up over ledge, then disappears into woods and reaches the scrub zone at 1 mile, where Red spruce (*Picea rubens*) with its thick bark shielding it from the cold and needles too thin for snow to rest on, becomes the predominant tree. The name for red spruce is derived from its red cones. The dark, four-sided, shiny needles, about half an inch in length, grow in curved from all sides of the branches.

Soon you will break through the trees and spy Dublin Peak, a prominent cap of rock at 3,060 feet, which many hikers mistake for the summit. A little more than an hour into the hike a flat ledge area (left) affords a good view to the north of lakes, open patchwork fields, and mountains stretching away to the horizon. To the east you can see the Pumpelly Ridge—the longest direct trail to the summit—that also climbs Monadnock's north side.

After briefly moving back under the cover of trees, the Dublin Trail emerges on the smooth, polished, and rocky upper ledges where the views are breathtaking. Take time to watch the play of light, and the cloud shadows drifting in jagged patterns over the emerald ocean of forest stretching toward a hazy, blue horizon.

At 1.9 mile you reach the Marlboro Trail junction. From here, just a 15-minute walk along a dirt base between behemoth boulders, a distance of 0.25 mile, separates you from the summit. (This approach to the summit is less demanding than it is in other trails). At the top, take time for eating lunch and appreciating the spectacular 360-degree view of the six New England states. Mount Washington is sometimes visible 104 miles to the north; you can spy parts of Rhode Island peeking above the horizon.

Sightseeing: At a 1,439-foot elevation, Dublin is one of the highest towns in New Hampshire. It is home to the offices of *Yankee Maga-*

zine and the *Old Farmers Almanac*, which are located on Main Street across from the town library. Although Peterborough has the distinc-tion of having founded the first tax-supported library in the county, Dublin had a free public library in 1822. Despite its rock-strewn soil and steep hills, Dublin began as an agri-cultural town. As a sideline to farming, some of the women braided palm-leaf hats to earn money for their wedding out-fits. Agents of the country merchants brought them the raw material, and later col-lected the finished hats. In 1840 Dublin entered the sum-mer resort business. Around the turn of the twentieth cen-tury, many artists gathered around Dublin Lake to vaca-tion, socialize, paint, sculpt, and write. Some of the fa-mous figures who lived for extended periods of time in the town or made it their per-manent home included Mark Twain, Admiral Byrd, imagist poet Amy Lowell, and artists Abbott Thayer, George deFor-

On the way to the top of Mount Monadnock.

est Brush, and Joseph Linden Smith. The popularity of Dublin re-mained well-established into the twentieth century.

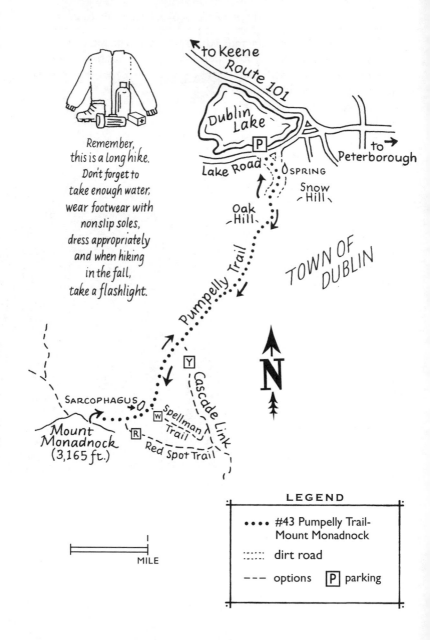

Remember,
this is a long hike.
Don't forget to
take enough water,
wear footwear with
nonslip soles,
dress appropriately
and when hiking
in the fall,
take a flashlight.

to Keene

Route 101

Dublin Lake

P

Lake Road

SPRING

Snow Hill

to Peterborough

Oak Hill

TOWN OF DUBLIN

Pumpelly Trail

N

Y

Cascade Link

SARCOPHAGUS

W

Spellman Trail

R

Mount Monadnock
(3,165 ft.)

Red Spot Trail

MILE

LEGEND

●●●● #43 Pumpelly Trail–
Mount Monadnock

⋮⋮⋮⋮ dirt road

--- options   P parking

43
Pumpelly Trail, Mount Monadnock

Rating: Challenging. The trail zigzags over open ledges of the
   northeast ridge of Monadnock and offers far-reaching views.
Distance: 9 miles
Hiking Time: 6 to 7 hours
Lowest Elevation: 1,479 feet
Highest Elevation: 3,165 feet
USGS Maps: Monadnock, Marlborough
Other Maps: New Hampshire Division of Parks and Recreation map;
   AMC Guidebook map; SPNHF Monadnock-Sunapee Greenway
   Trail Guide
Trailhead: Dublin, New Hampshire

With its sweeping views of New Hampshire, the craggy summit of
Monadnock is a prime spot for hikers to savor the splashes of orange,
yellow, scarlet and gold offered each fall foliage season. Monadnock
is 1,000 feet smaller than the White Mountains and much easier to
climb, but you still get above the tree line for an eye-popping view of
the countryside illuminated by the brilliant colors. The fall is a grand
time to take in Mother Nature's show but hikers should follow certain precautions. With the earlier sunset, pack a flashlight in your
backpack, and remember to dress appropriately because the temperature drops as you gain elevation. Fallen leaves on the trail make for
slippery conditions, so wear footwear with sturdy nonslip soles.

   While most hikers swarm up the direct approaches on Mount
Monadnock's southern face (such as the White Dot Trail, which is
the shortest route to the top), hikers willing to put in a little more
time and effort in exchange for relative solitude should consider the
Pumpelly Trail. Get your legs pumping early, however, if you plan to
hike Mount Monadnock's longest direct trail, which starts at the
southeast edge of Dublin Lake and continues 4.5 miles to the summit. The approach is more challenging than that of the White Dot

Trail, but you will find all the views and not as many people. You will also discover many interesting geological features, including the Sarcophagus, a large glacial boulder that looks like a burial sarcophagus or coffin when viewed from the east on the ridge. The abundance of dramatic geological features is not surprising since Raphael Pumpelly, a professor of mining at Harvard and a summer resident of Dublin, laid out the trail in 1884. The first third of the Pumpelly Trail is relatively easy but the terrain steepens at midsection. Once you reach the ridge, the walking becomes easier. A primary attraction of the Pumpelly Trail is the last mile, bare all the way to the summit with expansive views.

Access: From Manchester, take Route 101 west to Dublin. From the flagpole in the village continue 0.4 mile to Lake Road (left). Continue on Lake Road and park off the shoulder of the road after 0.4 mile. The Pumpelly Trail starts opposite a shorefront log cabin.

Description: The trail begins on a woods road under tall hemlock and turns right after 100 yards. Several minutes later, you will turn left at another woods road as oak, pine, and maple mix into the forest community. About 45 minutes from the start of the hike, the trail gets rockier and narrows. After turning left, you begin a steep climb through the woods over a jumble of knotted tree roots, boulders, and ledge that will make you feel like you are scaling a climbing wall. Five minutes into the climb will bring you to a ledge (left) a few steps off the trail with a good view of Dublin Lake, the saddled ridge of Crotched Mountain, and Mount Kearsarge further to the north. The rounded peaks of the Wapack Range, looking like a pod of humpback whales, sprawl across the horizon to the east. Thorndike Pond lies below at 1,159 feet. After taking in the view, return to the trail, which continues in the woods and emerges at a wide ledge for an enhanced view of the vista you took in moments earlier. From this point your route alternates through woods and open ledge with spectacular views of ponds, mountains, and low rolling hills glowing in gold, orange, and crimson. Thickets of red spruce (many twisted and no more than shrub size because of the high wind exposure) and

On the Pumpelly Trail, Mount Monadnock.

balsam cling tenuously to the gray ledge as warblers and thrushes flit through the firs. Shortly you will come to a ledge with a view of Monadnock's summit and false summit (Dublin Peak) to the right (west). Ten minutes later the yellow-paint-marked Cascade Link enters from the left. The Cascade Link descends to the White Dot Trail and State Park headquarters. You are 3 miles from Dublin Lake at this point. Cairns and paint blazes mark the trail now. Fifteen minutes more of walking brings you to the white-blazed Spellman Trail, which enters on your left. At the junction of the Spellman Trail, the trail turns right and dips into a wooded ravine.

As you climb out of the ravine you will pass the Sarcophagus, a mammoth, coffin-shaped glacial boulder that is also known as the "boat." Continue on the open ridge with views of the mountain and surrounding countryside. Ten minutes from the Sarcophagus, you will reach a large rock cairn with a wooden marker coming from its peak that marks the junction with the Red Spot Trail. Watch for shrubs such as mountain cranberry, low bush blueberry, Rhodora, withe bush, black chokeberry and winterberry as you continue through the scrub zone. The bare rock summit is 0.75 mile distant as you clamber over smooth, billowed schist.

At the top, enjoy the magic of Monadnock's unsurpassed 100-mile views of to all six New England states. Notice the physical features on the mountain—folded layers of quartzite and the large depression that bends from the summit and rises again at one northernmost prominence of Pumpelly Ridge. The true summit is marked by a bronze USGS benchmark. Bring a windbreaker; The peak is likely to be breezy, which can be either refreshing in warm weather or uncomfortable on cooler days. There are numerous places among the summit rocks where you can sit, including a cellar hole of an old stone building.

Sightseeing: Just 0.1 mile west of the junction of Route 101 and Lake Road is Old Pound Road (right). Continue a short distance to a cemetery and town pound built in the late eighteenth century. Most of the town centers included a town pound, a small enclosure that was built to contain loose animals until the owners came and paid a fee to retrieve them. Initially, animals could wander about with considerable freedom but as towns became more populated this practice ended. The poundkeeper's job was to lock up the four-legged escapees, and his salary was the fee he collected for his efforts. A short distance west of the town pound is the site of Dublin's first Meeting House (built in 1771).

44
Bald Rock, Mount Monadnock

Rating: Strenuous. The main section of the hike follows the Cliff
   Walk Trail past several historical landmarks to a prominent
   hawk-viewing area. Challenging stretches of ledge will prove too
   strenuous for young children. An optional extension is a steep
   1.0-mile trail to the summit.
Distance: 3.6 miles
Hiking Time: 3.5 hours
Lowest Elevation: 1,500 feet
Highest Elevation: 2,640 feet
USGS Map: Monadnock
Other Maps: New Hampshire Division of Parks and Recreation map;
   AMC Guidebook map; SPNHF Monadnock-Sunapee Greenway
   Trail Guide
Trailhead: Jaffrey, New Hampshire

Praised in poems, the inspiration for countless paintings and photographs, Mount Monadnock is a mecca for thousands of hikers every
year. The famous have found their way here—Thoreau climbed its
peak on four separate occasions and Emerson called it an "airy cita-
del." The second most-climbed peak in the world (the first being Ja-
pan's Mount Fuji), Mount Monadnock has a network of forty miles of
maintained trails, many of which lead to its 3,165-foot summit.

   Most hikers take the popular White Cross or White Dot Trails,
which begin near the warden's cabin just north of the Monadnock
State Park Headquarters area, where there is year-round parking. A
popular route follows the White Dot Trail up and the White Cross Trail
down (approximately a 4-mile round-trip; hiking time 3 to 4 hours).
The hike outlined here begins at another popular site, the Old Toll
Road Trailhead and follows the Cliff Walk Trail to Bald Rock, a prominent outcrop and hawk-viewing area. The 1-mile White Arrow Trail
offers an optional hike to the summit. There is a $3 per person service

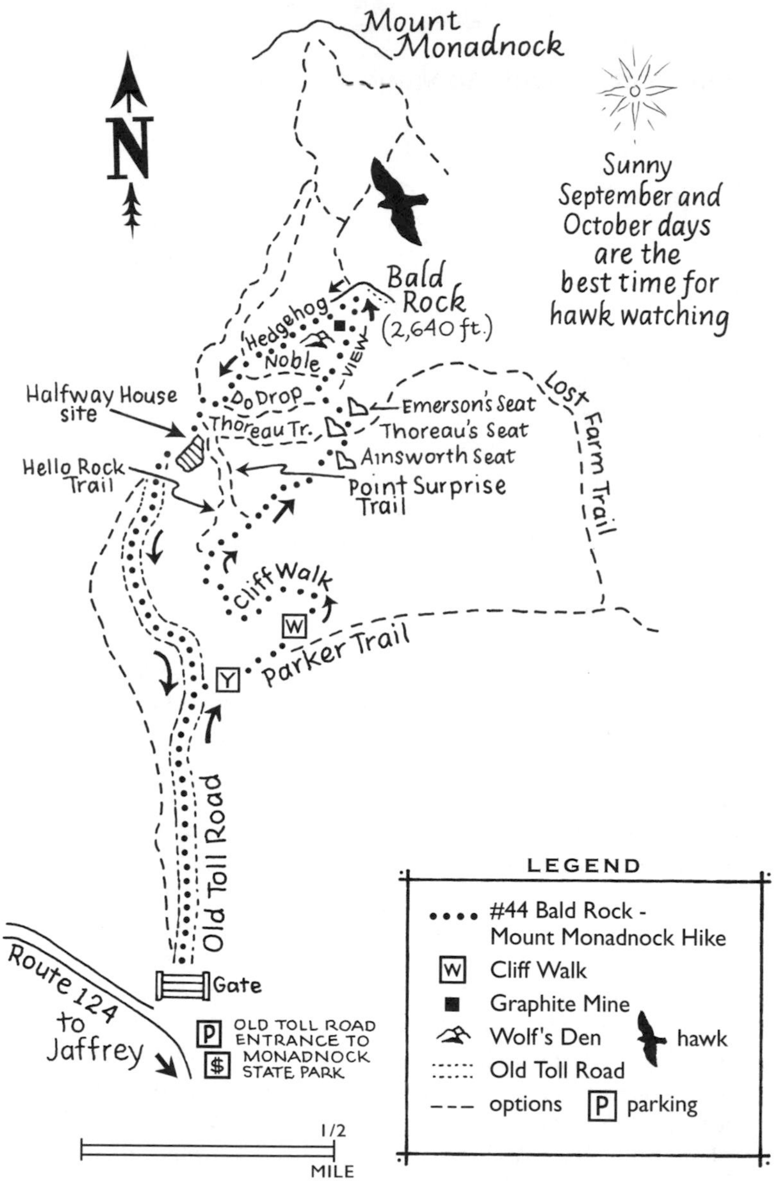

Mount Monadnock
N
Sunny September and October days are the best time for hawk watching
Bald Rock
(2,640 ft.)
Hedgehog
Noble
VIEW
Do Drop
Halfway House site
Thoreau Tr.
Emerson's Seat
Thoreau's Seat
Ainsworth Seat
Lost Farm Trail
Hello Rock Trail
Point Surprise Trail
Cliff Walk
W
Y
Parker Trail
Old Toll Road
Route 124 to Jaffrey
Gate
P
$
OLD TOLL ROAD ENTRANCE TO MONADNOCK STATE PARK
1/2
MILE
LEGEND
#44 Bald Rock - Mount Monadnock Hike
W Cliff Walk
Graphite Mine
Wolf's Den
hawk
Old Toll Road
options
P parking

charge; $1 for children aged 6 to 11; no charge for children aged 5 or under, nor for New Hampshire residents age 65 or over. Make sure that you bring plenty of water, warm clothing for fall- or spring-hiking, and a sturdy pair of boots—but do not bring your dogs.

Access: Take Route 101 west to Route 202 south in Peterborough. Continue to Jaffrey and follow Route 124 west for 5 miles. The Old Toll Road Parking Area is off Route 124, 3 miles beyond the main access to the park.

Description: The hike begins at an elevation of 1,500 feet on the Old Toll Road near a booth and beyond the gate at the north end of a 65-car parking lot. Maps of the trails are available at the booth. Originally, the Old Toll Road carried guests up to the Halfway House Hotel. Over the years a number of hotels were built on the site. Among the first guests was Ralph Waldo Emerson.

From the parking area, the road rises gradually through a mixed hardwood forest. In 15 minutes you will reach the junction with yellow-blazed Parker Trail. Turn right onto the Parker Trail. The walking is easy now, but boulders lining the steeply sloped woods to your left are an indication of the rugged ledge you will soon encounter. After 10 minutes, you will turn onto the Cliff Walk Trail on the left. (The Parker Trail continues to State Park Headquarters.) The Cliff Walk Trail is well-marked by white Cs painted on rocks; it follows long sections

The Cliff Walk Trail is well marked by white Cs painted on the rocks.

of ledge on the southeast side of the mountain. The trail rises immediately to a jumble of boulders and ledge. As you continue for the next 10 minutes over these giant rocks, the hiking gets very rugged and can be slippery in places. The strenuous trail alternates through hardwood and spruce forest and ledge, with many good outlooks to the south and southeast.

About one hour from the start of the hike, you reach the junction with Point Surprise Trail on the left. Just before the Lost Farm Trail junction, you will come to the first of several "seats" or lookouts. In this case, it is Ainsworth Seat, named for Jaffrey's "first settled minister." Two minutes ahead on the right, just beyond the Lost Farm Trail junction, lies Thoreau's Seat, a long, smooth rock outcropping. The Thoreau Trail enters from the left here. Like the famous naturalist, you may want to stop and admire the view that stretches southeast to the Wapack Mountain range, with a checkerboard pattern of meadows, farms, and lakes dotting the Contoocook River Valley below.

Up ahead on the trail to the right is Emerson's Seat. Just beyond the Do Drop Trail junction on the left, you will scale a steeply-sloped vertical ledge to emerge at a spectacular outlook. The Noble Trail enters to the left here. The craggy summit of Grand Monadnock looms to the north; in the distance to the southwest lie Gap and Little Monadnock Mountains. A few minutes more on the trail brings you to the Wolf's Den on the left, a jumble of ledges and caves. Nearby is the "Graphite Mine," a graphite vein that was worked about 1849. Flakes of graphite were collected here in barrels and rolled down a ramp to the Halfway House clearing.

A final section of flat ledge will require hand and toe-holds. Five minutes of scrambling will put you on the Bald Rock Ledges. Bald Rock itself is a large schist outcrop. Just below is an interesting rock pedestal called the Pulpit. On the eastern part of the ledge is a cube-shaped erratic inscribed with the words "Kiasticuticus Peak." Years ago, Bald Rock was the only open spot on the mountain, for Mount Monadnock was once covered to its summit with trees. The mountain's craggy shoulders and summit were eventually exposed by severe forest fires, some of them purposely set by early homesteaders

Mount Monadnock from Bald Rock. Photograph by Curtis Carroll.

to smoke out wolves threatening their sheep. Years of wind and erosion washed away the summit soil.

From Bald Rock you can see Monadnock's southwestern false summit, which is topped by a weathervane. Perhaps the most spectacular sight is the view of Monadnock's craggy summit rising from across the forested valley to the north. Bald Rock is used as a vantage point by the Audubon Society for its hawk counts because of the clear view if affords across the Contoocook River Valley. There is also less haze to look through here, compared with the view from the summit.

Hazy days that impeded good views are not caused by humidity, as commonly believed. The culprits are tiny air particles such as sulfates or organic and nitrate particles. Usually, regional haze is pollution that has been transported from hundreds of miles away. Most sulfates come from coal-burning power plants and most nitrates and organic-based aerosol pollution come from cars and smokestacks.

If you do see hawks, there is a good chance they will be Broad-wings, which are about the size of a crow, with broad, rounded wings and short tails that spread out like a fan. Broad-wings usually stay close to the ridges where thermals, columns of warm air, are forced up the slopes. Using minimal effort, these hawks spiral to great heights, then tuck their wings and descend in a long, slow glide to catch the next thermal. Sunny September and October days are the best time for hawk-watching, especially after the passage of a cold front with the wind freshening from the northwest.

When you are ready to return, locate the Hedgehog Trail to the west, which leads to the Old Toll Road. The steep, rocky path moves down a narrow opening to the left of Bald Rock, then enters a dark spruce woods. Look for a sign on a tree here. Use caution as the trail is full of rocks and roots. After ten minutes of hiking, the Hedge Hog Trail joins the Sidefoot Trail on the left. Continue downhill on the Sidefoot Trail and you will emerge after a few minutes at a large clearing. This is the former site of a series of Halfway House Hotels. The first was built in 1858 and known as the Mountain House and the last one burned to the ground in 1954. Look for an inscription on a rock face, denoting the hotel site near signs for Hello Rock, Point Surprise, and Thoreau Trail on the eastern side of the clearing. From Halfway House clearing, follow the Old Toll Road for the 30-minute walk back to the parking lot.

Optional Extension: If you have time, you can take the White Arrow Trail for 1 mile from the Halfway House clearing to the summit. Look for a sign at the northwest end of the clearing. Built in the eighteenth century and the oldest trail to the summit, the White Arrow Trail starts off steep and rocky, and continues that way to the top. In some places it is like walking up stairs, because in 1861 a geodetic survey team laid in about 400 stone steps to assist them in hauling their equipment to the top.

As you continue, notice unusual markings that look like turkey tracks or small crosses on the slabs of schist. These are sillimanite crystals that stand out due to the weathered surface of the rocks. They were formed during a period of folding when intense heat and pressure within the rocks changed the mineral composition. Many of these crystals were changed into mica. Shale metamorphosed into schist and sandstone became quartz, which you can easily see in the white streaks in the rocks.

One half-hour from the Halfway House clearing, you will emerge from the trees and suddenly see an open ledge looming above you that looks like it might be the summit. When you arrive, you will realize you are not at the top, but turn around and take in the spectacular view that unfolds to the south. The town of Troy, New Hampshire, Gap Mountain, Little Monadnock Mountain, the Wapack Range, and Mount Greylock are all visible. You can also see Bald Rock directly below you. From this high point, the path climbs and you will scramble over the rock outcrop for the final 30-minute ascent to the top, where you can observe Mount Monadnock's famous view of the six New England states.

On a fair day the view embraces an area 150 miles in diameter, where some 200 lakes and ponds may be seen. One hundred miles to the northeast, you can see the peaks of the Presidential Range, especially when they are snow-capped, with Mount Washington in their midst. On an exceptionally clear day, you can see the Atlantic Ocean and Boston's Prudential and John Hancock buildings 62 miles away. Mount Tom and Mount Greylock in western Massachusetts are discernable, as well as the long line of Vermont's Green Mountains to the west.

Nonprofit Conservation and Recreation Organizations

The American Hiking Society
1422 Fenwick Lane
Silver Spring, Maryland 20910
301-565-6704
www.americanhiking.org

Appalachian Mountain Club
New Hampshire Chapter
5 Joy Street
Boston, Massachusetts 02108
617-523-0636
www.amc-nh.org

Ashburnham (Massachusetts) Conservation Trust
PO Box 354
Ashburnham, Massachusetts 01430
978-827-6427
www.ashburnhamconservationtrust.org

Ashby (Massachusetts) Land Trust
PO Box 144
Ashby, Massachusetts 01431
978-386-5591

Audubon Society of New Hampshire
3 Silk Farm Road
Concord, New Hampshire 03301-8200
603-224-9909
www.nhaudubon.org

Beaver Brook Association
117 Ridge Road
Hollis, New Hampshire 03049-6425
603-465-7787
www.beaverbrook.org

Forest Protection Bureau
NH Division of Forests and Lands
PO Box 1856-172 Pembroke Road
Concord, New Hampshire 03302-1856
603-271-2217
www.nhdfl.org

Francestown Land Conservation, Inc.
PO Box 132
Francestown, New Hampshire 03043-0132
603-547-2515

Friends of the Wapack
PO Box 115
West Peterborough, New Hampshire 03468
www.wapack.org

Harris Center for Conservation Education
83 King's Highway
Hancock, New Hampshire 03449
603-525-3394
www.harriscenter.org

Marlborough-Roxbury Land Association
50 Clapp Pond Road
Marlborough, New Hampshire 03455-2301
603-876-4503

Monadnock Conservancy
PO Box 337
160 Emerald Street
Keene, New Hampshire 03431-0337
603-357-0600
www.monadnockconservancy.org

Monadnock Sunapee Greenway Trail Club
PO Box 164
Marlow, New Hampshire 03456
www.msgtc.org

The Nature Conservancy
New Hampshire Chapter
22 Bridge Street, 4th Floor
Concord, New Hampshire 03301-4987
603-224-5853
www.Nature.org

New Hampshire Sierra Club
40 North Main Street, 2nd Floor
Concord, New Hampshire 03301
603-224-4719
www.newhampshire.sierraclub.org

Silver Lake Trust
PO Box 222
Harrisville, New Hampshire 03450-0222
603-827-3867

Society for the Protection of New Hampshire Forests (SPNHF)
54 Portsmouth Street
Concord, New Hampshire 03301
603-224-9945
www.spnhf.org

Souhegan Valley Land Trust
PO Box 417
Milford, New Hampshire 03055
www.svlt.org

State of New Hampshire
Department of Resources and Economic Development
Division of Parks and Recreation
172 Pembroke Road
PO Box 1856
Concord, New Hampshire 03302-1856
603-271-3556
www.nhparks.state.nh.us

Trailwrights, Inc.
PO Box 1223
Concord, New Hampshire 03302
www.trailwrights.org

References

Appalachian Mountain Club. *AMC White Mountain Guide*. 26th ed. Boston: Appalachian Mountain Club, 1998.

Baldwin, Henry I. *Monadnock Guide*. 4th ed. Concord, N.H.: Society for the Protection of New Hampshire Forests, 1987.

Day, Freida C. *Historic Mont Vernon*, Vol. 1. Mont Vernon, N.H.: Mont Vernon New Hampshire Historical Society, 1990.

Day, Freida C. *Mont Vernon Hotels: The Golden Days*. Mont Vernon, N.H.: Mont Vernon New Hampshire Historical Society, 1994.

Doan, Daniel. *Fifty More Hikes in New Hampshire*. Woodstock, Vt.: Countryman Press, 2006.

Federal Writers' Project of the Works Progress Administration for the State of New Hampshire. *New Hampshire: A Guide to the Granite State*. Boston: Houghton Mifflin Co., 1938.

Flanders, John E. *Wapack Trail Guide*. West Peterborough, N.H.: Friends of the Wapack, 1993.

Frizzell, Martha McDanolds. *A History of Walpole*. Walpole, N.H.: Walpole Historical Society, 1963.

Jorgensen, Neil. *A Guide to New England's Landscape*. Chester, Conn.: Pequod Press, 1977.

Kibling, Mary L. *Walks and Rambles in the Upper Connecticut Valley*. Woodstock, Vt.: Backcountry Publications, Inc., 1989.

Kulik, Stephen. *The Audubon Society Field Guide to the Natural Places of the Northeast: Inland*. New York: Pantheon, 1984.

Lindemann, Bob, Mary Deaett, and Green Mountain Club. *50 Hikes in Vermont*. 5th ed. Woodstock, Vt.: Countryman Press, 1997.

Tanner, Ogden. *New England Wilds*. New York: Time-Life Books, 1976.

Thomson, Betty Flanders. *The Changing Face of New England*. New York: The Macmillan Co., 1958.

Whittemore, Suzanne. *In the Shadow of Monadnock*. Keene, N.H.: Historical Society of Cheshire County, 1993.

Index